EATING IN THEORY

Experimental Futures Technological Lives, Scientific Arts, Anthropological Voices
A series edited by Michael M. J. Fischer and Joseph Dumit

ANNEMARIE MOL

Eating in
Theory

DUKE UNIVERSITY PRESS DURHAM & LONDON 2021

Printed in the United States of America on
acid-free paper ∞
Cover designed by Aimee C. Harrison and
Courtney Leigh Richardson
Text designed by Aimee C. Harrison
Typeset in Minion Pro and Avenir LT Std by
Copperline Book Services

Library of Congress Cataloging-in-Publication Data
Names: Mol, Annemarie, author.
Title: Eating in theory / Annemarie Mol.
Other titles: Experimental futures.
Description: Durham : Duke University Press, 2021. |
Series: Experimental futures | Includes bibliographical
references and index.
Identifiers: LCCN 2020030114 (print)
LCCN 2020030115 (ebook) |
ISBN 9781478010371 (hardcover)
ISBN 9781478011415 (paperback)
ISBN 9781478012924 (ebook)
Subjects: LCSH: Eating (Philosophy) | Food—Environmental
aspects. | Food habits—Psychological aspects. | Food
habits—Netherlands.
Classification: LCC TX357.M653 2021 (print) |
LCC TX357 (ebook)
DDC 394.1/2—0dc23
LC record available at https://lccn.loc.gov/2020030114
LC ebook record available at https://lccn.loc.gov/2020030115

Cover art: Apple branch. Courtesy Guiter Dina/
Shutterstock.com.

CONTENTS

Empirical Philosophy

1

AMONG CURRENT GLOBAL PROBLEMS, those of ecological sustainability are particularly pressing. It is no wonder, then, that scholars from a wide range of backgrounds seek to get an intellectual grasp on them. This book seeks to help with that quest. It has no practical solutions to offer, but it does present some suggestions about how the theoretical tools of the social sciences and the humanities might be adapted to the pressing realities of environmental destruction. My contribution takes the shape of an exercise in empirical philosophy. Drawing on ethnographic stories about eating as sources of inspiration, I seek to enrich existing philosophical repertoires. This is urgent, since the theoretical terms currently in use in academia are equipped to deal with the problems of the past. Those problems have not gone away, but the terms crafted to tackle them are not particularly well attuned to addressing present-day human interferences with life on earth. This is because they are infused with a hierarchical understanding of 'the human' in which thinking and talking are elevated above eating and nurturing. What if, I wonder, we were to interfere with that hierarchy? What if we were to take bodily sustenance to be something worthy, something that does not just serve practical purposes, but has theoretical salience as well?

In this context, the term *theory* does not stand for an overarching explanatory scheme that results from a process of analytically drawing together a wide range of facts. Instead, it indicates the words, models, metaphors, and syntax that help to shape the ways in which realities are perceived and han dled. It connotes the intellectual apparatus that makes it possible for some thoughts to emerge and be articulated, while others are forced into the background or blocked altogether. If 'theory' opens and closes ways of thinking, the question arises as to what the theoretical repertoires currently prevalent in academia help to articulate—and what they silence. Here is my concern: the theoretical repertoires that contemporary social sciences and humanities draw on were pasted together in relation to humanist ideals such as seeking liberty from feudal overlords, protecting human beings from alienation, or dreaming up peaceful political arrangements. Over the past century, scholars have spoken for human dignity, argued against the ways in which industrial processes use people as resources, insisted that human subjects should not be treated as dumb objects in laboratory research, and defended rationality and due process in response to wars in which millions were killed. Time and again, it has been said that humans deserve more respect than many of them were—and are—granted. However, as human rights were, at least in theory, accorded to all of humanity, humans were, again in theory, disentangled from the rest of the world. Their ability to think and talk, or such was the idea, set them apart. This is *human exceptionalism*—the belief that somehow 'the human' is an especially deserving kind of creature.

Over the last few decades, human exceptionalism has been widely criticized. The critics do not deny that it makes sense to try to protect 'the human' from abuses like coercion, alienation, and violence, but they question restricting our empathy to humans. Other living creatures deserve similar respect, they say, and so do nonliving things on earth. Recent multispecies scholarship attends to elephants, dogs, tomatoes, earthworms, salmon, rubber vines, wheat, and many other forms of life; and, added to that, more-than-human work also reaches out to such varied stuff as rocks and rivers, water and oil, phosphorus and salt.[1] The scholars involved seek to query these phenomena on their own terms. But what are those terms? It is possible to talk about the *agency* of sheep, microbes, or molecules; or to celebrate the unique *subjectivity* of ticks, vines, or rocks. However, here is my concern: terms such as 'agency' and 'subjectivity' have been thoroughly informed by a particular understanding of 'the human,' the very humanist version which (building on earlier precedents) took shape in twentieth-century philosophical anthropology. It is from this observation that the present study departs: 'the human' inscribed in our theoretical apparatus is not *the* human, but *a* human of a quite particular *kind,* a human rising above other creatures, just as his [*sic*] thinking rises above his bodily engagements with the rest of the world. Hence, robbing 'the human' of his exceptionalism by spreading out his particular traits over the rest of the world is not enough. These traits, too, deserve to be reexamined. What is it to be human?

The intellectual apparatus of the humanist philosophical tradition permeates contemporary 'international' social sciences and humanities. In this book, I will primarily refer to work done in English. This is not to say that the theories embedded in adjacent languages are radically different. Both German and French have been crucial to the formation of the particular versions of philosophical anthropology about which I come to write. To acknowledge that I was raised and educated in the Netherlands, I will mobilize some Dutch sources, too. However, the commonalities and frictions between these linguistically adjacent tongues fall beyond the scope of the present book.[2] Overall, I keep the precise boundaries of my inquiry unexamined. All I seek to do is interfere with the traces of the hierarchization of 'the human' that are left behind in current academic work published in English. This hierarchization comes in variations. Sometimes, 'the human' is split into two substances, stacked on top of one another: a lowly, mortal body, and an elevated, thinking mind. Elsewhere, it is not substances but activities that are differentiated. In this case, metabolic processes such as eating and breathing are deemed basic; moving is situated somewhat higher; perception is above that; while thinking stands out as the highest-ranked activity. In other scholarly work, the senses are judged comparatively, which leads to a mistrust of smell and taste, touch being doubted, and sight and hearing being praised as providing information about the outside world. In this book, I explore this ranking in detail, but this short summary already indicates that, in one way or another, eating (pertaining to bodily substances, a metabolic activity, and involving untrustworthy senses) has been persistently downgraded. This informs my quest: What if we were to stop celebrating 'the human's' cognitive reflections *about* the world, and take our cues instead from human metabolic engagements *with* the world? Or, to put it differently: What if our theoretical repertoires were to take inspiration not from thinking but from eating?

To address this question, I analyze a few ways in which current intellectual repertoires are marked by hierarchical understandings of 'the human.' As points of contrast, I will, time and again, introduce exemplary situations of eating, as so many alternative sources of theoretical inspiration. These interventions are grouped together under a series of general terms. For chapter 2 this is *being*. Under scrutiny, this abstract term is filled with quite specific concreteness: that of three-dimensional, embodied human *beings* situated in surroundings that stretch out around them. An important icon of these beings is the walker. But while walkers (putting one foot in front of the other) move their bodies through their surroundings, eaters (as they bite, chew, and swallow) move their surroundings through their bodies. Which makes for another kind of *being* altogether. Chapter 3 is about *knowing*. Knowing is usually framed as following from a subject's engagement with objects of knowledge perceived from a distance. But if remote knowing may indeed be orchestrated, in eating foods, the known objects become incorporated into the knowing subject. This makes for the transformation of both object and subject. Established understandings of *doing*, the topic of chapter 4, are modeled on the agency implied in willful action, such as the voluntary movements of arms and legs. In eating, hands usually move food to mouths. Swallowing is a muscular activity, too. However, the digestion that follows cannot be similarly trained, and rather than being steered from a center, it constitutes a spread-out, churning kind of *doing*. Chapter 5 addresses *relating*. Twentieth-century scholars have explored how humans relate, or should relate, to each other. They stressed that giving is better than receiving or insisted on kinship and companionship. This insistence was predicated on equality between those who relate. Eating, however, is an asymmetrical relation. This shifts the question from how to achieve equality to how to avoid the erasure of what is different. In chapter 6, finally, I attend to socio-material politics and return to theory. Rather than fusing the lessons learned in this book into a coherent whole, I leave them standing as they are: a multicolored patchwork, a polyphonic song, or, if you will, a buffet meal.

This is a difficult book, if only because it moves between theoretical apparatuses and empirical configurations in an un-

TERMS AND THE REVOLUTION

In 1971, Dutch public television aired a philosophical debate about *human nature*. The two protagonists each spoke in their own language—Noam Chomsky in American English, Michel Foucault in long-sentenced French—while the Dutch chair spoke mostly English but from time to time shifted to French. There were subtitles and background explanations in Dutch. The latter were provided by Lolle Nauta, public intellectual and philosophy professor at the University of Groningen. I saw a taped version of this debate in 1977, in my first week as a philosophy student at the University of Utrecht. Ten years later, Lolle Nauta (who by then was my PhD supervisor) told us over a meal that we shared after a seminar with a bunch of colleagues that Foucault had been reluctant to participate. He only accepted the invitation once he learned that the proposed chairperson, Fons Elders, had been the first man to appear

usual way. The empirical stories told here do not lead to theoretical conclusions about eating itself; rather, they are meant to rekindle our understanding of *being, knowing, doing*, and *relating*. Over the course of almost a decade, I have read the relevant literatures and studied eating situations ethnographically. Based on this work, I have authored and coauthored articles about such issues as the importance of food pleasure in health care settings; tensions between contrasting nutrition science repertoires and ideas about dieting; and the ways in which the stakes of research projects affect the crafting of food facts.[3] In this book, my analyses have a different aim: they are meant to do philosophical work. Hence, my primary aim here is not to contribute to Food Studies or, for that matter, to Eating Studies. I gratefully draw on scholarship from those fields, but rather than being *about* eating, this book takes its cues *from* eating. It provides lessons for theory. It reconsiders the terms, models, and metaphors that, along with a plethora of socio-material infrastructures, make academic writing possible. Theory in this sense of the term does not describe the world; instead it takes the form of a toolbox that affords diverse—though not endlessly diverse—descriptions. Theoretical tools often stubbornly sustain themselves in the background of remarkably different positions in ongoing debates. However, they are not fixed. It is possible to *recall* them—even if recalling takes effort. This entails, first, digging up the past and carefully revisiting the concerns that were built into vested theoretical tropes, and then, second, to let go of those tropes and propose verbal openings that allow for other ways of thinking.

Eating in Theory is a book in the tradition of empirical philosophy, written in the form of short, dense chapter sections that hang together under chapter headings. You are now reading the first section of the introductory chapter, in which I summarize what *Eating in Theory* sets out to do. In the second section, I present a prototypical example of a hierarchical model of *the human*. I extract this from *The Human Condition*, a book published by Hannah Arendt in 1958.[4] In my brief analysis of this book, I cannot begin to do justice to what it was meant to achieve at the time of its writing. Instead, I hope to convince you that the hierarchical version of 'the human' embedded in its theoretical apparatus (and in that of many kindred books) indeed deserves to be shaken up. To introduce 'empirical philosophy,' the subsequent section explores the classic contrast between philosophical normativity and the empirical gathering of facts. The section that follows explicates how these opposites became pasted together by robbing philosophy of its alleged transcendence and tracing the empirical realities that inhabit prevailing theoretical tropes. This raises the question which theoretical inspiration alternative 'empirical reali-

naked on Dutch television, most probably a European first as well. The acceptance left Elders, now fully dressed, with the task of bridging not just the gap between English and French, but also that between two repertoires of thinking that went off on entirely different tangents.

This debate is currently viewable on YouTube, with subtitles in English (https://www.youtube.com/watch?v =3wfNl2L0Gf8). At the time, YouTube and related wonders, such as personal computers, smartphones, and the internet, were undreamed-of marvels. Dreams instead envisioned 'the revolution.' This has not quite materialized. Other transformations, yes. But not that one, even though *revolution* was more or less the only term both protagonists used approvingly. They disagreed about everything else— certainly the topic they were asked to comment on, *human nature*. Chomsky firmly believed in 'human nature.' He took it to be important to underscore that all humans, regardless of where they come from and what they live through, have an innate core in common. Trained as a linguist, he argued that this commonality was evident in the human ability to learn languages. The scientific theory to which Chomsky put his name was that all human languages have the same fundamental grammatical structure. He took this basic grammar to be innate. If his theory was scientific, it was also political. Chomsky argued that because humans were similar in nature they should be treated equally in society: social justice was long overdue. Foucault, by contrast, took 'human

ties' might have on offer. Such as, notably, realities to do with eating. But what is 'eating'? Empirical philosophy has not just brought 'philosophy' down to earth but also altered 'empirical.' The next section traces how reality came to be understood as multiple, as something that comes in versions.

In the last section of this chapter, I write a bit more about the stories of *eating* that animate this book. These are deliberately provincial. They are specific to the sites where I, and sometimes other researchers, studied them. These sites include rehabilitation clinics, nursing homes, research laboratories, shops, restaurants, kitchens, and living rooms, most of them situated in the Netherlands. I work not only with materials from eating practices I observed or talked about, but also with those I engaged in as an eater. In the field thus pasted together, *eating* takes a variety of shapes: ingesting, stocking up on energy, feasting, stilling hunger, taking pleasure, and so on. These variations form multitudinous intellectual sources of inspiration. Throughout the book, I call on one version of eating or another, picking whichever best serves my theory-disrupting purposes. But beware. While I interfere with vested theoretical reflexes, I do not offer a coherent alternative. This is a book of theory, but it does not present 'a theory.' Rather, it shakes things up and creates openings. Instead of reassuring answers, I offer eating-inflected intellectual terms and tools. I hope they are inspiring.

The Human Condition

This book has been germinating in me for some time. Its starting point dates back to 1977, when I was a first-year philosophy student at the University of Utrecht, in the Netherlands.[5] For our Philosophical Anthropology class, we had to read Hannah Arendt's *The Human Condition*. The subdiscipline 'philosophical anthropology' was tasked with describing 'the human' in a transcendental way, which meant beyond all particular (physically, socially, or culturally specific) humans. My teachers considered *The Human Condition* an exemplary specimen of the genre, one that all philosophy students ought to encounter. As an eager novice, I read the book with dedication. Making my way through demanding passages and a somewhat muddled overall structure, I gradually got a grip on it and was astounded. It did not surprise me that the book aimed to build an intellectual means of defense against totalitarianism. In the Netherlands in the late 1970s, the question of 'how to avoid another Holocaust' was vividly present as a normative hallmark, while the horrors of the gulag had gained enough public attention to get through to me. However, my feminist sensibilities revolted. While at the time many writers still unashamedly equated 'the human' with 'the man,' Arendt did not. She wrote about 'women' or, rather, in line with her ancient Greek sources, about 'women and slaves.' This left people who might be classified as 'women' *and* as 'slaves' in a somewhat awkward position, but I was willing to suspend judgment on that.[6] What astounded me was that Arendt agreed with her sources that 'women and slaves,' who in ancient Greece did all the work of daily care, were engaged in demeaning tasks. 'Free men,' by contrast, took political action, and this she praised. Why, I wondered, did Arendt go along so easily with the self-congratulatory way in which ancient Greek 'free men' celebrated their lofty politics, while scathingly denouncing the life-saving efforts of the so-called women and slaves?[7]

It has taken me some time to put the argument together, but the present book is my belated response to that early encounter with philosophical anthropology. Let me therefore say a bit more about *The Human Condition* as an example (one among many) of the hierarchical tropes in which 'the human' is cast in twentieth-century Western philosophy. Hannah Arendt wrote this book in the 1950s against the background of the Holocaust, the gulag, and less obvious forms of tyranny—among which she counted bureaucracy. The concerns of people submitted to colonial rule and their struggles for independence did not inform her analysis; they remained conspicuously absent. Arendt argued that the sciences offer no political protection against

nature' to be a delusion. He did not dwell on the shared human ability to speak, but he addressed the diversity between ways of speaking. He did not foreground grammar, but semiotics. In his academic work, he explored what different, historically specific linguistic repertoires allowed people to say and what they made unthinkable. Take the term *justice*. By calling for social justice, Chomsky considered himself a political radical, but Foucault did not see this as radical at all. To him 'justice' was not *an ideal state of affairs* to strive for, something to realize after the revolution. Instead, it was a *term that figured as an ideal* within the discursive structures of present-day societies. The notion of 'justice' was fundamental to the police (both in France and the US) and to justice departments working to impede the revolution.

Nauta, operating in didactic mode, tried to stay neutral and explain what animated both positions. He visibly enjoyed the task. By today's television standards, his accounts are movingly longwinded. Camera positions, cuts made and not made in the filming, body language, clothing, hairdos, and questions from the audience are all also markedly out of date. But at the time, they were unsurprising. At some point, Foucault, in a slightly patronizing, matter-of-fact tone, asserted that in the revolution those whom he called 'the oppressed classes' would 'obviously' use violence against those currently in power. Chomsky was taken aback, shocked. He asserted that

tyranny as they merely gather factual knowledge: they remain shallow and flatten out what is normatively at stake. Only the arts and philosophy, normative endeavors, could offer the imaginative response necessary to safeguard liberty in the face of totalitarianism. Seeking to provide a philosophical contribution, Arendt took her inspiration from ancient Greek sources, notably Aristotle. Along with him, she asserted that it was the true calling of 'the human' to engage in politics. Withstanding the lure of totalitarian rulers depended on rising above the banalities of the flesh. Arendt deplored the fact that the bodily incarnation of humans means they need to eat and drink: "To mortal beings this natural fatality, though it swings in itself and may be eternal, can only spell doom."[8] It was her quest to eschew this doom. It is in this context that she deplored the 'grinding tasks' of 'women and slaves,' which are 'merely' necessary for survival and keep humans tied to 'nature.' She called these endeavors *labor*.[9] Elevated above *labor* was *work*, which was performed by 'craftsmen.' This included making things, like houses or tables, which had a certain durability. Their solidity protected humans against 'nature' and their durability stood out against nature's capriciousness and fluidity. Highest among human occupations was *action*, which broke the endlessly ongoing repetition of life and death. In ancient Greece, engaging in *action* was the prerogative of 'free men,' who saw to it that their *polis* did not submit to the laws of nature but set its own laws.

Once Arendt had spelled out the differences between *labor, work,* and *action,* which in ancient Greece were performed by different social groups, she took the philosophical liberty of fusing them together as jointly forming 'the human condition.' In the philosophical anthropology she proposed, anthropos, the human, is a hierarchical composite. Lowest in the hierarchy is *animal laborans*—the 'laboring animal,' engaged in repetitious care to assure the food, drink, and cleanliness necessary for survival. Next comes *homo faber*—not an animal, this time, but a 'making man,' crafting the durable goods that help to safeguard humans against the perils of nature. The highest level in the hierarchy is the *zoon politicon*—the 'political being' whose creativity allows humans to organize themselves as a society. As the *zoon politicon* engages in action, he breaks with nature and its necessities. It is this break that held Arendt's normative attention. Breaking with nature, she contended, marks 'the *truly* human.' Arendt criticized political theories in which the *zoon politicon* is not similarly celebrated, notably the versions of nineteenth-century naturalism in which Marxism is rooted. Naturalists, wrote Arendt, sought to escape the Cartesian dichotomy between human consciousness and the material world by foregrounding eating. They theorized the human as "a living organism, whose very survival depends upon the incorporation, the consumption, of outside matter."[10] In this way, the material world no longer opposed the 'cogito,' but entered the human 'being.' Arendt wrote that while this may sound tempting, it is yet another manifestation the Christian inclination for granting too much importance to human life.[11] Survival is not what makes *us* human; freedom is.

Like 'the Greeks' whom she admired, Arendt had little patience for the chores necessary for survival. This impatience did not clash with her own apparent membership in the category of 'women and slaves.' Instead it fit her attempts to break out of the social position accorded to 'women.' Arendt sought, in an emancipatory mode, to live and work as 'a philosopher'—however difficult this was for someone all too easily considered to be 'a woman' in the eyes of others. As a philosopher, Arendt sang the praises of the *zoon politicon* contra totalitarian arrangements that kept people mindlessly focused on survival. However, by the time I read her work, some twenty years later, emancipatory ideals of equality between the sexes had been supplemented with feminist critiques on one-sidedly acclaiming the pursuits of men. Shaped by this new feminist ethos, I revolted against the idea of casting aside as lowly

he saw violence as unjust, something that, he underlined, he would turn against, no matter from whom it came. I do not remember whether this painful part of the exchange got through to me as a first-year student. But the academic side of the debate certainly caught my imagination. It struck me that rather than making arguments in given terms (as Chomsky did), philosophers could apparently also doubt terms (as Foucault did). They could put certain words between brackets, abstain from using them, and instead put them in their historical and social contexts. They could willfully ignore what otherwise seemed self-evident and suspend conclusions—even in the face of political urgency. Stop. Take a step back. For new things to happen, we might need to dream up new words.

Most of the sidelines in the margins of this book contain stories about *eating* that I import from the works of others. This is to compensate for the limits of my own, narrowly situated, fieldwork. It helps to underscore, that beyond my particular field, *eating* takes on a myriad of other shapes. However, this first sideline does something different. It is a caveat. It issues a warning that in this book I will *not* address the many *injustices* related to eating, however pressing they are. Along with that, I will bypass all kinds of other inequalities between people, grouped along class, gender, ancestry, color, country, culture, or other lines. Injustices and inequalities form real enough reasons for concern, but the present book I have written as a student of Foucault, not

the life-saving labor of people—women or otherwise—such as farmers, cooks, and cleaners. Arendt might have retorted that she sought to downgrade not some groups of people but, rather, the fleshy substrate of all people: "The human body, its activity notwithstanding, is thrown back upon itself, concentrates upon nothing but its own being alive, and remains imprisoned in its metabolism of nature without ever transcending or freeing itself from the recurring cycle of its own functioning."[12] However, in the late 1970s, it was already too late to take 'the recurring cycles of nature' for granted. These were noticeably under threat.[13] And what, I wondered, would become of pleasure if 'the body' was cast as a prison from which 'we humans' needed to free ourselves?

The Human Condition presents just one version of the hierarchical thinking that permeated twentieth-century philosophical anthropology. In the present book, I will revisit a number of others. In this way, we may come to recognize the traces they have left behind in our present-day conceptual apparatus, in the ways in which we imagine what it is to *be*, to *know*, to *do*, and to *relate*. This inquiry should help us reimagine what those verbs might mean. But if I seek to escape from (some of) the theoretical hold of our philosophical ancestors, I do not argue that they were wrong in some general sense, nor that I have access to a deeper truth that eluded them. Instead, I seek to situate their work in relation to the concerns they sought to address. This opens space for the question of what alters now that different concerns come to the fore: concerns to do with metabolism, ecology, environmental destruction. Hence, in this book I do not aim to contribute to the emancipation of this or that group of people—farmers, cooks, or cleaners. Instead, I seek to revalue their pursuits, the *labor* relevant to survival. This I approach by unraveling (things to do with) 'eating.' Mind you, the Western philosophical tradition is not univocal, and along the way, eating has been recurrently appreciated. Take the nineteenth-century naturalists whom Arendt reproached for seeking to escape Descartes's binary between *ego* and *world* by attending to ego's ingestion of the world. Or, for that matter, take Descartes. He may have insisted that his *thinking* (not his eating) proves his *being*, but in letters to his learned female friends, he used to dwell for pages on end on dietary advice.[14] Here I will leave out such complexities, take shortcuts, and simplify. I do not aim to do justice to the philosophical anthropologists of old. Instead, I seek to recall them: to revisit samples of their work in order to escape from its grip.

Facts and Norms

In philosophical anthropology, 'the human' was a general figure, abstracted from really existing ones. And although Arendt differentiated between *types* of humans, she too combined 'free men,' 'craftsmen,' and 'women and slaves' into a single entity, *the* human, whose condition she sought to define. In response to this, some scholars raised the concern that leaving 'the human' unspecified meant, by stealth, that only 'the man' was taken into account. In this way, philosophical anthropology concerned itself with no more than half of the species and elevated male standards into general ones. One author who voiced this concern was Frederik Buytendijk, who in the early 1950s published a book titled (I translate from the Dutch) *The Woman: Her Nature, Appearance, and Existence*.[15] The aim of the book was to give 'the woman' the recognition she deserved and to articulate her particular qualities. Buytendijk mused that 'the man,' though difficult to know, forms a puzzle that can be solved, while 'the woman' ('as is widely recognized') somehow remains a mystery that defies knowledge. Rather than seeking to tame this mystery, Buytendijk said, 'we' would do well to stop overvaluing masculine achievements and appreciate 'the woman' for her distinctive, elusive traits, including her passivity. We know, wrote Buytendijk, that 'the man' realizes himself in his activities, in getting things done. 'The woman,' by contrast, has the virtue of staying closer to nature. Poetically speaking, she resembles a plant, most

Chomsky. Hence, I do not critique realities that fail to live up to given standards, but seek to contribute to a collective search for other words, for other ways of speaking and writing. Since that 1971 debate, a lot has changed, but the question of what intellectual work should contribute to has not gone away. And that is fine. There is no added virtue in agreement at this point; these are productive frictions. At the same time, any single book can only do so much, and this one is about ways of wording and models with which to think. It does not outline 'human nature,' but recalls it. It does not serve justice, nor contribute to equality, but asks questions concerning other *goods*.

notably its flowers, which graciously display their beauty.

Not everybody welcomed this particular brand of praise. One of Buytendijk's opponents was the philosopher Else Barth.[16] In her thesis, written in the 1960s and published as a book in the early 1970s, Barth did not argue with the above (and similar) contestable declarations one by one. Instead, she countered the very project of characterizing 'the woman.' In doing so, she drew on the philosophical discipline of logic, in which at the time reasoning about particulars like q and p was being supplemented with reasoning about heterogeneous sets. Women, she argued, form a heterogeneous set and there is no logical operation that allows for the fusion of the varied members of such a set into a singularity that warrants the use of 'the.' The members of the class of 'women' do not share a long list of discernible, distinctive traits. Women only have their biological sex in common, nothing more. (Querying the pertinence of 'biological sex' came only later; see below.) If Buytendijk was worried that 'the human' was readily equated with 'the man,' Barth had another concern. This was that people classified as 'women' might have to live up to fantasies about 'the woman' cultivated by the likes of Buytendijk. She was not eager to be respected for being passive and resembling a flower. Like others calling for emancipation, Barth welcomed the societal opportunities that women had just about, but only just about, obtained. Possibilities such as studying philosophy and becoming professional logicians.

'The human' was not just a philosophical puzzle-slash-mystery, but also topicalized in a wide range of empirical sciences. In that arena, the question of how to split up 'the human' played out along more axes than those of two sexes alone. Particularly prominent were attempts to divide the single human species into contrasting biological races. Early on in the twentieth century, physical anthropologists measured physical traits, such as height, skull size, and facial angles.[17] Some hoped their findings would allow them to differentiate between groups of people originating in different continents. Others worked on a smaller scale: in the Netherlands, there were attempts to differentiate racially between people from different provinces or even towns. Despite all the effort invested in it, the project was never particularly successful in its own scientific terms. Even so, 'racial difference' was used to legitimize colonial rule. Then the Nazis murdered millions of people, whom they designated with racial terms as 'Jews' or 'Roma.' Afterward, 'race' became—in Europe—a forbidden word.[18] In the 1950s, geneticists asserted that genetic variation among people did not cluster into discrete groups. The differences *among* those who allegedly belonged to 'a race' were as significant as the differences *between* such groups. But the story did not end there. Ever more elaborate tools made it possible to map ever more genes, while ever more powerful computers allowed for ever more types of clustering. Attempts to classify people into biological races thus linger on, often along with out-of-date classificatory terms.[19] At the same time, the idea that beyond their differences, humans share a *common nature* also endures: the discipline of genetics prides itself in having mapped 'the human genome' as if there were only one. This singularization goes together with a pluralization that descends to level of the individual, at which genetic profiling distinguishes between single people on the basis of their unique genetic codes—identical twins exempted.

While geneticists tried to link biological differences between groups of humans to their genes, epidemiologists studied how human bodies are affected by their social and material surroundings. This, they hoped, would help in tracking down the environmental causes of disease. Research along these lines made it possible to conclude, for instance, that when people who lived at sea level traveled high up into the mountains, their hemoglobin levels increased. Or that men in Japan had fewer heart attacks than their counterparts in the US because the former ate a lot of fish while the latter coveted meat. Migrants who moved from Tokyo to New York and then adopted the eating habits of their new neighbors saw their chances of having a heart attack increase accordingly. Women in Japan, in their turn, were far less bothered by menopause than their North American counterparts—maybe thanks to the amounts of soy they ate. All in all, the conclusion was that human bodies, whatever their starting point at birth, come to differ depending on the circumstances in which they find themselves.[20] These few sentences summarize decades of research, shelves full of books, or, nowadays, servers full of journal articles. Here, they are meant to indicate that differentiating a single, categorical 'human' into different 'groups of humans' was both backed up and undermined, in various ways, by diverse strands of biologically oriented research.

At the same time, social, linguistic, and cultural anthropologists also explored how humans may differ and what they have in common. Very roughly speaking: social anthropologists asserted that people gather together in societies to assure that collectively they have enough food and fluids to subsist on, safe places to shelter from harsh weather and wild animals, and protection against people from other groups. If different societies functioned in different ways, the pertinent commonality was that all societies seek to sustain themselves. Linguistic anthropologists, in their turn, differentiated between groups of people on the basis of their linguistic repertoires. Different ways of speaking allowed people to think and say different things. However, once again this also generated a commonality, the assertion that all humans use spoken, signed, and/or written symbols to communicate with others, express themselves, and arrange their affairs. Cultural anthropologists, finally, focused on a further kind of meaning-making. They gathered the stories that people tell each other as they try to get a grasp on an otherwise bewildering reality. Some traced commonalities between diverse foundational myths. Others clustered people into 'cultures' and cultures into 'types' on the basis of structural similarities between their folklore. In one way or another, all humans were taken to make sense of the world and give meaning to it.[21]

There is a crucial difference between, on the one hand, all these empirical attempts to specify 'the human' and, on the other, the philosophical discussions about 'the human' that I recall in this book. While empirical researchers, whatever the differences among them, shared the ambition to represent reality *as it is*, philosophy took itself to be a *normative* endeavor. It did not represent reality, but instead sought to qualify it, judge it, critique it. Take once again *The Human Condition*. If, in it, Arendt claimed that 'the human' *is* a *zoon politicon*, she did not ascertain a fact, but proposed a counterfactual. Exactly because so many people were *not* particularly interested in politics, Arendt insisted that *political* is how a proper human *should be*. She considered the reality she witnessed around her to fall short of the standards it was meant to meet. Empirical sciences were not supposed to be similarly normative, which is why Arendt called them 'shallow.' She asserted that in representing reality, scientists merely repeat it, while philosophy is able to offer more, that is, critique. Buytendijk was deliberately normative as well. He argued against the elevation of male traits to standards for 'the human.' In his book, he engaged in a dialogue with Simone de Beauvoir, who in *The Second*

Sex, published a few years earlier, had also insisted that 'the human' does not come in one sex only. But if Buytendijk gracefully accepted some of De Beauvoir's points, he passionately turned against her emancipatory call for women's equality with men. This, he argued, unwittingly left 'the male' intact as a standard. 'The woman' deserved her own standards.

It is easy to understand that Barth was not enthused about the particular standards that Buytendijk proposed. After all, if 'the woman' was to be beautiful and passive like a flower, Barth would be disqualified in one way or another. Either her sharp reasoning meant she was not a true woman, or her being a woman meant she could not be a true philosopher. Such judgments the empirical sciences emphatically hoped to avoid. For them, someone who did not fit the rules did not commit a *transgression* but constituted an *anomaly*. Anomalies were not be corrected; rather, they suggested that the theory stipulating the regularities had to be adapted. Hence, confronted with 'women philosophers,' an ideal-type empirical researcher should have concluded that Buytendijk's assertion that 'the woman' is 'beautiful and passive like a flower' is simply not true. Thus, the word *true* shifts its location. It no longer belongs to a person who (being a philosopher) is not a true woman, or who (being a woman) is not a true philosopher. Instead, it now pertains to a sentence ('the woman' resembles a flower) that is not true (given the existence of women philosophers). In short, while philosophy cherished its norms *over* reality, the sciences had to adapt their propositions *to* reality. This meant that these two research styles did not combine. Scholars were warned never to mix them up. The *is* of empirical studies and the *ought* at stake in philosophy had to be kept apart. Empirical researchers needed to see to it that societal or personal norms did not unduly color their facts; philosophers encouraged each other to go beyond the facts. Only a *transcendental* position, they agreed, made it possible to gain distance from *immanent* realities and be critical of them. This, then, is the contrast between 'empirical' and 'philosophy' that dissipated in the ostensible oxymoron 'empirical philosophy.'

Philosophy down to Earth

Twentieth-century philosophy had normative ambitions. As the sciences, in their own different ways, sought to establish empirical facts, philosophy granted itself the task of transcending those facts.[22] This task was divided between different branches of philosophy, which each tackled its own set of normative questions. Logic asked how to reason well, political theory how to achieve a just society, epistemology how to know well, ethics how to live well, and aesthetics sought to define beauty. Normative questions were to be answered not by attending to empirical realities, but by engaging in abstract reasoning and rational argumentation. That was the idea. But all along, that idea was contested. Diverse scholars interfered in diverse ways with the divide between immanent and transcendent, empirical and philosophical. In this way, gradually, *empirical philosophy* emerged. I use the term here as per the suggestion of the Dutch philosopher Lolle Nauta, who used it for the research that, in the late 1980s, he allowed his PhD students (including me) to do under his critical guidance.[23] To give a sense of the intellectual ancestry of the genre, I will cut a trail that starts with Wittgenstein's undermining the idea that proper reasoning depends on clearly defined concepts. The trail then shifts to Foucault's attack on the notion of counterfactual norms and presents Nauta's detection of empirical realities in philosophical classics. Afterward, it moves on to Lakoff and Johnson's demonstration that metaphors form a great conduit for such realities, and finally arrives at Serres's idea that alternative empirical configurations may inspire alternative theoretical tropes. This trail is not meant to serve as a historical overview; it is cut with the purpose of introducing the research techniques at work in the present book.

To reason well, or so a wide range of twentieth-century philosophers stipulated, one must start by properly defining one's concepts. It has to be clear what exactly particular terms do and do not allude to. Wittgenstein underscored this normative position when, in his *Tractatus Logico-Philosophus*, he wrote, "The whole sense of the book might be summed up in the following words: what can be said at all can be said clearly, and what we cannot talk about we must pass over in silence." In the decades that followed its publication, Wittgenstein spent a long time outside academia, and once he returned, it was this very phrase that he began to hollow out. Why, he asked, do philosophers spend so much effort on clearly outlining their concepts, while elsewhere, in ordinary settings, people manage very well without conceptual precision? If two friends play a game of tennis in the morning and one of chess in the afternoon, they do not need to wonder what exactly the word *game* refers to. What is more, in ordinary practices, words often do not *refer* at all. Rather than functioning as a label, they form part the action. Take two builders. If one of them yells "Stone!" to the other, he is not denoting an object, but giving an order: "Hand me that stone!" Spoken in another tone of voice, this same word "stone" might be a request: "Could you hand me that stone, please?" Wittgenstein's *Philosophical Investigations*, published in 1955, is packed with such ultrashort stories about ordinary events which succinctly convey his theoretical messages. Taken together, they undermine the idea that normative rules for the use of language add something significant to the practices that elude them.[24]

Wittgenstein's stories are quasi-ethnographic snapshots of ordinary language use. They show that such language use does not meet the standards of clarity and consistency, but that this does not mean things necessarily fall apart in practice. People get by very well with fuzzy and adaptable speech. Hence, or so Wittgenstein argued, the norms of 'proper language use' that philosophers try to erect are superfluous. They have nothing of value to add to a reality that does not take heed of them. In the work of Michel Foucault, empirical studies were made to do philosophical work in a different way. Foucault did not say that the norms dreamed up by philosophers have little salience for social practices. Instead, he argued that the norms that philosophers take to be transcendental are always already part of the society from which they emerge. Hence, they are not counterfactual, but belong to the same discursive field as the realities they are meant to critique. Foucault supported his arguments with detailed empirical studies of French historical archives. Drawing on these, he demonstrated that over the last few centuries conceptual repertoires, social institutions, and material arrangements had been formed and transformed together. Norms came and went as part of discourses, that is along with the socio-material configurations that they helped to foster and legitimate.

A particular norm that Foucault worked on was that of 'normality.' He pointed out that in modern societies populations are governed not just by means of lawlike rules set by kings or governments, but also through divisions between 'normal' and 'abnormal' made by professionals—from linguists to physicians. While people who transgress rules may be punished for this, people who do not meet standards of normality instead try to improve themselves to avoid ending up in the margins. People from the French provinces learn to speak 'normal French' and submit themselves to standards decided on by a Parisian committee of experts. If they maintain their local linguistic variety, they remain stuck in the provinces. By analogy, if people are sick or insane, they tend to seek out professionals for advice, pills, therapy, or some other intervention, hoping that this will return them to normality. The norms of grammar, health, and sanity are therefore far from counterfactual. They do not afford critical distance so much as they allow for the normalizing governance of populations.[25] What follows? Foucault's analyses have widely been read as pessimistic declarations that, in one way or another, the doings of people in modern societies are all firmly disciplined. End of story. However, Foucault's work may also be read as an activist call to escape. Or, as he put it in an often-quoted phrase (for which I cannot find the reference): "My job is making windows where there were once walls." If historical investigations show that things used to be otherwise, this offers the promise that they might become different again. And maybe they already are, somewhere else. As criticism is inevitably caught in the terms of those being criticized, it may be wiser to go out, run, play. Experiment with alternatives.

Hence, while Wittgenstein undermined the salience of crafting transcendental norms, Foucault cast doubt on their transcendence. And while Wittgenstein recounted anecdotes from everyday life to show that language-in-practice does not bow to philosophical norms, Foucault used archival materials to demonstrate that norms do not oppose the societies in which they occur, but help to sustain them. Another way to undermine the idea that philosophical notions reside in the transcendental realm was to show that philosophical treatises inevitably contain traces of the empirical realities relevant to their authors. Lolle Nauta called these *exemplary situations*. He adapted this term from the *exemplars* about which Thomas Kuhn wrote when describing how scientific knowledge is taught. When students learn about Newtonian physics, Kuhn contended, they are provided not just with wide-ranging theories, but also with exemplary demonstrations. To get a grasp on what 'gravity' entails, they are shown a ball that rolls down an inclined plane; to gain a sense of 'force,' they observe a demonstration of a spring pulled out of shape and then returning to its former position.[26] By analogy, or so Nauta proposed, philosophical texts become easier to understand if we dig out the empirical incidents that inform them. If Sartre wrote that 'the human' is a stranger to other humans, Nauta suggested that the *exemplary situation* behind this was a Parisian sidewalk cafe where solitary people sip coffee or pastis while eying strangers. Similarly, while philosophers used to read Locke as an author who wrote about 'property' in the abstract, attending to the empirical realities at stake showed that his concerns were rather practical: Could English gentlemen own land in North America? When Locke argued that land ownership follows from working the land, and that the way Native Americans lived off the land did not count as 'working,' he was defending his personal right to own property in the colonies.[27]

Exemplary situations may infiltrate philosophical texts in many ways. They may travel along with an evocative term, as they do when Sartre writes about 'strangers'; or they may hide in a concern, as they do in the case of Locke's musings about property. Metaphors form another possible conduit.

Take the famous 'argument is war,' which forms the opening case in George Lakoff and Mark Johnson's book *Metaphors We Live By*.[28] Philosophers used to present their preferred conversational format, that of 'rational argumentation,' as a peaceful alternative to violence. But, Lakoff and Johnson pointed out, they talked about it in bellicose terms. One may *win* or *lose* an argument, *attack* an *opponent*, *defend* oneself against such an *attack*, be more or less *tactical* or devise a long-term *strategy*. After a lecture presented in a philosophy department, the discussion period was opened with an inviting *'shoot!'* The metaphorical transposition of war language into argumentative settings is not just a verbal ploy. Philosophers did not just talk about *winning* an argument; they also avidly tried to *win*—for *losing*, they feared, would turn them into *losers*. That is to say: this metaphorical register was at work in departments of philosophy around 1980 and not just in the US, where *Metaphors We Live By* was published that year. I remember all too well how it also permeated intellectual practices in the Netherlands. This has changed. These days, academic conversations are no longer primarily staged as quasi-wars, fights over which univocal truth deserves to rule. Instead, they are cast as a matter of *exchanging* ideas, as if the academy is a marketplace where goods are bought and sold. *Ownership* has become important. For instance, behind crucial terms in a text, the name of an author may get added in parentheses: "(Foucault, 1973)." In this way ideas become intellectual property, to be protected by trademarks. A remarkable shift it is, and it provides another example of an empirical reality that speaks from ways of wording and their metaphorical resonances.

The empirical realities embedded in philosophical theories may also take the shape of traveling models. The work of Michel Serres provides endless examples of this. For instance, Serres has pointed out that Western philosophy is infused with models of stable, solid structures, while lacking in fluid or fire-like equivalents.[29] As part of this, there is an investment in transitive relations that may be thought of as modeled on wooden boxes. If box A is bigger than box B, then B fits into A and not the other way around. But if A and B are bags made of cloth then B, the smaller one, may hold a folded A inside it. This means that cloth offers a model for intransitive relations. Or take time as an example. This is imagined in a linear way as stretched out along a solid ruler: the present has left the past behind, while the future is still to come. But what, or so Serres proposed, if we were to model time on a handkerchief? When the handkerchief is stretched out flat, once again the past is over and the time ahead has not yet imposed itself. But a handkerchief may also be crumpled up, this suggests that the past may still be at work in the here and now, while the future may be acute, threatening or calling. A final example, should philosophers define concepts in a clear and distinct way? Wittgenstein said that in ordinary practices people get by very well without such solidity. Serres, in his turn, wondered about the effects of hardening concepts: this, he said, stifles thinking. Reflections become subtler when their terms are supple; philosophy is more versatile when ways of wording are allowed to transform viscously. In a turn against an excess of solidity, Serres proposed alternative models to think with: muddy places where water and land mix, clouds first forming and then dissipating into rain, curving paths that twist and turn, fires that consume what they encounter.

Serres is inventive. He does not just indicate the empirical realities embedded in existing theories: he 'goes out to play.' He leaves ordinary practices, historical narratives, vested exemplary situations, well-worn metaphors, and solid models behind and experiments with alternatives. In this way, new things get articulated. These 'new things' are not better in any absolute or transcendental sense. They do not ultimately fit standards for proper philosophy that his predecessors failed to meet. Instead, they allow for other things to be remarked on, and they speak to different concerns. This way of working forms a source of inspiration for the present book. Twentieth-century philosophical anthropology fostered the hope that the ability to think and engage in conversations might help humans to rise above physical violence. But in thus celebrating rationality, philosophical anthropology downgraded physical *labor* and elevated humans above other creatures. This does not help when we seek to address concerns pertaining to ecological fragility. The Anthropocene requires us to revisit what we make of *anthropos*. Our theories are in dire need of other terms. Serres played with cloths, fluids, and fires as alternative models with which to think.[30] My theoretical inspiration in this book comes, by contrast and complement, from diverse exemplary situations that all have to do with eating.

Empirical Multiplicity

When the divide between them is bridged, when *empirical* and *philosophy* are pasted together, this transforms them both. Philosophy, as I just recounted, is brought down to earth. It is prompted to take lessons from ordinary practices; it is situated in the societal setting from which it emerged; and it may be read as infused with immanent exemplars, metaphors, and models. In line with this, reading philosophical texts no longer stands in contrast to probing historic archives or doing ethnographic research, but becomes its own kind of empirical inquiry. At the same time, engaging in empirical inquiry changes, too, and that alteration forms the topic of the present section. The short version is that doing research is no longer understood as learning about a reality that passively waits to be represented. Instead, the reality under study shifts and changes depending on the intricacies of the study. Different operationalizations bring to bear different versions of reality. There are diverse stories to tell about this transformation. The one that I have on offer here starts once again with Wittgenstein and his call to learn from the ways in which language is used in ordinary practices. It then moves on to Foucault's insistence on divergence between discourses. Finally, I will exemplify what it means to say that reality is multiple by coming back, as promised, to the idea that women 'have only their biological sex in common.' Biological sex, indeed, is not just one thing; it comes in different versions.

Back to the beginning. While at first Wittgenstein contributed to the search for solid concepts, his later work demonstrated that, in ordinary practice, people get by very well with fluid terms. What did that mean for empirical research? While philosophers had thought that they needed solid concepts to reason well, empirical researchers called on solid concepts to ensure that dispersed findings could be added together into a coherent whole. They feared that loosening up on conceptual rigor would lead on to fragmentation. Based on the insights he gained by analyzing ordinary practices, Wittgenstein suggested that between firm coherence and radical fragmentation, there are looser ways of hanging together. Among these are, for instance, the *language games* that stipulate the use of words in a given practice. When two friends are playing chess, the word *king* evokes a piece on their chessboard; when they talk politics, the word *king* recalls a head of state. These are seriously different *kings*, but this does not lead to confusion. After all, between playing chess and talking politics, the two friends shift language games. In one case, the word *king* is part of a linguistic repertoire that also includes *board*, *pawn*, and *checkmate*; in the other, other relevant terms are *constitution* and *good governance*. If research rules impose the use of uniform concepts, this means that some language games triumph and others are silenced. Whatever does not fit the winning definition cannot be articulated.

If Wittgenstein's language games are tied to practices, Foucault's *discourses* include the societal *conditions of possibility* that allowed for their emergence and their salience. For instance, by the mid-twentieth century, the French law treated men who had sex with men as criminals, while, according to psychiatry, they suffered from a neurosis. The juridical system dreamed up punishments for offenders; psychiatric clinics offered treatments meant to transform effeminate deviants into *real* men. (Incidentally: since gay men were considered to be effeminate they, quite like women, always risked, if outed, being disqualified as philosophers.) But though legal and psychiatric discourses varied, both discredited male homosexuality and wished it away. Foucault, seeking to underline that this was not self-evident, presented a contrasting discourse that he found reading ancient Greek sources. Interestingly, these sources appeared to celebrate sex between men. What is more, they did not cast men who engaged in homosexual acts as effeminate. A man's masculinity depended not on *whom* he had sex with, but on *how much* sex he had. The proper masculine thing to do, no matter with whom one did it, was to refrain from overdoing it. Whether a free man lay with women, slaves, or young boys, he was supposed to be moderate. Foucault's conclusion was that neither 'homosexuality' nor 'masculinity' are stable configurations. They are understood and lived in different ways from one era to another. Holding up moderation as a masculine virtue inspires different sexual practices than (legally) forbidding gay sex or (psychiatrically) taking heterosexuality to be an instantiation of normality.[31]

Hence, each in his own way, both Wittgenstein and Foucault suggested that diverse socio-material formations and ways of using words make diverse 'realities' possible. Along with the work of many kindred authors, this inspired new ways of understanding the sciences. Here scientific meddling with the difference between the sexes may serve as an example. When, in the 1960s, Else Barth turned against stereotypes of 'the woman,' she proposed that 'women' have only their biological sex in common. But do they? When reexamined this appeared to be an all-too-simple way of putting it. For 'biological sex' means something different in the *language games* of diverse biological disciplines, or, in other terms, is ordered differently in concurrent biomedical *discourses*. Take anatomy and endocrinology.[32] Anatomy depends on the practice of cutting up corpses in order to visually inspect their insides. In line with this, it suggests that the sex of bodies may be read from the spatial arrangement of their organs: a woman has a womb, a vagina, labia, and breasts. In endocrinology, by contrast, biochemical techniques are used to measure hormone levels in blood drawn from living people. The definition of woman now depends on levels of estrogen and progesterone that, between menarche and menopause, change in rhythmic alternation. These versions of reality do not necessarily add up: a person may have a womb but low levels of estrogen; or her breasts may have been removed, while her menstruation is still regular. As a technique for contraception, anatomy suggests the use of condoms or diaphragms to block the passage of swimming sperm. Endocrinology, by contrast, offers 'the pill,' which contains hormones that interfere with the gestation of eggs. Hence, anatomy and endocrinology do not simply represent 'biological sex' differently. They also interfere with women, men, and heterosexual practices in different ways.[33]

This, then, is the particular way of understanding 'empirical' that *empirical philosophy* allowed for. The term *empirical* does not call up a univocal reality that the sciences represent in complementary ways. Instead, different knowledge practices interfere with reality in contrasting ways. Disciplines like anatomy and endocrinology may well share the term *woman*, but the term evokes different realities. Between these realities there are both tensions and interdependencies—in other words, reality is multiple.[34] This means that stating, or denying, *in general* that women have their 'biological sex' in common becomes rather vacuous. Instead, the issue arises as to which specific version of sex is realized, where, and to what effect? What do various branches of biomedicine depend on, orchestrate into being, or push aside? Along with these questions, normativity comes down to earth. It no longer resides in a transcendental realm of counterfactuals, nor is it flattened out by indisputable factuality. Instead, it resides in the contrasts between different ways of ordering, different versions of reality, all equally immanent. Critique takes a different shape: one mode of ordering may come to figure as the counterfactual of another. In the absence of an external, transcendental, position, normative questions cannot be answered in absolute terms. But they can still be asked. Not just by philosophers, in the abstract, but concretely, here, now, by everyone engaged in a particular practice.[35]

Eating

While in this book I recall philosophical anthropology—remembering it so as to interfere with it—I take inspiration from eating. But what is eating? Like 'king,' 'man,' or 'woman,' eating is not just a single thing. The word figures in diverse language games; the activity is shaped differently in different discourses. Eating comes in versions. This book, then, will not reveal what eating *really* is. Instead, I will work with selected versions of eating, handpicked to serve my theoretical purposes. While musing about *eating in theory* for years on end, I have ethnographically studied *situations of eating* in a range of sites. Most of my fieldwork I did in places I could easily reach by bicycle or train from the urban settings in the Netherlands where I have been living all this time. In health care facilities, I learned that eating may be difficult to do if one has no appetite or a hard time swallowing. In laboratories, I came across versions of eating that included ingesting nutrients, savoring flavors, or feeling satisfaction. In restaurants, I ate foods from diverse cuisines. In conferences, I heard speakers argue about the health effects of different foods, or deplore the depletion of earthly resources. And so on. I also learned a great deal from reading diverse literatures pertaining to food and/or eating (see for this and other scholarly relations the references in the endnotes!).[36] Thanks to a generous grant from the European Union, I worked with a team of spirited colleagues who were studying eating in yet more sites and situations. From them I learned about mundane tasting, global hunger, excretion, avoiding food waste, irrigation, kitchen fats, earthworms, and attempts to lose weight. Putting our newly gained insights together during team lunches, dinners, and seminars, we gradually developed a kaleidoscopic understanding of 'eating' as a composite-in-tension. In this book I draw from this composite, time and again, whatever allows me to interfere in vested understandings of 'the human.'

The field research on which this book depends concerns all kinds of people eating, and in a few cases nonhuman creatures too. At the same time, I shamelessly write about my own eating. In part, this is a methodological shortcut. Me-the-eater allowed me-the-researcher easy access to all kinds of details that would be otherwise difficult to study. However, my use of the first person singular *I* is also a play on the tradition of philosophical anthropology. The philosophical anthropologists whose work I seek to recall, wrote *I* in order to take a first-person perspective. They prioritized the subject position because they were concerned about the ways in which both natural and social sciences studied people from the outside, as if they were objects. Their particular *I* was meant to be a tenacious reminder that 'the human' forms the center of his (maybe a *sic* again?) own individual experiences. Hence, when philosophical anthropologists wrote *I*, their story was not meant to be about themselves, but instead to have universal salience. Their topic was *the* subject. My topic is not *the* subject at all—there is no such thing. When I write about *my* eating, I seek to underline once more the specificity of every eater. *My* eating is marked by such idiosyncrasies as a reliable university salary, access to well-stocked shops, modest but sufficient cooking skills, and a taste for a few comforting food repertoires. Other people eat different foods, in different ways, with different costs to themselves and their surroundings. Sociology has ample categorizations on offer to pin down the differences between 'me' and 'other people.' These make it possible to write that we match or differ in class, gender, nationality, ethnicity, dis/abilities, and so on. Here, I will abstain from using these categories. I do not want to import them from the settings where they were coined and impose them on the materials I gathered. Sometimes they fit the eating practices I write about, but sometimes they do not. It would be possible to consider their pertinence in each case again, but that would readily derail this book and turn it into a different one.[37] Above, I wrote that I am not out to emancipate oppressed groups of people, but hope, in a feminist mode, to revalue the denigrated pursuits of those who engage in life-sustaining *labor*. In line with that, my empirical interest is also not in people and the differences and similarities between them. It is, instead, in eating practices that, when analyzed afresh, are theoretically salient.

The *I* in the pages of this book, then, does not evoke a universal subject, nor does it stand in for a focal point at the intersection of well-vested sociological categories. Instead it is a reminder of the specificity and situatedness of each and every eater. That this particular 'I' frequently is 'me' and that, at least in some ways, the author and exemplified eater in this volume share quite some overlap is rather arbitrary. It is a methodologically convenient incident.[38] One last caveat for now. This book is called *Eating in Theory*. But that does not mean that I have an alternative *theory of eating* on offer, let alone an alternative overall theory. The theory relevant to this project is not a grand scheme that holds smaller elements together in the way a large wooden box may hold smaller wooden boxes. It is rather like a cloth that may be wrapped around or, alternatively, is folded within what is being said and done. It is a repository of metaphors to write in, models to think with, ways of speaking and forms of responding. It is a style. It does not hover above the social sciences and the humanities, but allows for them. It affords them. This is not the kind of theory that one may build from scratch or transform in total, but it is still possible to interfere with it. That is what I set out to do here. I use stories about situations of eating to shake up prevailing understandings of *being, knowing, doing*, and *relating* in which a hierarchical version of 'the human' goes into hiding. Mind you, these interferences are just a beginning. They only become relevant if you happen to find them inspiring, run with them, and put one or two of them to work in your own writing.

2 Being

IN THE SUMMER OF 2012, I walked for ten days along the north coast of Brittany, following a short stretch of a long Grand Randonnée path. There are many such trails, marked by white and red signs and cutting through varied French landscapes. I was on holiday, but that did not stop me from being observant. Almost ten years earlier, on the other side of the Channel, the geographer John Wylie had walked the South West Coast Path in North Devon, England. His walk was not meant to be a holiday. He sought to "explore issues of landscape, subjectivity and corporeality."[1] In the tradition of British walking, Wylie's explorations let him experience a romantic self, "dizzied by extension and expanse."[2] In his retrospective musings, he expands on the trials and tribulations of walking over rough paths. He mentions slopes he had to climb and streams with slippery stepping stones. The difficulty of his walk prompts him to argue that walking does not simply embed the self *in* a landscape, because the walker, struggling to cope, also finds himself *up against* that landscape. He relates that he was not particularly fit and ended up with "bruised shoulders, aching hip-joints, kneecaps and, above all, heels and toes."[3] But his account also contains a celebration of troubles rewarded. Emerging from an intimate path in the woods, Wylie is overwhelmed by the immensity of the coast seen from the cliff edge. The splendor of this view prompts him "to be all eyes before a numinous configuration of wind, waves and contour."[4] On the continental side of the Channel, my Breton path likewise afforded me stunning views of lively water with rolling waves and marvelous rocks of different colors. In addition to all that splendor, I also happened to enjoy the walking itself and the small things I saw along the way: a remarkable gate, prehistoric gravestones, an interesting patch of flowers, a bird. I carried only a day pack and my trail was easy. If I was troubled at all, it was by hunger, thirst, and a recurrent sense of shakiness.

Most mornings, the shops in the villages from which I started out were still closed. More than a decade beforehand, I had stopped eating wheat, which had overnight dissolved a long-term nagging ache in my bowels and gradually improved my overall sense of health. But in a region where lovely wheat bread was the most readily available food, this made foraging difficult. Hence, for my lunches I made do with an apple and an egg grabbed from the hotel breakfast table, supplemented with a wheat-free muesli bar from my supplies. Not a lot for a walker. Hence, one memory of this holiday that stands out for me is an evening when, ravenous, I sat on the patio of a small restaurant and ate a large Breton buckwheat pancake with goat cheese and honey. I indulged in the delights that the various textures and tastes offered my palate, but even more in the feeling of reinvigoration that followed from my meal. What a blessing it was to eat! A memorable moment indeed. Wylie, by contrast, has nothing to say about eating. Or, to be precise: he *does* mention having lunch. "I stopped to eat and rest just past the Point." But immediately after the comma his geographer's attention moves to the *place* where he stopped: "by a recently erected stone and plaque commemorating the First World War hospital ship *Glenart Castle*, sunk by torpedo in the early hours of 26 February 1918."[5] Of course, landscapes become more interesting when one relates to their historical depth. But it still strikes me that Wylie mentions eating only in passing, as if it were intrinsically uninteresting.

There is a practical dimension to my surprise. Apparently, Wylie handles his foraging with ease, while for me juggling when, where, and what I might eat is a recurrent characteristic of extended walking—and not just because of the wheat. Beyond that, a theoretical disconcertment looms. How is it that so much writing on "issues of landscape,

WHITEMEN AND LIGHT FOOD
In his book *The Meaning of Whitemen: Race and Modernity in the Orokaiva Cultural World*, Ira Bashkow writes *whitemen* as a single word. That spelling best fits the understanding of the Orokaiva, a group of people in New Guinea with whom Bashkow conducted long-term fieldwork. Bashkow explains in great detail how Orokaiva people assess and appreciate the world, in line with his conviction that 'we anthropologists' should be "moving beyond our current obsession with self-critique, and opening ourselves to the manifold ways our undeniable power and wealth are actually

subjectivity and corporeality" manages to take eating for granted? For Wylie is by no means alone in showing little interest in the topic. In my duffel bag, that was transported for me by car from one small Breton hotel to another, I carried a hardback copy of *Ways of Walking*. This is an edited collection with twelve spirited chapters on walking in various contexts and parts of the world.[6] Once I had arrived in my sleeping spot for the night, I would dig it out and take true intellectual pleasure from it. But strangely enough, none of the chapters explores how walking relates to eating. Even the beautiful one about seminomads following their herds as they graze, does not attend to when, where, and what the humans ate. A similar absence marks the books that Wylie took along. "In my rucksack I carried, among other things, Deleuze's *The Fold*, Merleau-Ponty's *The Visible and the Invisible*, Lingis's *The Imperative*, Bachelard's *The Poetics of Space*. These materials circulated through footfalls, the sound of the waves, views along the chaotic, curving coastline, the sun setting over the sea."[7] No wonder Wylie's body suffered under so much weight. (This was at the very beginning of the twenty-first century, before it became technically possible to carry whole libraries in a single lightweight device.) But however heavy Wylie's books may have been, they shared a common omission. They all delegated food and drink to the background, as mere preconditions for what truly matters in human life: apprehending the world, acquiring an intellectual grasp and an emotional sense of it, as a subject moving through outstretched, all-embracing space.

One of the quests of twentieth-century philosophical anthropology was to bring cognition down to earth. Rather than presuming that *thought* resides in a transcendental realm, *thinking* was recognized as an immanent activity that humans engage in as part of their ongoing lives. Maurice Merleau-Ponty worked hard on this. He sought to tie the *cogito* to the *flesh*. While Descartes famously asserted that his *being* was proven by his *thinking*, Merleau-Ponty retorted that *I am* "to the extent that I have a body and that through that body I am at grips with the world."[8] The cogitating *I* that Descartes wrote about sought to disentangle himself from his physical location. Merleau-Ponty's 'body at grips with the world' was located somewhere, moved through surroundings, and this was important as it allowed for perception and hence cognition. Here is Merleau-Ponty again: "When I walk round my flat, the various aspects in which it presents itself to me could not possibly appear as views of one and the same thing if I did not know that each of them represents the flat seen from one spot or another, and if I were unaware of my own movements, and of my body as retaining its identity through the stages of those movements."[9] Merleau-Ponty proposed that he was able to perceive his flat as a unified dwelling because he could walk through it as an integrated body. His version of phenomenology, then, configured *being* in a particular way—as the being of an embodied human in the center of a three-dimensional world filled with varied entities. To stress the importance of this subject position, Merleau-Ponty did not call the subject 'he,' but 'I.' And this *I* was able to sense *my* body and perceive *my* surroundings, by changing *my* place while retaining *my* identity.[10]

What, I wonder, would happen to *being* if the exemplary situation that Merleau-Ponty uses to think with, walking through a flat, were replaced by another exemplary situation, eating a meal? Take, for instance, the case of my Breton restaurant meal of buckwheat pancake with goat cheese and honey. With each bite, I incorporated yet another fragment of the world that had still been outside me a moment ago. Gradually, the food disappeared from my plate, while I transformed from feeling shaky to feeling gratified. Water and a tisane added to my contentment. Once I was finished, I said 'thank you' to the waitress, paid the bill, rose from my chair, walked back to that day's hotel, went upstairs to the room assigned to me, read more of *Ways of Walking*, and enjoyed a good night's sleep. The following morning, I was able to pick up the trail again. In the course of that day, I returned food remnants and no longer welcome bodily excesses, in the form of urine and feces, to bushes and toilets.

understood and felt by others" (259). The Orokaiva *others* to whom Bashkow has opened up use 'whitemen' as a term for people who are light, not just in color, but also in other respects. Or, rather, not even necessarily in color, but certainly in other respects. The skin of their hands and feet is soft and not calloused from hard work. Their ties with other people are weak and they have few obligations. For how else would they be able to travel so lightly, so far away from home? They are not rooted. They do not eat heavy foods that they plant themselves, but light foods that they buy for money. According to Orokaiva, human beings take on the characteristics of the foods they eat. Orokaiva themselves mainly eat what they call heavy foods. Their main staple is taro, which makes their bodies grow strong, helps with sleeping, and ties eaters to the land from which they eat. On festive occasions, Orokaiva also eat pigs. People do not eat pigs raised in their own households; but only pigs distributed by others as gifts. This makes for its own kind of heaviness, that of outstanding obligations. If you have been given food by others, sooner or later, you have to feed them in return.

Eating is not situated low in some hierarchy for the Orokaiva. It is central to their world. "Histories of contact tend to emphasize guns, tools, and other durables as the primary media by which indigenous peoples came to know the nature and the mettle of whitemen. Yet from the perspective of Melanesian peoples, it was food that constituted the most sa-

What might these incidents teach us about *being*? Here is the bottom line: as an eater I do not first and foremost apprehend my surroundings, but become mixed up with them. The edible parts of those surroundings, in their turn, wherever they were located beforehand, become assembled inside me. I analyze this in more detail below.[11] In doing so, I discuss an additional exemplary situation that informs Merleau-Ponty's writings. For next to musing about walking through his flat, he thinks with the fate of soldiers with head-wounds for whom walking poses problems. I contrast the problems of those soldiers with stories about (sometimes easy, sometimes difficult) incorporations of food and excorporations of bodily excesses. These stories do not explicate what eating *is* in general, but what *may be*, what it was in the specific, socio-material circumstances of my fieldwork. The hope is that exploring situations of eating may help to reimagine *being* as a transformative engagement of semipermeable bodies with a topologically intricate world.

Neuromuscular and Metabolic

Merleau-Ponty sought to bring *thought* down to earth by situating *thinking* inside human bodies. He contended that thought does not develop in some abstracted conceptual realm, if only because thinking is a practical achievement tied to the perceptive and motor engagements of the embodied subject with his ('my') surroundings. To stay focused, I attend to just one of his books, *The Phenomenology of Perception*, published in 1945. In line with earlier contributions to phenomenology, Merleau-Ponty here criticized objective styles of knowing, propagated by both the natural and the just recently emerging social sciences. He argued that human experience does not pertain to 'the' world, an objective reality, but to 'my' world, which presents itself to me, a perceiving subject. At the time, perception was avidly studied in neurology, and Merleau-Ponty read up on this. The neurologists he cited were concerned with the difficulties people may have in integrating their perceptions and coordinating their voluntary muscles in order to function as an integrated whole. This concern with the neuromuscular system had been spurred on by the First World War. Extended trench warfare during that period had caused stunningly high numbers of young men to die, while wounding many others. In their clinical practice, neurologists were confronted with veterans who had bullets and shrapnel fragments in their heads. As it was received wisdom that damaged brain cells do not heal and are not replaced, most neurologists were therapeutic pessimists. Some, however, argued that even in cases in which neurological structures were irretrievably damaged, their functions may nevertheless be partially regained. They asserted that well-targeted training may stimulate other, undamaged, parts of the neural system to take over. Rehabilitation medicine took off.

Worth mentioning in this context is the neurologist Kurt Goldstein, who had pioneered rehabilitation programs for German veterans. At first, his work had earned him high esteem. In the early 1930s, when the Nazis came to power, he fled Germany, which had become dangerous for a man who was both an outspoken socialist and a Jew. Temporarily in Amsterdam, with no patients to look after, Goldstein dictated the insights his work had afforded him to a secretary. Merleau-Ponty arranged for the resulting book to be translated from German into French for a phenomenological series of which he was the editor.[12] The volume appeared much later in English (in 1995) under the title *The Organism: A Holistic Approach to Biology Derived from Pathological Data in Man*.[13] Goldstein's book brims with clinical stories that testify to the various ways in which the neuromuscular system coheres. Damage done to just a tiny area may have effects throughout the entire body, while lost functions may be regained by adapting structures elsewhere that are still intact. One of Goldstein's patients was a man whom he called Schneider. Schneider had trouble moving, could no longer answer simple questions, and was unable to link his perceptions together in a meaningful way. Merleau-Ponty

lient medium of intercultural communication given indigenous notions of the person, truth, and knowledge" (154). These indigenous conceptions gave precedence to what is hidden over what lies on the surface; they valued what people ate over the appearance of their skin. The whitemen who landed in Papua New Guinea ate rice, since, when dry, it cannot rot and is relatively easy to transport. Their proteins came in the form of canned mackerel and corned beef, jointly called *tinmeats* by the Orokaiva. These foods gave the strangers away. "When whites fed these foods [rice, tinmeats] to the carriers, policemen, and villagers who helped them, they were thereby revealing themselves to Orokaiva, showing what was inside of them, who they were" (154). Eaters of light food, that is who they were. All the more, as they kept their food hidden. "When Orokaiva saw that rice and tinmeats were the foods whites carried with them from the faraway hidden places from whence they came, hiding them in their patrol boxes and storerooms under lock and key, it only made sense for Orokaiva to identify these foods with the whitemen's innermost nature" (154).

I disentangle these few lines from Bashkow's rich analysis to underscore that it is not *human* to consider eating to be lowly, a mere precondition for more important things—such as thinking. This particular hierarchical ordering may haunt the Western philosophical tradition, but it makes little sense in many other places, such as among the Orokaiva. Bashkow, meanwhile, draws other

learned from Schneider's fate that there is a connection between a person's ability to perceive his body as an integrated whole and his ability to integrate the world around him: "Although Schneider's trouble affects motility and thought as well as perception . . . what it damages, particularly in the domain of thought, is his power of apprehending simultaneous wholes, and in the matter of motility, that . . . of taking a bird's-eye view of movement and projecting it outside himself."[14] If left to his own devices, Schneider bruised himself by bumping into tables and chairs. This brings into relief that it is quite an achievement that most humans are able to avoid bumping into furniture standing in their way. It is thanks to an integrated body scheme that *I* am able to orient myself in space and live in a meaningful world.

Since Merleau-Ponty's argument was with a philosophical tradition in which 'thought' is disentangled from fleshy realities, Goldstein had a lot to offer. The troubles of brain-damaged soldiers made it painfully clear that the cogito depends on an intact brain. The concern from where my comments start is not that this is wrong, but that it leaves a lot unanalyzed. For instance, eating. The integrity of human beings depends not only on an intact brain but also on regularly filling one's stomach. Obviously, Merleau-Ponty knew very well that humans only thrive as long as they eat, but he did not pursue the topic. Put in biomedical terms: Merleau-Ponty imported a *neuromuscular* version of the body into *The Phenomenology of Perception*, taking the body's *metabolism* for granted. Goldstein, living and working in an impoverished Germany, never forgot that people's vitality depends on their eating. With this in mind, he campaigned (in vain) for better veteran pensions. The rehabilitation programs that he helped to develop sought to equip wounded veterans with skills that might allow them to do paid work. The hope was that it would be easier for families to care for their brain-damaged sons, husbands, and fathers if those men were at least able to earn their keep. But if metabolic concerns informed Goldstein's rehabilitation practice, they did not permeate his neurological theories. And it was only the neurological theories that formed a source of inspiration for Merleau-Ponty.

On his walk through Devon, Wylie had lunch close to a plaque commemorating a hospital ship sunk by a torpedo in February 1918. The villages along my walking trail in Brittany also invariably displayed memorials for soldiers killed during the First World War. By the time I arrived, they had been dead for almost a century. I read out their names, cut into marble plaques. It made me all the more grateful to be alive and so much older, too, than these men were when they died. However, my hunger and shakiness vividly reminded me that bodies are always fragile, even in the absence of war. Without nourishment, I would fall apart, not in a few days, maybe, but still surprisingly fast. Hunger strikers, if they accept fluids, rarely survive for more than a month or two. Elderly people who starve themselves to dead tend to be gone in less than a week. Survival cannot be taken for granted. Current estimates state that one in eight inhabitants of the globe is undernourished, while many more are malnourished, which means they ingest enough calories, but not enough nutrients.[15] This is a sad reality that in a philosophical tradition invested in *thinking*—however embodied—is all too easily forgotten. *I am* only to the extent that I exchange stuff with my surroundings.

Outside/Inside Boundaries

The ability to move depends on having had enough to eat. But eating, in turn, depends on the ability to move—if not necessarily one's legs, then at least the muscles of one's throat. In order for food to feed a body, it has to be incorporated. The classic way of doing this is by swallowing.[16] When this is easy, a person swallowing may barely notice the muscular activity involved; this comes to the fore only when it poses a problem. That is why I went to a rehabilitation clinic not too far from my Dutch home to learn about swallowing. The care that I witnessed there builds on the work of people like Goldstein. It targets

lessons from his fieldwork. For one, these are lessons about *race*. Differentiating between races, he argues, is not necessarily tied to physical appearance. Race can be indicated by other things, such as what people eat. In this form, it may endure even in the absence of the people who are perceived to be different. These days, most Orokaiva encounter few white-skinned people in their daily lives. However, as they have come to associate *whitemen* with light food, it is now that food itself—rice, tinmeats—that indexes whiteness for them. Most of them are ambivalent about this *light food*. Its lightness is attractive in that it promises freedom from the heaviness of the soil and of social obligations. Light food's colorful packaging also serves as an attractive adornment to the piles of heavy foods that people offer to their guests on festive occasions. At the same time, light food is indicative of *whitemen's* most despicable trait: they do not share. If one of them is richer than another, the rich one does not give away his possessions to those who are poor. *Whitemen* even go so far as to leave others hungry while they themselves have enough to eat and money to buy more. Money! To acquire whitemen's food one needs money. "To Orokaiva, the notion that a person should need money simply in order to eat is deeply immoral" (181).

A second lesson Bashkow draws concerns cultural distinctness. He notes that many anthropologists shy away from affirming alterity because they presume that countering injustices depends on

people whose swallowing is hampered because their brains are damaged, not so much by bullets or shrapnel fragments as by traffic accidents or cerebro-vascular accidents (that is to say, the bursting or the blocking of a brain ar-tery). Rehabilitation starts from the therapeutic hope that with careful train-ing, the lost ability to swallow may be regained.

In her consulting room, the speech therapist of the Woodland Rehabilitation Clinic laid out the basics of swallowing for me.[17] She sketched a throat, cut open in a sagittal plane, with the windpipe in front and the esophagus at the back. "That," she said, pointing with her pen to the esophagus, "is where the food should go as we swallow. And there," she added, her pen now on the windpipe, "is where it shouldn't go." After some further exchanges, she took me upstairs to a man whom I will call Mr. Kramer.[18] The day before, when she had asked him if she might bring an observer, Mr. Kramer had nodded yes. Now, as we entered his room, his left hand lay flaccid on a cushion and his left leg, para-lyzed as well, was hidden under his bed covers. With his right hand he gave each of us a firm handshake. This he could do, but he could not control the muscles of his throat and hence could not swallow. Neither could he talk. Mr. Kramer's wife, who was keeping him company, seemed glad to talk. The speech therapist listened for a while to the sad stories she told about their recent difficulties and then turned to Mr. Kramer.

She looked at him, caught his gaze. And she spoke calmly and clearly: "There we go, Mr. Kramer. We will work a bit more on your swallowing. You up to that?" He nodded. She then gave instructions, putting into words what usu-ally goes without saying. "Please, close your lips, close your teeth, push up your tongue to your palate. And think 'I am going to swallow, I am going to swallow'." From where I was sitting on a stool at the foot end of the bed, out of the way, I could see Mr. Kramer was trying, and trying again. But he failed. With one of her hands, the therapist then gently massaged his throat from the outside. This, too, she did again and again, but to no avail. Her next recourse was to set an example that he might mimic. "Please, look at me, Mr. Kramer. I will swallow along with you." And she did—a few times, and a few more. Mr. Kramer's wife remarked that all these efforts made her swallow, swallow like mad, she said. But her husband looked defeated. He just could not do it.

When a bit later, the speech therapist gave up for the day, Mrs. Kramer be-gan to talk again. With a smile now brightening her face, she said that last night their two children had both come to visit. For the first time since the brain in-jury had occurred, they had had a good time together as a family. Her daughter had brought apple juice and home-baked cookies. Mr. Kramer had looked on with great longing and pointed with his healthy arm at the cookies. "So we gave him some," his wife said. "Just a bit for the taste." The therapist was aghast. She tried hard to stay calm, but to also make herself clear: "Well, Mrs. Kramer, your husband is missing out on a lot right now. He truly is. But please, don't do that again. For as long as he cannot swallow, whatever enters his mouth may end up in his lungs. They cannot cope with that, his lungs. It may sound harsh of me to say this, but, you know, we see people die from things like that."

Swallowing is a skilled movement that depends on the intricate coordination of various throat muscles. A wounded brain may be unable to pull it off: Mr. Kramer understood what he was asked to do, but he could not do it. Moreover, incorporation does not just mean that food travels from the *outside* to the *inside* of the body. There are further spatial differentiations one has to reckon with. In the throat, food has to be propelled to the esophagus and not the windpipe. In 'normal swallowing' this is done without thinking, although laughing or talking may interfere with it. If it does, the art is to cough up the food that went down the wrong way into the windpipe. In people unable to control their throat muscles, things easily go the wrong way. And misplaced crumbs cannot be coughed up again, as the ability to cough is most likely hampered, too. Lungs respond to alien stuff with inflammation, which breaks the continuity of

holding on to a universal human and inclusive humankind. But Orokaiva, Bashkow says, happen to cherish their own distinctness. They hold on to their own views in the face of whatever *ideas* others (including anthropologists) may have about them. Orokaiva readily make sense of strange ideas on their own terms. Strange *things* are more problematic. That is to say, some things have proven easy to incorporate in Orokaiva practices, such as axes that make it easier to work one's garden. Others, however, were more disruptive, such as houses designed for just one nuclear family, which disrupted earlier ways of living together. Currently, however, Orokaiva ways of living are threatened most by a recently imported *practice*. This practice is growing cash crops such as coffee, cocoa, and especially oil palms. People engage in this because it provides them with money, which allows them to buy rice, tinmeats, and other items of white food that, as just mentioned, they use to adorn their festive meals. But, at the same time, setting aside fields for cash crops diminishes the space dedicated to growing local foods that villagers do not sell, but eat themselves. It also shortens the time that land is allowed to recuperate by lying fallow. Growing cash crops is diabolical: "In making people dependent on market commodity prices and relations of production, it furthers their transformation from free people centered in a world that belongs to them, where their livelihood and place is secure, to vulnerable peasants in a world economy to which they are mar-

the cell linings. This allows microbes to find a way in, and pneumonia ensues. For patients whose condition is poor to begin with, this is an assault hard to overcome. Among those who have difficulties swallowing, pneumonia is a common cause of death.

Here is the lesson for being. Merleau-Ponty's subject is able to walk around his apartment as long as his neuromuscular body works as an integrated whole. Its integration allows it to remain distinct from its surroundings, to avoid bumping into tables and chairs.[19] The configuration of an eating *I* is different. In the rehabilitation clinic, it becomes apparent that this figure incorporates bits of her surroundings into her body by swallowing them. This is a delicate thing to do, as food that passes the bodily boundary formed by the lips, mouth, and throat should not end up in the lungs but be steered into the gastrointestinal tract. Hence, while a walking body hangs together as a whole, an eating body is spatially differentiated. Distinct body parts relate to foodstuff in different ways. The gastrointestinal tract may welcome cookies; the lungs do not. In eating, then, *I am* a semipermeable, internally differentiated being, getting enmeshed in intricate ways with pieces of my surroundings.[20]

Like other muscular movements, the movements on which incorporation depends falter if crucial parts of the brain are destroyed. Training may allow one to regain the ability to swallow. But Mr. Kramer had not yet achieved it. Hence, a tube was inserted in one of his nostrils, guided through his throat, steered into his esophagus, and then pushed all the way into his stomach. Through this passage he was being fed. When people like Mr. Kramer remain unable to swallow for an extended period of time, they may be equipped with another kind of tube, one that enters their body through a hole cut through the skin of the belly and then through their stomach wall. Through this tube viscous foods contained in a bag may be gently squeezed into their gastrointestinal tract. Leaking (especially leaking between skin and stomach wall) is to be avoided.[21] But here is a puzzle. Even if food has reached the gastrointestinal tract, it is not necessarily inside the body.

In Grey Home, a residential facility for the elderly, Mrs. Ormel was slowly dying. A care assistant I will call Stella cautiously entered Mrs. Ormel's room, allowing me to follow her. On the kitchen counter, a few packages of fortified banana-flavored drinking yogurt were waiting. Stella poured a small amount from one of these packages into a tiny plastic cup. "This stuff," she said to me, "is heavy on the stomach. It would even be heavy on the stomach for healthy people like

us. *If Mrs. Ormel were to ingest a lot of it,* ginal and easily replaceable" (238). How-
she would give it back again, throw it up." ever well-meaning the insistence on 'our'
But Stella explained, it contained "every- shared human nature may be, for Oro-
thing you need"—nutrients, minerals, fi- kaiva it is not particularly a blessing to be
ber. Then Stella sat down next to Mrs. Or- absorbed in 'humankind.'
mel's head, gently woke the old lady, and
talked her through swallowing a few sips
of yogurt. "Is it nice?" she asked encouragingly. Mrs. Ormel answered with a
barely perceptible nod. When, sip after minute sip, the tiny cup was finally emp-
tied, Stella promised she would be back with more later. And so she was, several
times over the course of her working day.

I mentioned this incident in a talk on the topic of good care that I gave a
few months later during a study day for managers and professionals of nursing
homes. The talk was my return gift for fieldwork access, but it turned out to be
a crucial part of the fieldwork. For when I had finished, a nurse specialized in
elderly care stood up to say that what Mrs. Ormel had received was bad care.
The care assistant may have had good intentions, she said, but when a person is
dying, the nutrients contained in fortified yogurt will no longer cross her bowel
linings. Moreover, in a dying person, who has little to no bowel motility, the fi-
bers, meant to speed up the food's transit, are more likely to cause a blockage in-
stead. A small glass of cordial would have done a lot more to quench Mrs. Or-
mel's thirst, while its sugars, so much easier to absorb, might have perked her
up a bit. The nurse did not blame Stella, but argued that someone higher up in
the home's hierarchy should alter the care plans and see to it that all the care-
givers be educated accordingly.[22]

I hope that someone 'higher up' took heed of that advice. Here this nurse's
intervention allows me to draw another lesson: it is not obvious where incorporation happens, where food goes from the body's outside to its inside.
If food has passed the swallowing throat, or reached the stomach through
a tube penetrating skin and stomach wall, it is inside the body's anatomical
outlines. But it is not inside what in physiological terms is called its *internal
milieu*. To get to there, it has to be broken down small enough to be transported across the bowel lining and the walls of one of the tiny blood vessels
that border it. In a situation like the one in which Mrs. Ormel found herself, a
body appears to have two boundaries, one between the outside and the inside
of its overall shape; the other between its external and its internal milieu.[23]
In practice, these boundaries may be ordered sequentially, with food first

crossing the first and then the second. But the two boundaries may also be in tension.

A colleague tells me about a company producing fortified yogurts. As long as insurance plans in the Netherlands pay for these yogurts, was the idea, dieticians were likely to prescribe them. However, if the insurance companies were to change their policies, the yogurt company would be in trouble since fortified yogurts are costly, and most 'end users' do not particularly like them. If people had to pay for them out of their own pockets, they might go for tastier foodstuffs. Consequently, the company convened a range of experts to explore possibilities for improving the yogurts' taste. There were cooks and food technologists, concerned about taste, mouthfeel, and safe swallowing. For them, the body's inside started beyond the throat, once the difficult task of opening and closing the mouth and then swallowing was accomplished. There were also dieticians and nutrition scientists, concerned with the nutrients that had to be provided to different patient groups. For them, the body's inside started beyond the bowel lining; food in the stomach and the bowels still found itself on the outside. For quite a long time, the expert meeting was utterly confusing for all parties. Since they defined inside and outside differently, the experts kept on talking past each other.

COLONIAL BODIES

In her book *The Body of the Conquistador* Rebecca Earle takes us back to early colonial times. She writes about people who, as they traveled, overcame their regional differences and started to call themselves 'Spaniards.' At the end of their traveling, they settled as colonists in lands recently stolen from earlier inhabitants. They first called these lands 'the Indies' and later 'Latin America.' The Spanish settlers experienced their bodies neither as closed off nor as stable. Instead, while their bodily boundaries were porous, the substance of which they were made readily transformed. "Colonial writers throughout the sixteenth and seventeenth centuries agreed that people who traveled from Europe to the Indies were liable to undergo a variety of transformations, in accordance with the nature and celestial influence of the climate and as a result of eating new foods" (25). That bodies might so readily change befitted

Here it appears that the throat and the bowel lining do not necessarily come after each other harmoniously as two boundaries that foods subsequently cross. In the design of fortified yogurts they are in competition. Which one of them should one to attend to, which group of experts should one listen to, which is the more difficult or relevant boundary to cross?[24]

In hospitals that are rich and well-equipped enough, it is technically possible to circumvent both throat and bowel lining. A special bag of nourishment may be attached to an intravenous drip and, through a mediating, boundary-crossing needle, directly reach into the bloodstream. But even food that has made it to the bloodstream is not necessarily inside the body. Not in a functional sense. There are further boundaries to cross. And not only for the nutrients in the IV drips.

Maria, a dietician whose work I am allowed to observe, tries to explain to Mr. Herder what is going on beneath his skin. She takes a piece of paper and starts to draw. First a cell. "Let's say," she says, "that this is a cell in your body. Now if you eat"—and on another part of the paper she draws a cross-section of a bowel—"the sugar that you ingest enters your bloodstream, here, in your bowels. There it comes." She makes yellow dots dance over the paper all the way from bowel to cell. "And now this sugar knocks on the door of your cells." She draws a yellow dot near the cell and continues: "But the door is closed. Imagine it like this. The doors of your cells are locked and sugar needs a key to be able to enter. That key is insulin. Your doctor told you that you have diabetes, right? That means that right now, in your body, this key, insulin, is not working properly. That's why the sugar remains in your blood, it cannot enter your cells. It has no key. That's why you are tired, why you get irritated. Your cells have no energy! You may eat plenty, but your food simply cannot enter your cells. Now this medicine that the doctor prescribed to you, that holds substitutes for the key. It holds a molecule that allows the sugar molecules to cross the cell walls. And then your cells can do their work again."[25]

In the situation of a person with diabetes, the boundary between the *outside* and the *inside* of the body that is hardest to cross is hidden beneath the skin. It comes in the fragmented form of ever so many cell walls. The dietician uses the metaphor of the missing key to hint at what it takes to cross these walls. She recites that if cells are not being fed, this affects a person's *being*. To the core. You are tired. You get irritated. You have no energy. You lack nourishment.

This is the lesson for theory. Eating offers a model of *being* that is very different from that suggested by walking. For insofar as *I am* an eating body, my boundaries are crossed. For the life of me, I bite off, or slurp up, things from my surroundings and incorporate them into my body. Alternatively, someone else may shovel, push, or inject them into me. They cross a throat, bowel linings, the walls of my cells. They move from the outside to the inside, here

a humoral medical tradition that was concerned not with anatomical form or physiological function but, rather, with the balance, or lack thereof, between the four humors—blood, phlegm, black bile, and yellow bile. "Individuals possessed a particular humoral balance that helped to determine their 'complexion,' a term that referred equally to their character and their bodily qualities. People in whom black bile predominated were likely to be thin, dark and melancholic. Those with a predominance of blood were generally ruddy, outgoing and optimistic. Personality and physical appearance, in other words, were both manifestations of the same underlying complexion" (26).

In this setting, 'race'—a term not yet in use at the time—was neither attributed at birth, nor connected to bloodline. It depended instead on climate and food. This was challenging for the settlers, for it was difficult for them to maintain their strength and their European complexion so far away from home. They could not escape the climate in which they were steeped. Once settled in the colonies, they were subject to unfamiliar air, water, and stars. It might yet be possible to eat 'Spanish' foods: bread made out of wheat, red wine, olive oil, and the meat of cows, pigs, or sheep. Not that all people in Spain had access to such foods: poor people did not. They subsisted on gruel and porridge; if they were lucky, they ate rye bread and root vegetables. "Plants such as onions or turnips that grew under the ground were particularly suited to peasants, rather than in-

or there, but not just anywhere. The eating body's nourishment may travel some routes but not others. As an eater *I am* externally entangled and internally differentiated. What kind of *being* is that?

Changing and Staying the Same

As I eat, my body incorporates bits and pieces of the outside world. These form the building blocks from which I build myself. Over time, my eating has allowed me to turn from a child into an adult, but at some point, I stopped growing. Only when my children were growing in my womb did my belly blow up impressively; once they were born, I shrank again. I kept incorporating food though and thrived on the energy it contained. My eating has allowed me to go for walks. It has allowed me to breath, read, write, clean, cook, stay warm, and otherwise burn energy. Energy is material, all right, but it is not a thing a person may look at, hold in her hands or brush up against.[26] Instead, energy engenders processes; it allows for action. That in the morning after my Breton meal I was able to walk again, I owed to the energy that the buckwheat plants had caught from the sun and stored in their seeds, that flowers had turned into the nectar from which bees had made honey, and that grass had provided to the goats whose milk had been turned into my cheese.

On the internet I try to learn how much energy my body needed to walk the paths of Brittany. There is a website that differentiates between the number of calories needed for walking on grassy as opposed to paved paths. Another website asks me how long I walked and at what speed and also wants to know about my weight. Yet other websites want to know my age or if I am a man or a woman. Hence, ways of calculating my needs abound. And so, too, do ways of calculating the calories different foodstuffs contain. By law, every food package has to supply the relevant numbers and there are booklets and webpages detailing the calorie contents of unpackaged items. A lot of averaging and generalizing goes into such numbers. The apps that proudly promise they can keep track of food intake and expenditure may hope to provide rough approximations only.

What is more, the relation between intake and output is not as linear as biophysical tables make it seem. Some sports trainers suggest that when a body gains in muscle mass, it burns more calories, even when at rest. Some nutrition scientists propose that, although bodies absorb all the sugar they ingest, their uptake of other foods is selective. Others state that bodies adapt their biochemistry to the amounts they are provided with: when these are small, a body goes into 'saving mode.' This means that losing weight by dieting is tough if only because a starved body stocks up on every calorie it can grasp.[27]

And so on. Energy use is a contentious topic that I merely hint at here. What these few notes are meant to indicate is that as *I am* I simultaneously transform. Or: my form may stay the same, but my substance changes. Hence, one might say that I transubstantiate (although that term is difficult to use freely, since it has a different meaning elsewhere). My food alters in the process. From stuff on my plate it becomes *me*. From a buckwheat pancake with goat cheese and honey, it converts into energy for walking.

That my body does not continue to expand to the extent that it keeps eating, I do not just owe to its energy expenditure. It helps that from my bowels I excrete masses that I do not allow to pass through my bowel lining. It also helps that with my kidneys I expel excesses from my blood. Hence, I owe my particular kind of *being* not just to incorporations but to excorporations, too.

One fine spring evening, I have dinner at M.'s place. He has cooked asparagus—white asparagus, grown in the southern provinces of the Netherlands and only in season for a few weeks. These are typically eaten with boiled potatoes, boiled eggs, melted butter, and nutmeg. Meat eaters tend to add ham. The asparagus that M. has on offer have been carefully peeled: no hard threads spoil their lovely texture. We eat and talk. Just before leaving M.'s house, I retreat to the toilet so that I may travel home unencumbered by the need to pee. Then already,

dividuals higher up the Great Chain of Being, whose foods should come from correspondingly elevated locations such as the top of a tree" (60). In the homeland, then, *being* was also tied to what one ate. Low people ate low foods; high people ate high foods. In the Americas, acquiring sustaining, wholesome, Spanish high foods, that is, wheat bread, red wine, olive oil, and meat, was all the more important. For eating such foods would prevent Europeans from transforming into the people who ate local foods and whom they called 'Indians.' Simultaneously, there was hope for the 'Indians,' if only they would eat European food. "For early modern Spaniards food was much more than a source of sustenance and a comforting reminder of Iberian culture. Food helped make them who they were in terms of both their character and their very corporeality, and it was food, more than anything else, that made European bodies different from Amerindian bodies. Without the right foods Europeans would either die, as Columbus feared, or, equally alarmingly, they might turn into Amerindians. With the right foods, European settlers in the Indies would flourish and Amerindians might perhaps come to acquire a European constitution" (2–3).

Hence, while present-day histories of food recount the marvels that crops originating in the Americas, such as chocolate, tomatoes, peppers, potatoes, and maize, offered to the rest of us, the early settlers' concern was instead to try to grow foods from the Mediterranean in the New World. In many places, they succeeded.

less than three hours after our meal, I can smell the characteristic results of having digested and absorbed asparagus acid. It rises up from my urine. My body has barely incorporated this stuff, and yet already biochemically transformed it, and I piss it out again. "Hey, M.," I say when I return to his living room, "your meal makes for interesting fieldwork!"

Not all edibles that I incorporate feed my body. Even a part of what I absorb into my bloodstream I immediately expel again. Asparagus acid is a case in point. As it does not serve me, I excrete it. Its smell readily gives this away, while other molecules in my urine are less remarkable. I flush them without further ado. On to the next meal. Things are not so easy for people whose excorporations pose problems.

In a clinic for people with kidney disease, I sit in with the dieticians. They help patients eat enough to sustain themselves, but not so much that their kidneys cannot manage the excesses. In their consulting room conversations, the dieticians disaggregate foods into different components, each requiring different kinds of care. Sodium, or so I learn, is straightforward. It is hard on the kidneys and should be banned from one's diet, which is difficult to do, but an easy rule. Phosphorus, likewise, is to be minimized: "Maybe you can have hard cheese on your toast in the evening, Mr. Hodra, rather than the cream cheese you currently use. Hard cheese contains less phosphorus." Protein is more complicated. Diseased kidneys have trouble excreting the urea that is formed when protein is broken down, and urea is poisonous to the human body. This means people with kidney disease should minimize their protein intake. At the same time, they need to eat enough of it, as protein is a crucial building block in regenerating bodily structures. If bodies do not ingest enough protein, they retrieve it from their muscles, which quickly weaken as they are broken down.

The balance is difficult to achieve. The dietician tells me about a patient who lost his job because he was too often absent due to his disease. Recently divorced, he did not eat well because he was unable to cook. His bad physical state also undermined his appetite. But as long as his body remained in its current bad overall shape, he did not qualify for a transplant. To strengthen it, he had to eat better, but he could not afford lean meats, such as chicken. "It is sad," she said. "I would like to prescribe him chicken, but that is impossible. So I end up pre-scribing him fortified yogurt. His health insurance reimburses that."[28]

To remain strong, bodies need to renew their building blocks. If not prop-erly sustained, they weaken. But if they eat more than they can handle, that is harmful, too. Strengthening is a complex task: it depends on procuring and preparing food and on eating enough but not so much that your body cannot manage the excesses. In eating, then, endurance and change go together and diverse bodily boundaries are subtly and stubbornly negotiated.

When are my excesses no longer part of me? Does my urine exit me as soon as a kidney expels it from the interior milieu of my bloodstream to the exterior milieu of my bladder? Or only once I pee and push it out of my blad-der, across the sphincter at the end of the urethra? Then there are questions to ask about the fibers that I ingest but never absorb and that, along with the mi-crobes that thrived on them, I excrete through my anus: were they ever a part of *me* to begin with? Or do they never stop being so? If on the way from M.'s house to my own, I had wet myself, the smell of my urine, even if excreted, would have been taken for *my* smell. When I catch a bit of feces in a container and hand this over to a laboratory technician to be tested, she carefully glues a label with *my* name on it to mark its contents as *my* feces. The outcomes of the lab tests will be inserted in *my* files and passed on to *me*. What, then, about the remnants of which I relieve myself when flushing the toilet? Might they, in one respect or another, also still be *me*?[29]

Here is the lesson for theory. Eating suggests a model of *being* in which the body that *is* overflows into her surroundings. Some elements of that which was outside me I incorporate. These I use to keep myself together or, alternatively,

This saved them from the fate, so they thought, that had befallen the ancestors of the Amerindians. For Amerindians, too, were descendants of Adam and Eve. That they differed from Europeans meant that the local climate and local foods must have transformed their bloodlines and weakened their complexion. The notion of 'bloodlines' suggests a kind of heredity. "At the same time . . . a distinctive and inherited complexion could transform into something else. The consumption of particular foods, or other changes in regimen, might induce a 'second nature,' since new customs could radically alter the body" (203). Some Europeans risked undergoing such alterations. They ate the 'filthy things' the locals ate. "That some settlers, particularly in more peripheral parts of the empire, in fact consumed lizards, snakes and even insects was therefore extremely worrying. The Spaniard investigated by the Mexican Inquisition in 1543 for dining 'with Indians, sitting on the floor as they do . . . eating *quelites* [fresh herbs] and other Indian foods and the worms they call *chochilocuyli*' was one of a number who blurred the boundary between colonizer and colonized by their failure to respect fundamental culinary frontiers" (126).

The facts that the concept of 'race' had not yet been invented and that people's complexion could change, both over long historical periods and in the short run as well, did not mean that the Spanish saw everybody as equal. Amerindians were considered to need supervision and to be misjudged regarding many

I retrieve energy from them.[30] What I no longer need, I excrete through one of my various exit portals. All in all, I hold on to my form by transforming what I eat. My food transubstantiates me, while allowing me to stay the same. In this unsettled kind of *being*, the boundaries between outside and inside are traversed again and again, while continuity depends on never-ending change.

Where I Come from, Where I Go

Merleau-Ponty proposed an *I* able to avoid bumping into chairs and tables while walking through his apartment. Tim Ingold (one of the editors of *Ways of Walking*) takes the subject for a walk outdoors. To exemplify his approach, I here quote from an essay called "Footprints through the Weather-World."[31] Ingold is not keen on built-up environments where "life is lived on or above the ground and not in it. Plants grow in pots, people in apartments, fed and watered from remote sources" (126). Outdoors, things are different. "Plants grow *in* the ground, not *on* it, as their roots penetrate deep into the soil, while their stems and leaves mingle with the open air, rustling in its currents" (125). It is in this outdoor setting where Ingold situates the *I*, the subject. In a phenomenological vein, Ingold then describes hills from the perspective of the *I* who climbs them. "The ground is perceived *kinaesthetically*, in movement. If we say of the ground of a hill that it 'rises up,' this is not because the ground itself is on the move but because we feel its contours in our own bodily exercise" (125). The world through which a walker moves, Ingold contends, is not extrinsic to his mindful body, but helps to form it. Hills climbed and grassy paths formed by walking get inscribed into the body of a walker. This is an incorporation of sorts, but one of a neuromuscular kind. It remains in line with Merleau-Ponty's suggestion that the crucial ingredients of human *being* are walking, perceiving, and knowing. What Ingold adds to this are the hills, the wind, and the rain that, as a walker, one may struggle against. "For the walker out of doors . . . the weather is no spectacle to be admired through picture windows but an all-enveloping infusion which steeps his entire being" (131).

In the social sciences, weather has been understudied: "Given its centrality to life and experience, the absence of weather from anthropological accounts of human ways of being and knowing is little short of extraordinary" (132). Ingold attributes this to the fact that vested conceptual frameworks hold no space for weather. It is easy to agree with this, but why does Ingold take "being enveloped with weather" as somehow more real, more indicative of human *being* than seeking refuge in an apartment? It rhymes with his reverence for wandering and his contempt for being transported by train or car. "Transport carries the passenger *across* a pre-prepared, planar surface. The movement is a lateral displacement rather than a linear progression, and connects a point of embarkation with a terminus" (126).[32] In Ingold's take, transport has a delusionary character, since passengers who are carried around remain passive and therefore unchanged. No hills and grassy paths get inscribed into their bodies. This contrasts to the walking of a wayfarer, in which "the growth of knowledge . . . is part and parcel of his own development and maturation as an embodied being" (136). In the end, it is knowledge that Ingold is interested in: "knowledge [that] is not classificatory but storied, not totalizing and synoptic but open-ended and exploratory" (135). An interesting kind of knowledge indeed. But what about the eating on which it depends?—where are the 'conceptual frameworks' that help bring *that* to the fore?

The walker that Ingold presents us with moves through a world that stretches out around him and etches into his soul.[33] As he climbs, he feels the hill rising, the wind pushing back, the rain on his face. This kind of *being* involves a physical negotiation with one's surroundings and that is part of its appeal. I happen to be sensitive to that appeal. However, I also care to acknowledge that I owed the possibility to walk in Brittany to an impressively well-organized set of train rides. For city dwellers, 'wayfaring' tends to require motorized preparation. As indeed we are "fed and watered from remote sources," our food has traveled, too. The restaurant meal mentioned earlier

things—crucially, about what is good to eat. Some Amerindians even ate human flesh, and Spaniards considered this remarkable, not primarily because it was sinful but because it indicated poor taste. "Foods such as spiders and human flesh were thus strongly marked as 'Indian.' These were things that only Amerindians were supposed to eat, thereby demonstrating their uncivilized status and need for oversight" (126). In the eyes of the Spaniards who wrote the texts that now form the historians' archival material, the Amerindian Others were 'uncivilized.' Their eating habits were considered a strong indicator of this. Their purported lack of civilization made it acceptable for Spaniards to overpower the people and to colonize their lands. In the Latin American colonial context, then, the idea that *you are what you eat* was never an elegant way to avoid a racism that focuses on innate bodily traits (like skin color and other physical markers that so obsessed later racists). Instead, it suggests an inherent distinction between wheat-eating overseers and insect-eating people in need of oversight. This should serve as a warning that it is not inherently good to align *eating* with *being*. The effects of particular ways of wording depend, again and again, on myriad further specificities.

most likely contained local ingredients. Buckwheat is widely grown in Brittany; there are goat farms, and I saw plenty of beehives along inland paths. But eating from one's *terroir* is not obvious. A lot of the food available in urban settings travels from remote and disperse sites.

The food sold in the city where I make a living comes from all corners of the planet via intricate trading routes. There are apples shipped from New Zealand—those cultivated in the Netherlands are preserved in cool warehouses and trucked to the stores. There are beans imported from Kenya, dried apricots from Turkey, pineapple from Costa Rica. Most of the cheeses are Dutch, but there is also French brie, Italian parmesan, and Greek feta. There are individually wrapped bars advertised as 'natural' that contain 'nuts, fruits, and grains' that come from the US, although the label does not mention the ingredients' origins. The package with fair-trade chocolate sprinkles reveals that the cacao used has been sourced from 'Africa, Latin America and Asia.' Interesting.

At this point, my concern is not with the goods and evils of the global food trade.[34] Instead, I seek lessons about the situatedness of *being*. And this we may conclude: as I eat, I am not simply where I am. I am not just here. I may stay put, but the food that I ingest has traveled toward me. Even if hide in my flat, then as soon as I drink a cup of tea, I fold into my body stuff imported from China or Sri Lanka. Thanks to the chocolate I savor, bits of 'Africa, Latin America, and Asia' come to be juxtaposed inside me.[35]

Ingold's outdoor walker, struggling up against the wind, is where he is. My urban eater, by contrast, gathers together in her body edible samples from faraway places. Her eating situates her in a complex topological space. Despite sophisticated track-and-trace systems, it is hard to create a map of this space. But as stuff of various provenances convenes (mixes, gets mashed up) inside my eating body, my *being* is not a dot in a wider expanse round about me, but rather more closely resembles a vortex.

The way in which philosophical anthropology imagines 'the human' to relate to his surroundings is not attuned to the complex topological reality of my eating, nor, for that matter, to those of my excreting. For my metabolic remnants do not form a circle round about me either. Their spatiality is of a more intricate kind.

On a fine Saturday summer morning, I bike to the wastewater treatment plant that processes the sewage in my region. The plant is holding an open day. The place is not crowded and I get a private tour. The guide shows me that the effluent arriving at the plant first goes through a filter that blocks all materials larger than one centimeter in length or width. Once caught, these are assembled into a container and trucked to an incinerator. The effluent then moves on through a sedimentation tank, to let smaller solid particles settle. This sediment is sold to companies who use it to build roads. There I go, discarded bits of my body end up in roadbeds.

The murky water flows on to a closed-off tank that houses anaerobic bacteria, which process the sulfur. This greatly reduces the nasty smell for which sewage cleaning plants used to be famous, but, at least in the Netherlands, no longer are. Its sulfur content reduced, the wastewater is propelled into larger open tanks inhabited by some eighty species of bacteria, I learn. Jointly, these metabolize the organic materials present in the water. As the guide puts it, they do our work for us *They feed on whatever excesses and remnants my neighbors and I provide them. There I am, once again, now being eaten in my turn. Once they have multiplied and grown in mass, the bacteria are transferred to digestive tanks to be fermented by fungi. The gas freed in that process is used as fuel to power the treatment plant. In this way, former bits of me become fuel, not for another organism, but for combustion engines.*

The residue from the fermentation process, by now low in organic material, are trucked to another plant where they are burned. I keep on burning. The ashes that remain are used, once again, in road building. All the contaminants that the various filters and the eighty species of bacteria have not purged from the wastewater, then flow away into a river, out into the sea. In this way, I, or discarded bits of me, may end up anywhere in the world's oceans.

There is a lot more to say about wastewater treatment plants.[36] This particular one was built to reduce the organic overload in waterways, and while doing a fine job with that, it is incapable of making the scarce minerals in my urine and feces available as fertilizers. It also cannot retrieve micropollutants, such as medicines, recreational drugs, and their conversion products.[37] There are a lot of practical issues to tackle here. For now, however, I have a theoretical question: What does the dispersal of my remnants teach us about *being*?

Here is the lesson for theory. When it is modelled on eating, *being* is not just local. Composed out of elsewheres, my body gets spread out to sites nearby and far away. Bits and pieces that used to be part of me—are they still *me?*—fuel machines, form the foundation of roads or make their way into the oceans. I am by no means everywhere, but neither am I just here. The metabolic body suggests a model of *being* as neither fully here nor completely there, as here and there, multisited, dispersed.

The World through Me

When writing the *Phenomenology of Perception*, Merleau-Ponty sought to amend vested philosophical postulates. Rather than theorizing *thought* as if it were an abstraction, he focused on *thinking*, a vital activity of living people. Taking his cues from neurologists who had worked with soldiers wounded when they lifted their heads out of the trenches, Merleau-Ponty insisted on the importance of bodily integrity. As an integrated, bodily being, a human subject could make sense of his living space while moving through it. Expanding on this work, Ingold transferred the subject from the confinements of an apartment, out into a more challenging, hilly, terrain, where, in walking, he pushed against wind and rain. But while this made the world around the subject more lively, Ingold held on to a neuromuscular version of the body, in which wandering allows for knowing.

Building on this and breaking with it, I propose that we take inspiration from practices of *eating*. The stories about eating I told do not pertain to 'the human,' but to specific humans, caught in particular situations. In writing these stories, I use terms that have local salience in the settings about which I write. I do not draw on the work of particular scientists, say, the gastroenterological equivalents of the neurologist Goldstein. Instead, I listened to a variety of experts who talked to me while engaged in their daily doings: speech therapists, care assistants, nurses. When writing auto-ethnographically, I used vernaculars in which I am immersed and literatures I absorbed. Hence, what

I present is nothing like a universal for human eating, but it is eating all the same. Situated eating, tied to particular sites and situations: How does this help to rekindle *being*?

Merleau-Ponty's subject walks around his apartment as a well-integrated whole. As he avoids bumping into tables and chairs, he remains substantively distinct from his surroundings. His apprehension, his movement patterns and his cognition are affected by his surroundings, but his flesh is not. My eating body, by contrast, far from remaining distinct, incorporates bits and pieces of the outside world. And while externally entangled, internally I am differentiated. A gastrointestinal tract here, lungs there, welcoming different kinds of matter. The boundaries pertinent to this internally differentiated body are semipermeable and, with skillful bodily techniques or targeted tools, they may be crossed. Throat, bowel linings, cell walls. Skin, stomach wall, blood vessel. Anus, kidneys, urethra. Taking one route or another, bits of the world transit from my body's outside to its inside. Or, a short or long while later, from its inside to its outside.

But if there is traffic across bodily boundaries, there also is transformation: as I eat, my food stops being food and becomes a part of me. I may use my new ingredients to strengthen or rebuild cells, tissues and organs or burn them up. Across one boundary or another I expel what is unwanted. The eating body as it is storied here, then, offers a model of *being* in which the inside depends on the outside, while continuity depends on change. A model of *being*, too, in which what was far away may be absorbed inside me, while what was inside me gets widely dispersed. Here is the one liner: while, as a walker, I move through the world, when I eat, it is the world that moves through me.

3 Knowing

IN *The Phenomenology of Perception*, Merleau-Ponty insists that "all knowledge takes its place within the horizons opened up by perception."[1] This is in line with his quest to bring *thought* down from the transcendental heights to which philosophy had elevated it and tie if firmly to the *thinking* body. Perception, after all, is a physical affair. This had to be acknowledged: "We shall need to reawaken our experience of the world as it appears to us in so far as we are in the world through our body, and in so far as we perceive the world with our body. But by thus remaking contact with the body and with the world, we shall also rediscover our self, since, perceiving as we do with our body, the body is a natural self and, as it were, the subject of perception."[2] Here 'the subject,' the instantiation doing the knowing, is not abstracted from the human body, but grounded in it. The world perceived by this 'natural self' is a meaningful totality, rather than one composed out of fragments separately available to the different senses. For an embodied subject, Merleau-Ponty contended, a carpet is not an amalgam of a blue color that I *see* (sense datum 1) and a woolen texture that I *feel* (sense datum 2), which only get added together as I put my mind to work. Instead, as I walk around in my apartment, I perceive a familiar, integrated gestalt, a carpet that is pleasantly colored and comfortable to my bare feet. My bodily senses allow me, an integrated subject, to perceive phenomena in the outside world in an integrated manner. However, Merleau-Ponty only mentioned the contributions of some senses, notably those of seeing, hearing, and touch. Taste and smell were conspicuously absent.

This is not an accidental absence. It relates to the fact that, for Merleau-Ponty, eating and breathing are mere necessities of life, things that 'we humans' *must* do to survive. More truly human achievements are layered on top of survival. To articulate the distinction he is after, Merleau-Ponty imports the German words *leben* and *erleben* into his French. In the book's English translation, these are rendered thus: "Living (*leben*) is primarily a process from which, as a starting point, it becomes possible to live (*erleben*) this or that world." The translator at work here has translated *erleben* as 'to live'; the alternative, 'to experience,' would have marked the contrast with *leben* more clearly. For, as Merleau-Ponty continues, "we must eat and breathe before perceiving and awakening to relational living, belonging to colors and lights through sight, to sounds through hearing, to the body of another through sexuality, before arriving at the life of human relations."[3] It is in this way, then, that eating and breathing are cast as mere preconditions; truly human living involves 'perceiving and relational living,' which come to us in the form of colors, lights, and sounds. We may touch the "body of another." But tasting and smelling fall outside the scope of *The Phenomenology of Perception*. While it is the core argument of that book that thinking is a fleshy affair, only some fleshy affairs are deemed to be relevant to thinking. Seeing and hearing, yes. Touching, okay, that too. These senses allow for *erleben*. Tasting and smelling, by contrast, are merely matters of *leben*. The split that other philosophers made between a mind and body is shifted down a bit—but only a bit. It now runs directly through the 'higher' and the 'lower' capabilities of the human body.

This is another instance of the hierarchy within 'the human' with which in this book I seek to interfere by exploring eating (breathing deserves a book of its own).[4] The distinctions involved are deeply engrained in the Western philosophical tradition: that taste and smell are humble senses is not Merleau-Ponty's invention. In *Making Sense of*

TASTE TERMS

The sensuous characteristics of foods are not appreciated similarly everywhere. What in some cultural settings stands out as a treat is considered disgusting elsewhere. One and the same *taste* is rarely to everyone's *taste*. Indeed, the English word *taste* is intriguing. As a noun it travels from an attribute of food—that apple has a good *taste*—to the aesthetic preferences of specific eaters—apples are to my *taste*. As a verb, *to taste*, may indicate a subject's achievement—I *taste* the apple—or something being done by an object—the apple *tastes* good. This term

Taste, Caroline Korsmeyer notes that Plato and Aristotle ranked "bodily senses such as taste below the higher, more rational and cognitive senses."[5] Their reasons were that "sight and hearing operate with a distance between objects and organ of perception, and as a consequence they serve to draw attention away from the body of the perceiving subject to the object of perception external to the body. . . . The senses of taste, touch and smell, in contrast, are experienced as 'in' the body, locatable in the fingertips, the mouth, the olfactory passages."[6] Plato and Aristotle were interested in gathering knowledge about the world around them, and hence respected seeing and hearing, which they took to make such knowledge possible. Touch was intermediate, but taste and smell definitely were unsuitable vehicles for knowing the world. This was because, though these senses engaged with external objects, they happened on the inside and thus primarily made subjects more acutely aware of their own bodies—not of the world around them. Korsmeyer, seeking to positively revalue the sense of taste, is compellingly radical. She contends that this revaluation implies the upheaval of the entire Western philosophical tradition. Or, in her words: "One cannot simply add taste and the other bodily senses to philosophy as it has evolved and correct theories accordingly to be more comprehensive in their treatment of sensory worlds. . . . Philosophy is (or at least used to be) built upon attention to the eternal over the temporal, to the universal over the particular, to theory over practice. Taste is a sense that is not suited to advance the first term of any of these pairs."[7]

When I first read these words, I was enthused by them. Like Korsmeyer, I side with scholars who seek to shake up the Western philosophical tradition and hope to advance the temporal, the particular, and the practical over the eternal, the universal, and the theoretical. Also like Korsmeyer, I thought that attending to the sense of taste, highly relevant to eating, might help with this. But then I started to wonder about her tactics. Here is the problem: Korsmeyer deplores the hierarchy of the senses, but accepts the tradition of distinguishing those that are distal from those that are proximal. She even asserts that this distinction makes immediate experiential sense. She writes about seeing and hearing as obviously distal affairs, and about tasting, smelling, and touching as self-evidently folding the subject in on him- or herself: "While from the experience of the distal senses one may even share Plato's fantasy and aspire to leave the senses behind and ascend to purely intellectual understanding, the proximal senses keep the percipient in a state of awareness of his or her own flesh."[8] But who is the 'one' evoked here? Korsmeyer pursues the project of outlining 'the human' without situating 'him or her' in a specific setting. Moreover, while she turns against the traditional hierarchy of the senses, she holds on to the terms in which this hierarchy was framed. Without any apparent hesitation, she accepts that seeing and hearing are linked to the intellect, while touch, smell, and taste belong to the sensuous body. Korsmeyer appreciates 'the sensuous body' a great deal more than the philosophical tradition with which she battles, but she does not contest the nature ascribed to it.[9]

But is seeing necessarily a perceptive engagement by which a subject learns about the surrounding world? Maybe not always and maybe not everywhere. Maybe not even always and everywhere within the so-called Western tradition.[10] Take Wylie. He walked along the coast of Devon to learn more about 'landscape, subjectivity and corporeality.' There, he found himself to be "all eyes before a numinous configuration of wind, waves and contour."[11] The views that impressed themselves on Wylie did not primarily offer him knowledge, whether of Devon, his path, or the sea. Instead, they moved him. He was "dizzied by extension and expanse."[12] Wylie was interpellated not as a knowing subject, but as an appreciative one. In line with the Romantic tradition, the grandiose vistas he saw made him feel small, just a fragile speck in a world largely indifferent to him. Hence, in this case, seeing does not result in an integrated apprehension of a phenomenon but, rather, in awe. Casting Wylie's seeing as perceiving neglects that it offers sensations. 'Being all eyes' does not primarily provide the Romantic walker

thus intriguingly disturbs a few vested dichotomies. But that does not mean that the term *tasting* indicates a deeper truth about the relation between human bodies and their foods. Instead, it is a peculiar, particular, English word. 'Tasting' draws together people, things, and activities in a way that differs from what occurs in other languages. There are differences *within* languages, too. Take the Dutch word *lekker*—an untranslatable that resembles the English *delicious*. Some people use *lekker* to connote pleasures of the palate; others say *lekker* when their belly is agreeably filled. Some people restrict the use of *lekker* to moments when they praise foods; others protract it to include sex, the weather, a fine workflow, and beyond. And if uses of taste-related terms differ from one site to the next, so, too, do the perceiving and the sensing that inform that use.

Anthropologists of the senses tell stories of differences between the ways in which people sensuously engage with their foods. In line with my writing tactics in this book, I will not aim for an overview here, but instead offer an example to elucidate this point: Jon Holtzman's book *Uncertain Tastes: Memory, Ambivalence and the Politics of Eating in Samburu, Northern Kenya*. Holtzman lived with a few groups of Samburu. In their social structures, he tells, food is of huge importance. It forges ties. For instance, "the formalizing moment of the marriage— the performative act when Samburu assert that a marriage has truly come into being—is the slaughter of the marriage

with knowledge of the outside world, but more likely brings tears to those eyes.[13]

If seeing can move the subject, tasting, in its turn, does not necessarily fold the body in on itself. Take the taste laboratory that Gry Jakobsen described in her thesis, "Tastes: Foods, Bodies and Places in Denmark."[14] There tasting was organized with the aim of assembling knowledge about food objects. Panel members were trained by being offered test samples from a 'reference tray.' They were asked to specify the 'sensorial characteristics' of these samples while disregarding whether or not they liked them. By talking about their perceptions, panel members coordinated their palettes. When a new product was to be tested, they would begin by jointly calibrating the words they were going to use to describe it. In their own separate tasting booths, which had standardized light and a set temperature, they scored the 'sensorial characteristics' of consecutive 'food samples' on a scoring sheet. Each step was orchestrated. "The minute control of the relation between panelist and sample follows the sample all the way from its plastic container into the mouth of the panelists: Where should the teeth enter the egg white, and which teeth should be employed when chewing? How deep should the spoon be dipped in the honey? Where on the tongue should the liquid solution of cheese be poured? How many times should the bread be masticated?"[15] The panel members were required to test one sample after another, and yet come to each sample as if they were still fresh: "The leaders encouraged expectoration, that is, the spitting out of the masticated sample, followed by cleansing the mouth by masticating cucumber and crisp bread and sipping water, which is also expectorated."[16] All these efforts, says Jakobsen, turned the panel into an *intercorporeal machine* able to perceive the sensorial characteristics of food objects.

Seeing may stir up the soul, and tasting may be done perceptively.[17] Hence, the problem with the vested understanding of the senses is not just with their hierarchy. It is also with what they are assumed to achieve. It is with the opposition between perceptive outward knowing and sensitive inward feeling. To interfere with this, I will, in what follows, analyze a few situations in which perceiving and sensing come together in different ways. Using Jakobsen's description of laboratory tasting as a point of contrast will help to outline how this changes *knowing*. She writes that the setup of the laboratory afforded panel members the opportunity to accurately perceive the sensorial characteristics of food samples. In contrast to this, I will present situations in which eaters ingest their food without attending to its sensorial characteristics, or, for that matter, their own bodily sensations. This reveals that knowing—be it perceiving or sensing—requires active engagement. Next, in the laboratory, panel members set aside their likes and dislikes. I contrast this with situations in which knowing and valuing food go together. Such evaluative knowing may take a judgmental form, or be part of an effort to improve the food in question. A third dissimilarity: in the laboratory, panel members spit out the samples they tested. In the eating situations I describe, food is swallowed. This affects both the perceptive abilities and the sensations of the subjects who are eating. The model of *knowing* that emerges is neither objective nor subjective, but transformative.

Perceptive Sensations

Those currently working in the biology of the senses argue, like Merleau-Ponty, that the brain does not separate out 'sense data,' but integrates diverse sensorial signals into meaningful perceptions of the outside world. Along with sight, hearing, and touch, they tend to include taste and smell. The popular science book *Neurogastronomy: How the Brain Creates Flavor and Why It Matters* provides an accessible example of this. The specialty of its author, Gordon Shepherd, is retronasal smelling (smelling in the back of the nose).[18] Accordingly, it is not surprising that he insists on the overriding importance of smell for the brain's ability to construct (his term) a flavor out of the multisensorial inputs it receives. Retronasal smelling happens

ox (*rikoret*) which provides food for those attending the wedding" (72). But the ties forged by food are not only friendly. They can also facilitate damaging those to whom one is related through eating: "You can readily curse someone who has served as a herder for you for many years because of the extent to which they have benefitted from your food" (73). But if the ties forged by eating form a passage for curses, this means that herders can retaliate: "Because their herding labor has contributed to your well-being, their curses may also be potent" (73).

The 'you' that figures in those sentences is a man who owns a herd. Within households, such men are fed by women who cook and dole out the food. "Women (ideally) determine the exact quantity that their husbands and each child can eat, adjusting the amount upwards each day until they no longer finish the food" (134). Having served their husband and children first, a woman is supposed to make do with what is left in the pot. However, as nobody else has insight into the portions that a woman ladles out, she alone controls what is 'left over.' There are further elaborate ways that Samburu balance generosity with cheating. For instance, between men, sharing one's food is officially the appropriate thing to do. But that does not mean it is always done. "One of the important ways to avoid the profound jealousy surrounding food is to never eat in front of others without offering them some and, further, to never even let your eating be known" (134). If men are hanging out together,

when food, chewed and mixed with saliva, reaches the throat. At this point, volatiles waft up and enter the nose from the back. Even though this takes place in the nose, flavor is experienced in the mouth, due to the 'touch system' that tells humans that their food is located there. The touch system also actively contributes to flavor perception in other ways: "By manipulating the food in our mouths with our tongue, we carry out feature extraction on the *mouth-sense* of the food—whether it is smooth or rough, dry or moist, hard or soft, and so on."[19] Flavor likewise encompasses colors (seen before taking a bite) and sounds (heard while biting off and chewing). The taste buds on the tongue, in turn, add the ability to distinguish between sweet, salt, sour, bitter, and umami. In Shepherd's rendering, then, multisensorial inputs allow human brains to integrate various 'sensory stimuli' into a perceptive aggregate indicative of the food's 'flavor.'

In laboratory research into perception, the senses used to be kept separate. Shepherd, by contrast, tells stories of intriguing, cleverly designed experiments that demonstrate how the senses collaborate. He illustrates his propositions with examples from daily life that he presents using laboratory language. For instance, he writes about the tomato ketchup that his readers, presumed to be living in the US, may put on their french fries: "You couldn't design a modest sauce to be more flavorful. It stimulates directly three of the five tastes (umami is already stimulated by the meat flavor of the fries). It stimulates retronasal smell with volatiles from tomato concentrate, spices, and onion powder (to say nothing of the unknown artificial compounds hidden under the blanket term *natural flavoring*)."[20] As in the Danish taste laboratory where Jakobson did her fieldwork, *knowing* is staged as something that follows from perceptions that allow a subject to discern the sensorial characteristics of the object, here fused into flavor. Such *knowing* is done by the subject, but it is about the world. It seems to be an immediate result of a subject-object encounter.

But here is my problem. When Shepherd asserts that fries with ketchup are being smelled and tasted, he projects laboratory insights onto events taking place elsewhere. This occurs frequently: laboratory experiments are supposed to offer up generalizable facts about bodies. This assumption lightly skips over all the efforts that go into orchestrating such facts into being. The specificities of the situations where people actually eat fries with ketchup tend to be different. No trained panelists around; no tasting booths either. The surroundings may be noisy or messy. Shepherd has not investigated such situations. His ketchup story is merely a thought experiment. Ethnographic studies of actual eating practices suggest that, outside laboratories, people may never notice that "volatiles from tomato concentrate, spices, and onion powder" are wafting up the back of their noses. They may, even if they are eating food full of flavor, perceive nothing at all.

On a cold February evening, I join an introductory session held by a coach who supports people trying to lose weight. The participants sit in a circle. As we all introduce ourselves and say what has brought us there, I admit to being an ethnographer rather than a client. I ask if anyone has objections to me using their stories and I promise that I will not use their names. Everyone is fine with this. While confessions will be made, nobody plans to tell anything they desperately want to hide. Then the coach asks everyone to muse aloud about situations in which they tend to overeat. One person answers, "When I eat mechanically." Others join in and admit that they, too, often chew and swallow without attending to, say, the crispiness of their crisps or the taste of their brown bread with cheese. They keep eating crisps because they have opened the bag. They chew their bread and cheese absentmindedly while they are busy disciplining their children.

Here is a first lesson for *knowing*: outside the laboratory, in the wild, eating subjects may perceive the food objects they eat, but then again, they may not. The mere encounter between tongue, nose, and food is not enough for perceptions to happen. In the distracting settings of daily life, tasting may easily

someone who gets hungry may silently retreat. "If you decide to go eat when you are with a group of age mates, resting or playing *ntotoi*, you should never announce why you are leaving or even that you are leaving. You may simply suggest that you are going to the bush to urinate or defecate, and only later will your friends realize that you never returned" (133). Returning is not in order, for once back, you might need to urinate. This is bound to make your friends realize that you left to drink a calabash of milk your wife had set aside for you.

Samburu used to live as nomadic herdsmen. Throughout colonial times, they managed to hold on to their large herds. They would drink the milk of their cattle, supplemented with herbs and greens from the bush. If need be, they drank cattle blood. On festive occasions, there would be meat from a slaughtered animal. Young men would not eat into the supplies of their families, they would fend for themselves by hunting—although a courting woman might leave them a calabash of milk. Since the end of colonialism, all of this has changed. Hunting has been squeezed. Cattle numbers have dwindled due to infections and the shrinking of available land. Human populations, by contrast, have increased. Accordingly, wherever possible, maize is now grown as an added staple. Young men go out to work, and the money they earn is used to buy rice, even if rice is not considered particularly nourishing. Tea with milk and sugar has been welcomed as new 'traditional food.' Alcoholic beverages have

be skipped over. The participants in the counseling session address this, they recognize it, it is a problem for them, a situation they deplore. But there it is. When eating is pushed to the background, when other activities call for attention, perceiving food may simply not happen.

To confront us with what perceiving food can be if done attentively, the coach hands out a chocolate truffle to everyone present. First, we have to look at it calmly, from every direction. Then we are encouraged to smell it. Only after some serious smelling can we take a bite. A small bite. Notice what happens. What are your sensations? Can you tell them apart? We have to concentrate on our own bodies, and only once all the truffles are swallowed are we invited to talk again. Someone says that she thought the truffle looked quite ugly; someone else disagrees. Someone remarks that she liked the cracking sound of the chocolate coating. Someone else says that she did not at all fancy the cream beneath the coating—something she would never have noticed if she had eaten the truffle in her usual way, hastily. Someone admits it was a great truffle, but she could not help feeling bad about eating it—she was, after all, trying to lose weight.

Perceiving is not the natural effect of the encounter between an eating subject and a food object, but a possible event occurring as a part of a complex socio-material practice. It is something that may happen, or not, something that may be done, or left undone. An obnoxious cherry pit or the nasty taste of mold might jolt a nonperceiver into attending, but in routine situations the 'sensorial characteristics' of foods may well go unnoticed.[21] The coach of the workshop encourages the participants to pay attention, to prompt themselves to savoring what they eat. She assures them that doing so will help them to lose weight.

After the exercise, the coach insists that it is only when you attend to your food that it is likely to give you satisfaction. When a body is satisfied, it tells itself it has eaten enough. It stops eating. You do not have to force it to stop; it wants to stop. This makes attentive eating very different from calorie counting, which requires the eater to take control. The coach asks who has tried calorie counting. Almost everyone has. Someone says, "It always makes me feel bad. Then I eat something and I think, oh, boy, another 200 calories. What a shame." The coach nods. "Yes. And how can you enjoy your food if you think 'another 200 calories?' Then you focus on the calories. You don't taste. You don't take pleasure." In all its distracting obsessiveness, calorie counting risks blocking satisfaction. "If you really enjoy what you eat, you won't gobble up an entire package of cookies. *You only do* that *if you eat without paying attention."*

The coach hopes to cultivate her clients' ability to attend to everything they eat.[22] Such attention takes a different shape from the perceptive style cultivated in the laboratories just mentioned. In the laboratory that Jakobsen writes about, perceiving was meant to gather facts about food objects, while the researchers in the laboratories Shepherd draws on investigate what allows humans to perceive such objects. By contrast, the coach encourages her clients to simultaneously attend to what their food has on offer and to the sensations particular to their own bodies. Her concern is with people's bodily response to food that tastes good: a sense of satisfaction.[23] It is this sense of satisfaction that, or so she contends, will allow a person to feel when she has eaten enough. Here, then, perceiving the world and sensing the self are not played out against each other, but coincide. This suggests that *knowing* may be turned outward and folded inward at the same time.

Sensations of the body result not only from encountering food and eating it, but also from lacking it and needing it. The coach addresses this and encourages her clients not only to realize when they have eaten enough, but also to attend to their hunger.

The coach tells a story about one of her clients, a lawyer, who was regularly hungry as she drove home from work. Since

also been introduced, and women may earn money by brewing them. It is altogether a considerable transition. Among the losses deplored is the possibility of becoming intoxicated by food—especially meat. "The excessive strength the Samburu associate with meat consumption leads them, particularly murran [young men], to be seized by *Itauja* (literally 'hearts'), a form of trance. Samburu do not attribute such trancing (which involves violent shaking similar to epileptic seizures) to a supernatural cause, such as spirit possession. Rather, it is an intense emotional response in such contexts as circumcision rituals, marriages, or commonplace dancing of murran and their girlfriends—or brought on by excessive strength from having eaten well" (64).

I promised a story about the sensuous relations to food. These snippets illustrate that, in Holzman's rendering, in Samburu life, these were not prominent. Eating was primarily about other things: social ties, fairness, fending for oneself, seduction, marking special moments, strength, intoxication. When Holtzman asked about taste, he was told that, as long as it was properly handled, in the old days all food tasted the same: it was always *good*. No wonder, then, that the Samburu language is meager in taste terms. "Only five main words are used to describe the tastes of foods and these are fairly vague. *Kemelok* is often translated as 'sweet,' yet its meaning is less a physical sensation of sweetness than the positive experience of eating something tasty. Thus, *kemelok* is used to describe not only honey but also

she sought to lose weight, she did her very best not to act on this hunger by eat-
ing. Instead, she made work-related phone calls in order to actively forget about
her hunger. And indeed, such distractions made her hunger fade away. "But
though neglecting hunger may feel virtuous, it only shifts your body into saving
mode," said the coach, "so that the next time it gets food, it stores up supplies."

Here is what we learn about *knowing*. In the daily life settings of the workshop's participants, perceiving food objects and registering the bodily sensations related to them may be done actively or forgotten. What is more, perceiving food objects may slide into having sensations, whether of pleasure,
satisfaction, or hunger. In this way, well-established distinctions between the
world-out-there and the self-in-here get blurred. Instead, a person who pays
attention may get to know something *about* her food that is only pertinent *in*
relation to her body, that is to say: whether or not it is enough.

And 'enough' is just one of characteristics of food relevant to a particular
body that may or may not eat it. There are many more.

Take the time when I thought I was drinking decaf and then felt a rush of caf-
feine. This rush told me something about myself—I was unduly stimulated—
but also about the coffee—it was not decaf. Or take the time when I had eaten
a meal in which something was off. Probably it was the fish. Indeed, it surely
was the fish—the very thought of eating fish ever again made me feel even more
nauseous than I already was. This feeling permeated my entire body, but at the
same time it provided me with distinct knowledge about the fish: it had been
off.

The perceptive sensations relevant to these situations were simultaneously
in my body and *about* the food I had just ingested. When researched in laboratories as physiological facts, caffeine rushes and nausea tend to figure as
effects of particular foods on susceptible bodily systems. However, in the situations just rehearsed, it makes more sense to call them bodily *techniques* a
subject uses in grappling with the outside world.[24]

In this way, *knowing* is no longer modeled on a brain fusing the input of
the alleged 'five senses'—whether hierarchized or not.[25] Instead, it comes to
involve many more bodily sensitivities—including those that detect caffeine
rushes or become overwhelmed by nausea. This shifts *knowing* from something that results from 'the body' integrating its perceptions into the specific,
situated engagements of a person with stuff she happens to eat, here and now.
This meal was satisfying *to me*, but for *you* it might not have been enough. This

coffee gave *me* a caffeine rush, but *you* might hardly have noticed it. This fish made *me* nauseous while maybe you— well, if *you* are a human with a microbiome and sensitivities similar to mine, it might have disagreed with you as well. But if you are, say, a scavenger bird, it would not have made you sick at all. Were you a microbe, then you might have dug into it with gusto—or, more precisely, it was exactly because a bunch of microbes disagreeable to me had been feasting on it that the fish made *me* throw up.

Knowing, then, need not be understood as inherent to a natural body, *my* body, perceiving the world around me as an integrated whole. Instead, the stories of eating related here suggest that *knowing* may also come about when, in a specific situation, a specific person attends to selected bits of the world that, as she ingested them, affect her in this or that not-quite-predictable way.

Valuing Engagements

If we take inspiration from the stories about eating related above, the distinction between perceiving the world and sensing the self becomes blurred. The same goes for the distinction between establishing facts and evaluating.[26] In the taste laboratory Jakobsen studied, the *intercorporeal machine* comprised of separate tasters was supposed to establish facts about the foods on offer, putting aside the extent to which they liked those foods. When provided with sam-

especially tasty meat. Even fermented milk may be described as *kemelok*, if it has been soured well. . . . Apart from *kemelok*, only one other taste word describes a positive sensation. *Keisiisho* denotes saltiness, particularly in sour milk. All other taste words are, to varying degrees, negative. *Kesukut* is used for fresh milk that has started to go sour but that has not curdled. This is considered to be a serious defect in milk, though not one that renders it undrinkable. A parallel term for meat, *kesagamaka*, describes meat that has started to go bad—though meat has to become quite putrid by Western standards before people will refuse it. *Ketuka* refers to food that is tasteless, such as meat from animals that have not been fed salt. Today, porridge eaten without additives such as fat or milk is also referred to as *ketuka*, or may be described as tasting like *nchata natotoyo*, a dry stick. An additional taste term is *kedua*, or bitter, though this is not applied to food per se but is used for medical herbs and bile" (62).

This long quote makes clear that what a person tastes depends on more than 'the human body' alone. Foods eaten help to form the sensorium. A linguistic repertoire attuned to them helps in distinguishing between locally relevant flavors. People who herd cattle and hence live with animals providing them with 'good food,' may not need all that many words to specify the 'good.' Just one or two suffice. The goodness of fresh milk may then be contrasted with the slight disappointment resulting from drinking milk that has

ples of honey, the tasters assessed such traits as acidity, sweetness, juiciness, creaminess, and color. The results were later on to be used by food producers to fine-tune their recipes. These practical purposes, however, were carefully kept far apart from the moment of perception. In many other sites and situations, this is different.[27]

One fine day in August I make tomato soup for myself and E., my daughter. She has come home to work on her MA thesis, and I am trying to tame the present book. The latter is tantalizingly difficult: time and again I lead myself astray. But cooking a simple, soothing meal for the two of us—that I can do. For the soup I slowly fry onions in olive oil. Then I add a bunch of tomatoes, a few small pieces of ginger, a cube of vegetable bouillon and some water. Once this concoction has simmered for a while, I let it cool a bit. Then I send it through a passe-vite. This tool allows one to squeeze a mixed, more- or less-viscous mass through small holes. It filters out the skin, the seeds and any other hard pieces, while turning the rest of the ingredients into a pleasantly textured, puréed soup. As I heat this up, I take a spoon and taste it.

This particular kitchen-bound tasting was not meant to assemble bare facts about the soup such as its acidity, sweetness, juiciness, creaminess, or color. Instead, I wanted to know if the soup was *good*. Rather than being factual, my tasting was valuing. The valuing was not of a judgmental kind. I was not acting as if I were the judge of a cooking competition, out to grade my own achievements.[28] Instead, I hoped to find out whether, then and there, the soup needed further care. Maybe I had to add some lemon juice and sugar; some pepper or salt, or—who knows—some thyme or basil? This kind of *valuing* is not meant to establish evaluative facts such as 'this soup is good' or 'this soup is disappointing.' Instead, I did it to find out what more I could do for my soup, and hence for my daughter and myself—its prospective eaters.

Appreciatively assessing the taste of one's soup may help to improve it. This means that tasting is not just receptive, not necessarily a matter of accepting the world for what it is, but may be part of actively interfering with it. And it is not just the soup that is amendable to improvement. Tasting may contribute to improving other things as well.

We sit down to eat and talk work for a bit. How has your writing been going? What about yours? At some point, E. interrupts her own intellectual musings and inserts a reference to the soup. "Delicious! Is there ginger in it?"

There is a lot to unpack in this short phrase. For a start, *delicious* entails a positive evaluation of the soup. But more is going on here. Asserting that the food is delicious may be a way of giving a compliment, as in 'You are a good cook' or 'You did a good job today.' But in the present case, it was more likely not about me being good, or having done well, but, rather, a recognition of my work: 'Thank you, Mom, for cooking.' With her appreciative remark, E. made her own contribution, if not to the soup, but to the overall mood and our mother-daughter relation.

Added to E.'s 'delicious' there was an inquiry into the presence of ginger. This may seem factual—is there ginger in the soup, yes or no? But once again, more is going on. By remarking on the soup's gingery taste, E. made it clear that her

started to sour. The satisfaction provided by fine meat contrasts with the warning against meat that is going bad. Mentioning that meat lacks salt marks a lack of care on behalf of herders, who should have provided their animals with salt to lick. The bitterness of healing herbs completes the vocabulary pertinent to traditional Samburu life. In contrast to this, the flaws of present-day Samburu food are encapsulated in the word used to characterize unadorned porridge—a mealy dish made from maize. This, even if prepared well, does *not* taste good. It tastes of nothing. In the absence of a specific term in the language for this particular negative appraisal, an analogy has been found. *Dry stick.* That is what modernity tastes like to contemporary Samburu.

'delicious' qualification was not empty. She was not saying 'thank you' mechanically, while absorbed in thoughts about her thesis. No, she was truly paying attention to the soup; she detected ginger in it. In addition, she presented herself as a good daughter once again by signaling that she might want to take cooking lessons from her mother. If ginger made this particular soup into a success, she might want to add it to her own future soups as well. Maybe in practice she wouldn't—but that was not the point. The point was to signal appreciation. Of the soup, the cooking, and of my motherly care overall. These objects of appreciation are not clearly distinguished: each slides fluidly into the other.[29]

The *knowing* relevant to these domestic situations does not result in the facts (about foods or physiology) coveted in laboratories. But neither does it take the judgmental form of cooking competitions: the point is not to ascertain whether the soup *is* good or bad. Instead, I taste the soup in order to find out if it is good enough—for me, for my daughter—or if I should try to improve it. E., in her turn, praises the soup as a way of thanking me, and thus contributes to the overall mood. Hence, our evaluative knowing hovers around us, attaching first to one object, then to another. At the same time, apprehending the world intertwines with our attempts to tweak it—or at least a tiny part of it—so that it gets closer to what figures locally as *good*. It is caring.

But if improving the taste of food may contribute to the quality of a situation, improving a situation, may, with some luck, improve the taste of the food.[30] In nursing homes, this insight is used to encourage people with dementia to eat better, which in their case does not mean less, but more.

Research has indicated that elderly people in nursing homes tend to eat more if the ambiance of the setting in which they eat is improved. Hence, in Blue Home, the tables are set with colorful placemats. The hot meal is not passed out on individual plates, but served in serving dishes meant to be shared. In this way, eaters no longer need to state their preferences in the abstract—do you like peas or carrots?—but can select what they want to eat in a more immediate manner—look, smell, here are two kinds of veggies, which one of them would you like, here and now? The room is supposed to remain quiet, with no people wandering about or walking in and out. If at all possible, care personnel sit among the inhabitants and encourage mealtime conversation. One of the nurses is admirably good at this. She asks: "Where did you go on holiday, Mrs. Stevens? To the mountains, you say? Oh, that is great. Was that in Austria, maybe?" Or she looks encouragingly into people's eyes, asking such questions as "Is it nice?" or "You do like sausage, don't you?"[31]

If the diligent nurse at work in Blue Home asks the elderly in her care if they like their food, she does not hope to find out whether the food is good or whether it suits the eaters. Instead, she shifts their attention to their food, so that they might take more pleasure from it. The content of her questions is inconsequential, the sheer fact that she asks a question, pays attention, cheers things

EFFICACY AND AESTHETICS

In my fieldwork sites, the ways in which foods impress themselves upon bodies are disaggregated. Nutrients are taken to have substantive, physiological *effects* that either allow for or hamper bodily functions, while flavors are taken to be *noticed* by the senses. As they speak to the senses, flavors may carry information that encourages eating (yes, nourishing) or instead warns against it (beware, danger!). In daily parlance, however, flavors tend to figure as 'merely' aesthetic, accidental qualities, frivolous extras that provide pleasure. There is a lot more to say about this, but here, rather than engaging in further unpacking, I fold these complexities together to introduce a contrast with an elsewhere. For it is not self-evident that *effecting* and *being noticed* must be torn apart. In the Chinese tradition, for one, the flavors of food have direct bodily effects. As Judith Farquhar puts it in her book *Appetites: Food and Sex in Post-*

up. Just like colored placemats, chatting improves ambiance and hence may contribute to people's appreciation of what they eat. Objects are apprehended jointly.[32] Caring for any one of them contributes to the quality of the others.

Here is the lesson for theory. If the situations recounted here are taken as exemplary of *knowing*, then *knowing* would be an evaluative engagement in which various objects are appreciated in combination. Soup, ginger, motherly efforts. Placemats, atmosphere, chatting. This appreciative *knowing* does not just slide between objects; it also affects them. Perceiving and sensing are part of active attempts at improvement. Tasting the soup, saying it is delicious, laying out placemats, asking "Is it nice?": all such engagements are caring. The objects of knowledge are adapted to the subjects who eat them. What we have here is the model of *knowing* in which mutual attuning and substantive transformations intertwine.

Changing the Subject

In the process of appreciatively getting to know them, objects may be transformed. I may add a bit of lemon and honey to the soup, so that it comes to taste better to those who will eat it. My daughter may compliment the soup, thus humoring me. The nurse in Blue Home may contribute to improving the local atmosphere and consequently make eating more appealing. And it is not just the qualities of food objects that may readily change, but likewise the perceptive abilities and physical sensations of the subjects who eat them.

V. and I first get to know about vegetable scoring cards in an interview with a dietician. These cards form the heart of a serious game meant to attune children to the sensorial qualities of vegetables. They list a great many vegetables, showing pictures and providing names. Each of them has a row of boxes next to it. A child who is not too keen on vegetables receives the card. The game is that every time she eats a vegetable, she may put an X in one of the boxes next to it. When she reaches box 16, she is allowed to give a final verdict and grade the Brussels sprouts, broccoli, green beans, and so on, using the grading system current in Dutch schools. In this way, the vegetables end up with a grade between 1 (very bad) and 10 (perfect). The crucial advantage of this technique, the dietician tells us, is that children do not have to listen to adults insisting that some vegetable or other is good. Qualities are not objectified. Instead, children may develop their own preferences and take their dislikes seriously. However, she adds, "But I tell

socialist China, "In the idioms made available by Chinese language and herbs, we can see bitter experience rendered treatable with sweet drugs and pungent substances used to set the stagnant fixities of old pathology into more wholesome motion" (66). In daily parlance, Chinese people associate the tastes of their foods with opportunities to heal. In medical treatises, these associations are developed in great detail. For instance, a *pungent* taste has the function of "moving qi, moving blood, or nourishing with moisture" (156). The effect of *sweetness* is that it replenishes the body and strengthens the effects of drugs used to treat depletion disorders. It may also sooth acute pain. *Sour* helps to contract and constrict and hence it counteracts excessive excretion. The function of *bitter* is that it is draining and drying. *Salty*, finally, "softens hardness and disperses lumps" (156). The English words are approximations that differ from what is evoked in the context of Chinese medicine. This short list should all the same get across the point that flavors do not need to be understood as the accidental qualities of foods, information about foods' other properties, or embellishments that only afford aesthetic appreciation. In the Chinese tradition, the flavors of foods have direct effects on the health of the person eating them.

That flavors have physiological effects is rooted in a long and complex tradition. To exemplify this, I invoke another book, *Food, Sacrifice and Sagehood in Early China*, written by Roel Sterckx. It presents

them to not be too fast with their negative appraisal. They should give the vegetable a fair chance."[33]

Here, knowing and valuing are cast as interdependent: by getting to know the vegetable, you learn to like it. A vegetable is not inherently tasty or revolting. Rather, the question is how its sensuous qualities impress *me*—this particular child confronted with Brussels sprouts, broccoli, or green beans at the dinner table. The vegetable scoring card invites children to do the grading; the price the children have to pay for their recognition as a discerning subject is that they 'give the vegetable a fair chance.' They should seriously engage with it by eating it at least fifteen times. The expectation of the adults proposing this game is that by trying a vegetable again and again, children will warm up to it. If in some cases they do not, if in the end the Brussels sprouts remain stuck at a 5, an *insufficient*, that is okay. In the meantime, at least, the broccoli and the beans (plus the carrots, tomatoes, zucchini) have changed the subject. They have attuned the child to their flavors.

Here is the lesson for *knowing*: engaging perceptively with an object, while at the same time valuing it, may change the subject. When tasting is organized as an interactive game, the subject may gradually learn to appreciate the object. But if foods may warm an eater to their traits, they may also spoil the subject-object relation.

During a conference lunch break, we are walking through the streets of a university town. A colleague who has just heard that I am studying 'what it is to eat' tells me a heartbreaking story. At the age of eleven, she entered a pancake-eating competition organized during a festival in the Dutch village where she grew up. The goal of the competition was to eat 'as many pancakes as you can.' She loved pancakes and she loved winning. So she ate and ate, and she won. She won! However, since that day, pancakes no longer agree with her. Worse, they disgust her. The smell alone is enough to make her feel sick. Even when occasionally she finds herself in a situation where there is nothing else to eat, she cannot bring herself to take a bite. An empty stomach is not enough to overcome her aversion.

This is a strong case of a spoiled relation. In milder cases, the disgust may gradually fade. After eating fish gone bad, one may throw up, be sick for a day or two, but then, after a few weeks maybe, happily eat fish again. Here, however, the disgust has firmly settled in. By gloriously winning the competition, the eleven-year-old self of my interlocutor unwittingly spoiled her own pancake eating for a lifetime. Or had she? Maybe it makes more sense to blame the pancakes.[34]

Here is the lesson for theory. Interacting with a food object may increase a person's perceptive skills, but also her appreciative propensities. The *taste* of foods is bound to affect the *taste* of those who eat them. One's liking may increase or decrease. This may be reversible or not. It may happen slowly, over repeated sessions, or remarkably fast, on a single occasion not so festive after all.

Foods may shape the appreciative propensities of eaters in various ways. For one, a range of preparation techniques can come to be aggregated into a cultural repertoire, a 'cuisine,' while, at the same time, a group of people are clustered together as those who recognize this cuisine as integral to their 'culture.'

In Blue Home's ward for people with dementia, the residents are having lunch. For most of them, this consists of either peas or carrots, with either meatballs or chicken, and either fried or mashed potatoes. They have a choice between two traditional Dutch meals and three constitutive elements thereof. Mrs. Klerks, however, is eating bami goreng, *which is originally an Indonesian dish. Ba indicates the presence of meat,* mi *is a wheat noodle, while* goreng *means that these ingredients have been fried up with any combination of vegetables and*

a range of textual materials from the Han state during the Warring States period. In that context, Sterckx writes, eating was communal, and not just among the living. The dead received a portion of every meal as a sacrifice. "Sacrificial rituals were the cornerstone of everyday religious life in Warring States and Han China. The presentation of offerings, raw or cooked, animal or vegetable, was an activity that extended from the household to the local community, state, empire, and the cosmos at large. Obligations related to the sacrificial economy punctuated, in various ways, the public and private existence of people across most segments of society" (123). In everyday family meals, it was enough to make a small offering. On special occasions, larger collectives presented large offerings to spirits in the hopes that they might join the festivities. "The sacrificial procedure involved all human senses in an amalgam of music, dance, fragrance and visual spectacle. The sacrificial space represented a symbolic arena to which the spirits were to be lured by sensory means" (83). To lure the spirits, the food on offer was colorful and tasty. "Food was among several sensory tools that offered a conduit for communication with the spirit realm" (83). Immediate ancestors, quite like living eaters, were bound to appreciate the flavors of food offerings. Distant ancestors were more likely to prefer 'ethereal ingredients.' "Spirits operate in a world beyond taste, a world in which sensory memory is increasingly detached from human sensation and worldly flavors" (85). Conse-

sometimes shrimp or egg. Another indispensable ingredient is the sambal, *a spicy red pepper paste. Mrs. Klerks visibly enjoys her food and shovels one spoonful after another into her mouth with dedicated concentration. Before long, her plate is empty. One of the nurses tells me that Mrs. Klerks does not eat so well (that is, so eagerly) every day, not when she is handed 'ordinary' (that is, Dutch) food, but she invariably does when the meal she is offered is* Indisch.[35]

Indisch is the Dutch adjective for things to do with colonial Indonesia. Mrs. Klerks grew up there as an Indo—someone with mixed Indonesian (usually Javanese) and Dutch ancestry.[36] In the 1950s, after Indonesia had finally gained its independence, Indos were made to feel unwelcome there, and many of them migrated 'back' to the Netherlands, where they had never been before. Dutch social workers, tasked with facilitating their integration, taught Indo women how to cook meals around potatoes, with the argument that these were cheaper than rice. Despite such efforts, most of those concerned did not warm to Dutch food, but held on to variants of their traditional cuisine, adapting the ingredients that were available. These days, care institutions try to be 'culturally sensitive,' which in Blue Home means that, a few times a week, Mrs. Klerks is served the *Indisch* food for which she has a taste.

But in the Netherlands, it is not only Indo people who eat *Indisch* food. Since the 1950s, Indonesian restaurants have opened; cookbooks have been published; and most of the necessary ingredients are now readily available in Dutch supermarkets.[37] *Bami goreng* and *nassi goreng* (*nassi* is rice) have become standard fare not only in many Dutch households, but also in the Dutch army and other institutions with central kitchens.

For reasons of efficiency and economy, food served in the Blue Home is prepared in a kitchen situated in Riverview, a large home for elderly who are able to spend their days in their own rooms. While observing there, I help by clearing tables in the restaurant. This allows me to ask Cisca, a member of the restaurant staff, if she thinks the food they are serving is good. Cisca answers: "Yes, it is mostly okay and sometimes even tasty. Especially the bami goreng. *The cook has a good hand with it." On days when the kitchen serves traditional Dutch fare, Cisca (keeping an eye on her money and cooking a hot supper for her husband and children at home anyway) brings homemade sandwiches for her own lunch. But Thursdays are an exception. Then, one of the two daily hot lunches on offer in Riverview is* international, *sometimes Italian or Mexican, but most often* Indisch. *If Cisca notices a few days beforehand that there is going to be* bami goreng *on the menu, she leaves her sandwiches at home and pays for the treat. Delicious!*

When cooking *Indisch*, the kitchen staff make extra portions, which are frozen so that the Indos among the eaters may enjoy them on another day. But Cisca is not an Indo, she doesn't mention family ties with Indonesia as her reason for liking this dish. Instead, she praises its quality and the expertise of the cook. Cisca frames her own liking of *bami goreng* not as a matter of culture, but as a matter of recognizing its especially good quality. Cisca knows one *bami goreng*, a delicious one, from another that is just ordinary. In her own modest way, she is a connoisseur.[38]

In both these stories, *knowing* about a dish helps to form the appreciative propensities of those who do the knowing. Dishes in a certain taste *range* may attune a group of eaters to themselves. Jointly, such dishes and their eaters then form a 'food culture.' This fosters a sense of belonging in, and a divide between, 'food cultures.' However, it is also possible to differentiate between the taste *gradients* of dishes, with some being okay and others truly delicious. The people who acquire this distinctive ability, those *in the know*, jointly distinguish themselves from other, less discerning eaters. In both cases, the objects of knowledge are formative of the subjects knowing. They shape their tastes and cluster them into categories.[39]

quently, the success of luring spirits with sensuous stuff was uncertain. Maybe they would appear, but then again, maybe not.

But if flavors might or might not lure spirits, what did they do for humans? In the texts that Sterckx analyzed, this is not described; it is instead apparent from what they prescribe. These texts addressed an idealized human, that is to say, a man both a ruler and a sage. This person was advised to train his senses to the utmost. "An advanced sensory disposition formed part of the general type casting of sagehood and skill in early China" (168). There was no hierarchy of the senses. In the Greek tradition, seeing and hearing were celebrated as senses that provided knowledge of essential, effective things, while smelling and tasting were considered sensuous and merely offered pleasure. In the Chinese tradition, knowledge was not pitted against pleasure, other contrasts mattered. Crucially, moderation opposed excess. In line with this, all the senses were considered to be involved in appreciating the world. The eyes enjoyed beautiful sights; the ears derived pleasure from harmonious sounds; the nose liked fragrant smells; the mouth savored fine tastes; and the body valued rest and relaxation. It was acceptable for a wise man to enjoy all these pleasures, he just had to avoid overindulgence. It was among his tasks to remain modest and balanced. "Rulers, like cooks, ought to strive for balance, guard what is essential, and take heed not to neglect the inner qualities of things at the expense of overindulg-

However, if foods may alter the tastes of eaters over the course of years, this may also happen over a much shorter time span.

Once her MA thesis has been submitted, E. works for a few months in Paris. When I visit her there, she has made a reservation for us in a gluten-free restaurant. This is a treat. No careful pondering of the menu to discern hidden wheat, no toing-and-froing with the kitchen, no risk of a bellyache. We order and then wait. After hours of wandering about in the city, I am hungry. When the guests at the table next to us get their food, the smell is enticing. I surreptitiously glance at their plates with great longing. "Don't stare, Mom." Finally (it feels so long . . .) we are served. This time around, I compliment the food, and these compliments extend to both the restaurant and my daughter, who has made the effort to find it and make a reservation.[40]

Dessert arrives and E. take a bite. She frowns. "Hmm, this is strange." She has never had almond milk panna cotta before. A few bites later, I ask whether she wants to swap dishes, but by then she has changed her mind, or rather, she has changed her senses. "No, thanks, I am beginning to warm to it." My own response to my dessert, a pear tart, is rather different. The first spoonful I love. But after just a few bites, the tart loses its allure. Its flavors have not changed, I have. I may have been hungry before our meal, but this is my third course and I am, to put it bluntly, full.[41] *This greatly reduces the ap-*

peal, not just of the pear tart, but of other foods as well. The dishes served to a new round of neighbors do not smell enticing at all. I try to block them from my attention to avoid feeling aversion—even nausea. When I pay at the counter, I have no inclination whatsoever to buy the gluten-free cookies on display there. No cookies for me. Not for tomorrow or the day after. It is difficult to believe that I might want to eat anything at all ever again.

Here the attuning (of E. to almond milk panna cotta) proceeded quickly, but so too did the spoiling (of the relation between me and not just a fine pear tart, but any food). A bit of habituation may facilitate one's liking. But eating—ingesting, digesting—may also seriously diminish it. Moreover, it is not only one's perceptive capacities that transform, but so too do one's sensations, one's feeling of what is good to eat or not, appreciated from within. No wonder that in the taste laboratory where Jakobsen did her fieldwork, the leaders encourage 'expectoration,' spitting. The laboratory, after all, was exploring the 'sensorial characteristics' of food samples, and to achieve that aim, the tasting subjects had to encounter each new sample afresh. In the restaurant, by contrast, one did not spit. There people were meant to appreciate the flavors on offer and, at the same time, assuage their hungry bodies.[42]

Here is the lesson for theory. Foods incorporated may transform both the discerning skills and the appreciative inclinations of their eaters. Eating changes the conditions of possibility on which getting to know a dish depends. Eating may warm a subject to the taste of her foods, or impede any further tasting. Getting to know a dish may lead on to valuing it ever more positively or, alternatively, make appreciating yet another bite altogether impossible.[43]

The food changes in the process. After being chewed and swallowed, almond milk panna cotta loses the ability to seduce. If, nauseated, I had vomited up my three-course dinner, a dog might have liked the results, but not the other guests in the restaurant. Since I kept my meal inside, it worked its wonders in transforming *me*. It may have spoiled my appetite, but it also provided me with enough energy to walk out of the restaurant to the metro, through its lengthy corridors and back out into the streets again, all the way to E.'s apartment.

ing in outwardly apparent pleasures" (70). Overindulgence was a sign of weakness. So, too, was hoarding meat or holding a banquet when the harvest had been bad and ordinary people went hungry: "Social conditions need to be met before the sage-ruler can find full pleasure in sensory satisfaction. His organs are only capable to 'sense' to the fullest when the state is well ordered" (179).

The ruler-sage had to contribute to the state being well-ordered. Such order allowed the ruler-sage to sense to the fullest. In this way, he could appreciate, in moderation, what was being offered to his senses. Including foods. Eating tasty foods, again in moderation, was bound to feed the ruler-sage's abilities, helping him to rule wisely. No contrast here between essential, substantive (physiological) effects and 'merely' accidental (aesthetic) pleasure. Food provided a person with nourishment thanks to its flavor, which carried vital energy, qi. "The intake of flavor through the medium of qi induces clarity of mind that will enable one to govern" (64). In pre–Common Era China, the efficacy of food did not contrast with the pleasures it might offer. Instead, through the medium of qi, effect and appreciation went together.

I like this. My overall argument does not depend on it: the situations of eating I encountered in my provincial fieldwork are sufficient to rekindle vested imaginations of knowing. But even so, the otherness implied in the advice provided to the ideal Chinese ruler-sage is gratifying. Essential and accidental do not need

Living and Experiencing Intertwined

Merleau-Ponty suggested that leben, surviving, allows for what truly matters, erleben, experiencing. In the situations I have described here, living and experiencing are not similarly piled on top of each other. For when the weight loss coach encourages people to enjoy their food, the relation is the other way around. Their pleasure may allow them to lose weight: intensifying their erleben could improve their leben. The same holds when people with dementia are lured into eating more, or when children give vegetables a fair chance and come to like them. In both cases, pleasure is organized not as an extra layer added to vitality, but as a contribution to vitality. The meals I shared with my daughter allowed us our leben, but we could have lived with more ease (buying ready-made soups) or more cheaply (Paris has lots of fast food outlets). The added pleasures of a fresh soup and an accommodating restaurant were not essential for survival. But it makes little sense to split sharing a meal into ingesting nutrients and enjoying the tastiness of the food or the warmth of the companionship. In some situations, health and pleasure, or brain and belly, may be disaggregated, but not always and not everywhere. In practice, it is very well possible for leben and erleben to level, serve each other, intertwine.

But if leben, living, is not situated below erleben, experiencing, this interferes with the hierarchy in 'the human' that marked twentieth-century philosophical anthropology. The situations of eating related here allow for further interferences, too. For in eating, we saw, distal perceptions of the world-out-there do not have to stand in stark contrast to proximal sensations of the self. The food being eaten and the eating body can be perceived, sensed, felt—known—together. The model of *knowing* that ensues is site- and situation-specific. I may, here, now, as a specific subject, with a specific perceptual and sensorial history, attune to—get to know, come to like—this particular soup. In doing so, I do not just put my five senses to work, but a far wider array of signaling and appreciative systems, including appetite, satisfaction, motherly love, or nausea. As perceiving overflows into sensing, so, too, does establishing facts overflow into valuing. I know there is caffeine in the coffee (which I may like or dislike, or which may unduly increase my heart rate). The fact finding may be part of a relational plot (is there ginger in it, Mom?). The valuing, in turn, does not necessarily end in a verdict, but may lead to an intervention: if the soup tastes as if it needs more pepper, I add that. What we have here, then, is a model of *knowing* that is not about passively apprehending the world but, rather, about actively engaging with it.

The engagements involved are consequential. Both the subjects and the objects of the knowledge relevant to 'my eating' transform each other in the process. The objects change both the discerning abilities and the appreciative propensities of the subjects. The fit between object and subject may improve (a child who did not previously may learn to love broccoli) or worsen (a child who loved pancakes may come to be disgusted by them). A certain range of foods may attune a group of eaters to their shared taste so that they form a food culture. Or discerning eaters may learn to distinguish foods in terms of quality. Attunement between foods and eaters may take a long time, but foods may also transform the sensibilities of eaters in the course of a single meal. Within a few bites, almond milk panna cotta may turn from slightly weird into quite good. Within an hour or two, a food may shift from smelling enticing to being too much. Food, once ingested, make further food lose its sensorial appeal.

And if subjects change, so, too, do the objects. In the model of *knowing* that speaks from the situations of eating just recounted, the subject involved may improve the food object first—cooking and spicing it—but then rob it of the characteristics that made it so attractive. Once chewed, food no longer looks enticing. Once swallowed and mixed with stomach acid, it no longer tastes good either. Once in the bowels, where microbes help break it down, its smells become revolting. In eating, then, the knowing subject does not main-

to be disentangled; pleasure does not have to be despised; it may be enjoyed in moderation. I am not out to romanticize life in the states from which classic Chinese texts emerged. But their particularities help *me*—here, now—to escape from what was presented as self-evident in the intellectual traditions imposed on me. They offer me a 'Foucauldian moment.' What effect, I wonder, do they have on you, reader? How do you appreciate them?

tain distance from the object of knowledge. Instead, subject and object interfere with each other, change each other, intertwine. Rather than representing, other relational modalities are at stake. Learning to be affected, affecting. Taking pleasure, improving. Belonging, distinguishing. Caring, meddling. Satisfying, feeding. Chewing, appreciating. Listening, attending. In this model, *knowing* is not *of* the world, but *in* it. It is altogether transformative.

Doing

IN HIS 1999 BOOK, *The Expressiveness of the Body*, Shigehisa Kuriyama unravels what he calls in the second half of his title *The Divergence of Greek and Chinese Medicine*. This results in fascinating stories about the ways in which physicians from these two medical traditions diagnosed their patients. Both would feel pulses, but while Ancient Greek physicians tried to detect rhythmic pulsations, classical Chinese physicians sensed flows of energy. Both would look at their patients' bodies, but while Greek physicians would see muscles and address their ability to move, Chinese physicians would attend to the color of a person's skin and tongue to assess his liveliness. The Greek medical tradition was fascinated with "the articulation of intentions and the exercise of muscular will."[1] In the Chinese medical tradition, by contrast, "humans resembled plants not just in 'vegetative' processes, such as growth and nutrition, but in their moral development, in the way they grew and revealed themselves as persons."[2] To illustrate the difference between the Greek and the Chinese body, Kuriyama juxtaposes two images. One is a 1543 print from Vesalius's anatomical atlas. It shows a well-trained man after his death, whose muscles are made visible by clearing away the skin, connective tissue, blood vessels, and nerves with tweezers and knives. The other is a 1342 drawing by an unnamed Chinese medical artist. This shows a rather plump, living man in a loincloth, on whose body the artist has drawn a single meridian and its pressure points, all of which are named. Kuriyama points out that each of these drawings would have posed a profound puzzle for doctors versed in the other tradition. The Chinese did not use knives to separate muscles from other tissues—they did not even have a word for 'muscle.' The Westerners, in their turn, never detected meridians and considered images depicting them to be absurd.

Kuriyama's comparative analysis convincingly shows that 'the body' is not self-evidently given to those who seek to know it. Different medical traditions each know a different body. Here, I leave Kuriyama's analysis of the Chinese tradition to one side and work with his analysis of the Greek understanding of the body. This, he says, pivots around the muscle. "In tracing the crystallization of the concept of muscle, we are also, and not coincidentally, tracing the crystallization of a sense of an autonomous will. Interest in the muscularity of the body was inseparable from a pre-occupation with the agency of the self."[3] Here we encounter the 'free men' of ancient Greece again, though not, as in Arendt's rendering in *The Human Condition*, engaged in political discussions. This time, they are working out in the gymnasium. They train their muscles and thereby acquire control over their movements. Kuriyama argues that, in the Western tradition, all voluntary action was modeled on this feat: a free man can start and stop the movements of his legs, arms, neck, and torso at will. This is even more dear to his self-understanding than his superiority over *others* who are not free men. "The history of the Greek muscular body involved, early on, the history of how Greek men defined themselves vis-à-vis various Others—animals, barbarians, women. But it subsequently became entwined as well with the evolution of another, less-studied aspect of self-definition, namely, the relationship of self to change." Some changes would just occur; others the self could bring under voluntary control: "Henceforth, the heart of all readings of the body

SITUATED BODIES

In *Metabolic Living: Food, Fat and the Absorption of Illness in India*, Harris Solomon presents lessons he learned while conducting fieldwork in a mixed neighborhood in Mumbai. There, as in so many other places around the globe, overweight and obesity are on the rise. Along with this, there is an increase in the incidence of metabolic syndrome, a combination of arteriosclerosis, high blood pressure, and high blood sugar levels that lead to type 2 diabetes. Metabolic syndrome is a worldwide problem, but Solomon's medical informants no longer take 'the body' to be universal. They have adapted internationally set standards to *Indian* bodies. More particularly, they have lowered the thresholds between Body Mass Indices (BMI) they consider to be *normal*, *overweight*, and *obese*. The BMI is derived by dividing a person's weight in kilograms by the square of their height in meters. Its significance has been

would be framed by the dichotomy opposing processes that merely happen, naturally or by chance, and actions initiated by the soul."[4]

A few pages further on, Kuriyama puts it like this. There is, he writes, "a fundamental schism in Western self-understanding: the split between voluntary actions and natural processes."[5] It is a helpful formulation of the Western understanding of the self that I seek to leave behind in this chapter. Chinese and other non-Western traditions harbor plenty of models of *doing* that elude the split between 'voluntary actions' and 'natural processes,' and I might have sought inspiration there. However, I have made it my quest to insist on 'otherness' *within* the so-called West. And while ancient Greek 'free men' were talking politics or training their muscles, so-called women and slaves labored to provide food and drink. This labor involved the *cultivation* of allegedly natural processes, and this demands effort, but does not offer control. And it is not just foods-to-be which are cultivated, but the eating body, too. This is why in trying to remodel *doing*, I seek inspiration from situations to do with eating. However, at this point, there is a complication. For in my field, 'the split between voluntary actions and natural processes' appears to be a tenacious one. It runs right through 'eating.' In public health admonitions in the Netherlands (as in many places elsewhere), eating (this or that food) is set up as a *choice*. Laboratories that study 'eating behavior,' in their turn, take eating (this or that food) to result from *causes*. In this chapter, I do not take either of these orchestrations as being truer to life than the other. Instead, I contrast both of them with situations where eating (this or that food) takes the form of a *task*. A task does not just happen; it is something that needs to be *done*. But this *doing* is not a matter of centrally controlled action, but of what might best be termed *caring*. Of negotiating, tinkering, trying, and trying again.[6]

The tinkering care that allows for my eating, or so I come to argue, is not just 'my' *doing*. When 'I' eat, my eating is made possible by others and, what is more, even partly done by others. The collective actively involved in my eating includes other people who grow, transport, or sell my food, but also nonhumans such as the kitchen fires that partly digest it. Hence, 'my' eating suggests a model of *doing* that does not just elude centralized control but also defies individualism. Cultivating 'my body' depends on the efforts involved in cultivating ever so many other f/actors. What is served by this eating?—what is it for? In 'the human' theorized by twentieth-century philosophical anthropology, eating allowed for the 'vital goodness' of the creatures doing the eating. Vitality, being alive, was cast as the natural prerequisite for the subsequent building of culture. Eating (along with breathing) made

seriously contested, but it is a stubborn number. As BMI has been used in all research publications to date, it remains a point of reference. An Indian committee of experts, however, took the risk of flaunting the possibility to engage in historical and international comparison. They argued that the globally established cut-off points for BMI do not do justice to the reality of Indian bodies: these are at risk of developing metabolic syndrome with lower BMIs than bodies in other locations. Hence, the committee lowered the cutoff points for healthy, overweight, and obese BMIs. Within a day, millions of people found themselves classified as deviant.

In a Mumbai hospital, Solomon sat in with professionals caring for people who were overweight or obese. Treating these patients is tricky. There are no safe, effective pills that assure weight loss, and only very few people get slimmer through dieting. In Mumbai, exercising is easier said than done, as the temperature is high and the air is polluted enough to cause health problems of its own. Surgery also appeared to be disappointing. If it worked at all, it tied people to severe eating restrictions they had hoped to escape. Outside the hospital, however, Solomon found that issues to do with weight were not high up on the list of pressing concerns. His neighbors were more worried about the adulteration of food. Alcoholic beverages were diluted with ethanol and other cheap, potentially deadly substances. Milk powder had meal mixed into it; chili power was contaminated with grounded brick. Even if that was not go-

it possible to live and to then, as a high point, have cognition (Merleau-Ponty) or political discussions (Arendt), or strive after moral ideals (as Hans Jonas argued).[7] In his book *Philosophy of Biology*, Jonas posited a hierarchy within the human that mimicked the hierarchy between different living creatures. He ascertained that plants merely seek to live, which means they metabolize; that animals, in addition to metabolizing, move about and empathize; while only humans, on top of these lower-level activities, are able to envision 'moral rightness.' In Jonas's schemes, eating is natural and, in eating, 'the human' resembles a plant. I will, once again, mobilize a few contrasting exemplary situations with which to think. These are situations in which eating does not simply serve the 'vital goodness' of the eaters involved but is, rather, torn between different kinds of good—and different kinds of bad. Instead of being a *mere* matter of life and death, then, in the related situations, 'my' eating is suspended between different ways of living and of dying.[8]

The Task of Eating

Getting to eat this or that food tends to be presented as a 'voluntary action' or as a 'natural process,' depending on the setting. In public health admonitions, the first approach is favored; in laboratory research, the latter. In this section, I exemplify them both, and then present instances of eating I came across in

Dutch clinics and kitchens, in which eating instead constitutes a *task*. The 'voluntary action' example that I present resonates with many public health campaigns analyzed in medical sociology, so I am saying nothing new here.[9] Rather than adding a novel insight, I make an already-established one relevant to the analysis of *doing*. As an example of public health at work, I quote from the Dutch Nutrition Center's website, which seeks to promote "healthy and sustainable choices of consumers."[10] The center suggests that people should eat some foods rather than others, but it calls its encouragements not 'encouragements,' but 'information.' The idea is that 'consumers' will make good choices, if they have access to 'independent information that is scientifically supported.'[11] This, then, is what the center provides. As a contrast to the advertisements and infotainments in which the food industry loudly praises the miraculous qualities of its packaged foods, cool facts might be heralded as welcome antidotes. But the facts under consideration are not just factual. They are made to serve the goals of 'health' and (this is a recent add-on) 'sustainability.'

Addressing its viewers as you, *the site goes into teaching mode: "Varied food is needed to keep your body healthy. If you keep eating the same foods, then it is difficult to manage to ingest all [the] nutrients [you need]."[12] To explain what 'varied' means, the site presents a drawing of a wheel with five food clusters.* You *are advised to choose foods from each of these clusters every day. The clusters correspond to what in nutritional science are called 'nutrients.' Take, as an example, cluster 3: "This cluster includes meat, meat products, fish, milk, dairy products, cheese, eggs, and meat replacements. Eating these products helps you to incorporate necessary nutrients such as proteins, fish fatty acids, iron, calcium, and B-vitamins."[13] If you are eager, or prepared, to fine-tune 'your choices' yet further, you are offered more nutritional information, allowing you to engage in detailed dietary calculations. "On average, healthy people need 0.8 grams of protein a day for every kilogram bodyweight. That amounts to some 56 grams of protein for a person of 70 kilos."[14] And so on.* You *may learn that proteins are composed of amino acids, that some of these are essential, and that they must be ingested in the right combination.*

That *you* are presented with all this information suggests that the professionals of the Dutch Nutrition Center do not expect *you* to ingest the appropriate quantities of protein *spontaneously*. Instead, the facts provided should allow you to do so *consciously*. They should afford you the opportunity of making well-informed choices. The appeal here is to a 'voluntary actor' who, if only

ing to kill anyone, it was still frightening. Produce delivered to shops in bulk and subsequently weighed out on the spot for customers was regarded with suspicion: it was too easy to adulterate. Packaged foods seemed more trustworthy. But then again, the plastic packaging presented its own health risk. Hence, while public health warnings all focused on the risks of consuming excessive calories, in daily life other substances demanded attention: "The plastic enrobing packaged foods, and the brick in the chili powder the plastic is supposed to deter, destabilize easy answers about what it means to be sick from food" (227).

In Mumbai, food gives rise to health concerns of different kinds. But the local salience of food reaches way beyond health. Solomon exemplifies this with the case of *vada pav*. *Vada pav*, a local delicacy, is "a chickpea-battered, deep-fried, spicy mashed potato patty (the *vada*) tucked into a slightly sweet soft bread roll (the *pav*)" (69). To public health authorities, *vada pav* "was a 'killer' primarily because of its high calorie count, and the killing could be stopped only by stopping its consumption. The figure of the obese person—especially the obese child—anchored many stories about the risk of *vada pav* to Mumbaikars" (71). But this risk was not easy to mitigate because other things mattered more. If a school stopped offering *vada pav* in its cafeteria, children would go outside and buy it on the streets. If a dietician told clients that eating *vada pav* was 'out of the question,' these clients might answer that by five

they—you—were to put in the effort, might take calculated control. The site draws on facts about bodily needs established by nutrition scientists on the basis of laboratory measurements of their research subjects. And *you* may now use these facts to calculate, rationally, from outside your own body, as if you were your own laboratory technician, what *you* should eat.

But while this advice draws on laboratory research on 'bodily needs,' there are also laboratories that study 'eating behavior.' These configure 'behavior' not as an action based on a choice, but as an effect that follows from a cause. Detecting causal chains at work in 'nature' however, depends on the ability to orchestrate them into being. Natural scientists craft the 'nature' they study in the laboratory. In science and technology studies, this has been amply demonstrated, so once again I am relating nothing new. Instead, I reiterate a few salient snippets from this tradition that are relevant to *doing*. My cues I take from a research article published by an interesting research group that generously allowed both me and two members of my team into their laboratory for interviews and observations.[15] I quote from the 'material and methods' sections of one of their articles so as to be precise and specific about their research practices. That I singled out this article for analysis does not signal that I consider it bad, rather the opposite. I greatly appreciate its ingenuity and the elegant way in which it undermines the public health discourse around 'food choices' just recounted. But that does not mean that causal stories are as generalizable as they are all too readily taken to be.

The article "Protein Status Elicits Compensatory Changes in Food Intake and Food Preferences" reports on a study regarding what the researchers call "the effect of specific diets on food preferences." The question addressed was whether, like animals, human beings whose diets have been short on a specific nutrient unwittingly adapt what they eat to compensate for that lack. The focus was on protein. "The objective of this study was to investigate the effect of a low protein status compared with a high protein status on food intake and food preferences."[16] To meet this objective, the researchers meticulously controlled what their research subjects ate for almost two full weeks. These research subjects, university students, knew that the study focused on nutrients, but they did not know which nutrients. They committed themselves to eating everything they were provided, but nothing more. On weekdays, the research center invited them in for a calibrated hot lunch and to receive supplies. "The home meal package contained two bread meals with toppings for dinner and breakfast and beverages, fruits, and snacks. On Fridays, subjects received a home meal package with foods and beverages for the entire weekend plus instructions for the preparation of these foods." And here is the crux: half of the participants were fed with twice *the amount of the protein they were deemed to need; the other half with only* half *this amount. Between the two groups, total calorie counts were the same. After two weeks, the effects of protein overfeeding versus protein underfeeding were tested. All the research subjects were sent home with a bag that contained substantially more food than they were likely to end up eating. They were asked to eat whatever they felt like and to not share out the rest, but instead to return it to the lab. The researchers carefully measured the leftovers. The result: "There was a spontaneous 13% higher intake of protein after a low-protein diet than after a high-protein diet, whereas total energy intake was not different."*

The researchers flagged this as an interesting finding: like mice and other animals that had been investigated in earlier studies, 'low protein status humans,' too, spontaneously stock up on proteins when given the chance. Hence, just like other animals, humans do not make 'informed choices' about eating this or that food; they do not calculate their 'food intake.' Not necessarily, at least. For in the scenario of the experiment, the researchers had made the calculations, while the research subjects obliged them by first eating the foods they were provided with, and subsequently attend to their spontaneous desires,

o'clock in the evening they had hunger pangs and were 'called to' eat it. They did not regard the oats, puffed rice, and salads dieticians recommended as serious food, let alone for 'a man with work to do.'

Vada pav stills hunger that less-coveted foods cannot. But there is more to it than that. Solomon recounts the history of vada pav. In partition times, the habit of eating spiced potatoes with bread traveled along with Hindus migrating from Sindh, a city located in what is now Pakistan. In Mumbai, the dough was closed around the potatoes to make it easier for workers in the mills to eat the snack on the train to work. Once the mills shut down and the workers were laid off, they tried to sell vada pav on the street. Building on this, the Shiv Sena, "a regional political movement that promotes the rights of Hindu Marathi-speaking people," tried to turn vada pav into an icon of Hindu Mumbai belonging (69). The Shiv Sena provided sellers with stalls painted in Shiv Sena colors and it organized competitions to establish which recipe would be served by the vendors in these stalls. When the police and municipal officials decided to restrict the informal economy and began to chase off vada pav sellers, the Shiv Sena offered protection. But not for free: "It began with a few rupees each day but over time would indebt street vendors to the Shiv Sena in amounts of hundreds or even thousands of rupees a week" (81). Solomon also tells about street vendors who managed to stay clear from politics and the debts that came

which appeared to be in line with their bodily needs. Here, then, eating this or that food is not configured as an action over which an individual should take 'control.' Instead, what is orchestrated into being is a behavior following on from a 'natural process.'

The two ways of understanding eating just rehearsed are in tension. Public health information encourages people to make responsible 'food choices' based on counting the nutrients they ingest. But why? If one's 'food preferences' indeed change with one's 'protein status,' it seems unwise to try to overrule this finely balanced physical feedback system with exterior calculations. *You* might as well go with what you *feel* your body needs.

But here is the caveat. A 'low protein status' does not all by itself cause a 'higher intake of protein.' The relation between this alleged 'cause' and its alleged 'effect' depends on particular conditions of possibility. Orchestrating these into being in the laboratory was hard work.[17]

For a start, not everyone could participate in the study: "We recruited healthy, normal-weight subjects aged 18–35 y." To clarify what this means in practice, here is who could not join: "Exclusion criteria were as follows: restrained eating [Dutch Eating Behavior Questionnaire: men, score of 2.25; women, score of 2.80], lack of appetite, an energy-restricted diet during the past two months, change in body weight of 0.5 kg during the past two months, stomach or bowel diseases, diabetes, thyroid disease or any other endo-crine disorder, prevalent cardiovascular disease, use of daily medication other than birth control pills, having difficulties swallowing/eating, hypersensitivity to the foods used in the study, being a vegetarian, and, for women, being preg-nant or lactating."

That long list indicates that many people were not considered for the study and that, accordingly, the results might not hold for them. It is impossible to know whether they do: 'non-normal' people (deviants, the diseased, preg-nant and lactating women, vegetarians) were not included. What is more, the circumstances created by the study are not easily re-created elsewhere. An-other crucial condition of possibility for the 'spontaneous 13% higher intake of protein' reported in the article is that there are foods containing protein. That the 'eating behavior' of the research subjects in the laboratory appears to be an effect of their 'protein status' owes a lot to the fact that the research-ers provided the students, for free, with all their meals.

In the research center, ingredients were bought and calculated; lunches were cooked; home meal packages packed. The materials and methods sections does not detail who did what, but all this is obviously a lot of work; and it costs money, too. Some grant must have paid for it. The research subjects were ac-tively involved as well. They came to the center for their lunches; in the evenings and mornings, they peeled their fruit; opened their packages with ham (high-protein intake group) or jam (low-protein intake group) and put these on the slices of bread that were included in their home meals. They ate what they were provided. For some (especially the international students), it may have been dif-ficult to enjoy eating cold sandwiches for both breakfast and dinner. But still, by and large, the students involved in this research project were pampered. They received free food every day for two full weeks and, at the end, a big bag with lots of meat. (That vegetarians were excluded greatly simplified both the calcu-lations and the catering.)

Laboratory research foregrounds particular aspects of the reality it grapples with and obscures others. Researchers who study how healthy volunteers re-spond to a lack of protein gain no insights about those who do not fit their 'inclusion criteria.' The people in question could be studied, deviant group by deviant group, but that would demand a range of different research set-ups and a lot more grants. Researchers obviously know this. This is why they spell out the conditions orchestrated in their lab in their 'materials and meth-

with it. They all used their own combination of spices and preparation techniques, so that the *vada pav* tasted different from one stall to another. All of the sellers with whom Solomon talked took pride in their ability to make a living. Some tried mass producing *vada pav* to bring in more cash. This was not easy. As one person attempting to mass produce *vada pav* put it, "'With street food, even if it's vegetarian, those bacteria give the food a taste of non-veg, a taste that no chef can give.' The challenge, then, is to corral the disorder of the infectious streets without sacrificing the taste" (91). Food, Solomon underscores, is not just about health. It contains more or less complex histories, has a more or less enticing taste, costs, or may be a source of, money. Moreover, eating, not so much in terms of calories as in terms of engaging with *this* or *that* food, can constitute a way of living, offer a sense of belonging, and provide an eater with a deep feeling of satisfaction.

ods' section. The effects of variables kept stable may be listed as topics for 'further research.' However, such specifications tend to disappear when 'facts' are generalized and made to travel without the 'methods' on which they depended. Calling something a 'natural process' suggests that it is *not done*, that it merely happens; but this hides what *has been done* to make it happen. In the present case, it erases a lot of diligent work by laboratory researchers, technicians, cooks, as well as the students involved in the study as eaters.[18]

It only takes a small amount of fieldwork outside controlled laboratory settings to reveal that what people eat and do not eat in the wild depends on more than their 'protein status' alone. Eating depends, crucially, on food. But even if there is enough food on offer, people whose bodies need protein do not necessarily eat them spontaneously.

Rita Struhkamp did fieldwork in a Dutch rehabilitation clinic, and in one of her articles she wrote about the care of 'Fred,' a young man with a spinal cord injury. Fred had ready access to food, but little desire to eat. He was undernourished, and as a result he had developed sores on his skin.[19] By the time Rita encountered him, he had hardly any subcutaneous fat left, and his sit bones pressed directly against his skin, which had trouble regenerating. When talking with Helen, his doctor, Fred said, "I know I should eat better, but the problem is that they serve dinner at noon here. You see, I don't feel like having my hot meal right in the middle of the day! And then sandwiches at 5 p.m., that's also much too early. I don't feel hungry at that time." Fred longed for more accommodating surroundings. "'It's much easier at home,' he continues. 'At home I can have something to eat whenever I fancy it.'" Helen asks what he would eat at home. "'Pizza,' is his prompt answer. Helen laughs and suggests that Fred should see the dietician, but Fred is not particularly eager: 'Oh, she'll give me these horri-

ble nutritious yogurt drinks, which I really hate. They're simply disgusting and they turn my stomach. I'm not going to take them!'"[20]

This tells us that humans who lack proteins do not stock up on them *in general*, if only they are given a chance. Some of us do—for instance, the 'normal eaters' included in the above study. But if eating were always and everywhere a 'natural process,' a behavior following from internal cues, Fred would eat all right, for his body direly needs it.[21] What to make of the fact that he does not? It might be possible to figure out which internal feedback processes have gone awry and how it is Fred has lost his appetite. However, in the clinic there is neither time nor money to do this. What is more, such investigations would be unlikely to suggest another treatment than, in one way or another, helping Fred eat more. But how to do that? Telling Fred to make better choices does not work. The clinic's professionals have long since learned that admonishing people to take control of themselves is unlikely to improve things. Hence, in the clinical setting where he finds himself, Fred's eating is configured neither as an effect following from a cause nor as the result of a choice. Instead, it stands out as a *task* that must somehow be accomplished.

The pertinent question in relation to this task is how to accomplish it. Who might do what to solve the immediate problem? The dietician might prescribe fortified yogurts, but alas, that will not work, for Fred insists that they are disgusting. Maybe, then, if Fred cannot stomach hot lunches, he could be granted access to a microwave so that he might heat up his meals when he feels like it. Or what about allowing him to order in pizza? And so on.[22] In the clinic, in conversation with Fred, or so Struhkamp relates, professionals tried to establish the conditions under which Fred would be able to accomplish the task of eating the food, including the proteins, needed to repair his skin.

Here is the lesson for theory. In a situation like Fred's, *eating* is neither a matter of voluntary control nor embedded in causal chains. It is a task that is difficult to achieve, but that, by creating

INTERFERENCES

In *The Weight of Obesity: Hunger and Global Health in Postwar Guatemala*, Emily Yates-Doerr explores the interferences between globally oriented health experts and local traditions related to food in and around the city of Xela, in Guatemala's Western Highlands. In Guatemala, as in Mumbai, incidences of 'metabolic syndrome' have recently increased. This does not mean, however, there is no longer hunger. Public health researchers based in Guatemala found that excessive weight and hunger are not simply opposites. They are related. For a start, people who were undernourished

suitable circumstances, and with the support from others, may yet be accomplished. The *doing* staged in this way is not confined to a moment—of choice—nor is it linear—like a causal chain. Instead, it is of a caring—iterative, adaptive, tinkering—kind.

In the laboratory study cited above, the 'research subjects' are provided with food; and so is Fred in the clinic. On the website of the Dutch Nutrition Center, likewise, *you* are encouraged to *choose* healthy and sustainable foods, as if such foods are simply available and happily waiting to be chosen. This skips over a range of concerns that are prominent in many other settings, such as where to buy food; how to pay for it; where to find the time, the skills, and the equipment to cook it; and so on. *You* are provided with information—as if a lack of information is what stands between you and eating well.[23] In many daily life settings, however, other things are going on. This is blatantly obvious in situations of poverty. See studies about the hunger among slum dwellers, war victims, refugees, and others who have difficulties eating 'healthy foods' due to lack of money or availability.[24] But even the welfare state inhabitants addressed by the Dutch Nutrition Center do not simply 'choose' food. They work for it. Some of them do so under dire circumstances and against the odds. But even for people who have a fine salary, easy access to information, and well-supplied food stores around the corner, getting to eat may stand out as a *task*. There is, in one way or another, a lot to *do*.[25]

Take that spring day when I made a spinach frittata. I had leftover potatoes; the spinach on offer in the supermarket looked particularly appealing; I knew my dinner guest would like this frittata; I had cooked it before. All this may go into why I made that particular dish on that particular day, but then and there, this why question was not so prominent. The how question took precedence. Take out the chopping board and a knife; cut the potatoes into pieces; put these in a pan; fry them in olive oil; add cumin, pepper, and salt. According to the label on its bag, the spinach had been 'washed in ice water three times.' Lucky me, I did not have to do that. Instead, I made the spinach shrink in another pan; put it in a colander; pushed out the fluids; transferred it to the chopping board; cut it. In a large bowl I mixed three eggs, enough to hold the vegetables together, added some salt and pepper; added the diced spinach and poured the resulting mixture into the pan with the now fried potatoes. (I had stirred these around a few times in between.) I lowered the heat under the pan to give my frittata some quiet cooking time.

You get the picture. Described in this way, the *I* is not making choices for which she needs information. Nor is she being propelled by hidden causes. Instead, she is cooking dinner. For this she needs money, time, skills, ingredients, a kitchen with equipment, and so on. These all work along with her, but still she labors hard to align them. Hence, framing my eating spinach frittata as either a choice or a natural inclination shifts aside the effort involved in dreaming up that this would be today's meal and then putting it on the table.[26]

The Western philosophical tradition holds human beings to be suspended between an 'autonomous will' that incites actions and 'natural processes' that underpin behaviors. But what goes on in the clinics and kitchens visited here suggests another model for *doing*. For in such settings, getting to eat this or that food is not *primarily* the consequence of a choice, nor *generally* the effect of a cause. In the situations I just presented, eating stands out as a *task*. Accomplishing that task takes time and effort. The *doing* involved is iterative, it is of a probing, wandering kind. If the microwave does not help Fred eat, maybe ordering in pizza will. Or the other way around. If I had found myself out of olive oil, I might have used butter to fry my potatoes. Instead of fresh spinach, I could have used the frozen variety. Had my guest not turned up, I might have eaten the second half of the frittata the following day. Adaptations form the hallmark of caring kinds of *doing*.[27]

early on, as young children or while still in their mothers' wombs, have an increased risk of becoming overweight later in life. What is more, a person may be malnourished despite ingesting a lot of calories. "The basic premise of malnutrition's 'double burden' is that in environments with abundant processed foods, people will consume high quantities of macronutrients (lipids, proteins and carbohydrates) while still consuming insufficient amounts of micronutrients (vitamins and minerals), resulting in simultaneous prevalence of over- and undernutrition in the same populations, the same households and even within the same body" (44). But what should be done? In the global health meeting halls, where the disconcerting numbers are made visible for all to watch, this seems evident: change the numbers. Lower the intake of staple foods and fats and increase the amounts of fruits and vegetables that people eat, and, by all means, encourage exercise. But where are the switches and the controls? On the cybernetic pictures that adorn scientific articles, they are easy to point out. If you push on this arrow, what goes on in that box will alter. But outside, among the messy realities of complex daily lives, things are not so simple.

Yates-Doerr lived with diverse families in and around Xela. She went to the market with the women of the households, spoke with them and their friends, and sat in on classes and in clinics providing advice on nutrition. This is how she learned that introducing a numerical take on life in Xela leads primarily to confu-

Here is the lesson for theory. *Doing* does not need be torn between a determinate will and causal determination, between action and behavior. It may also be configured as a *task*: willful and responsive, creative and adaptive, infused by desire and attuned to the circumstances. It might be interesting to think with this model of *doing*, emerging from the clinic and the kitchen, elsewhere, too.[28]

Doing Spread Out

In the Western philosophical tradition, 'natural processes' just happen, while 'voluntary actors' exert control over their actions. There is no place in this dichotomy for actively doing nothing, for *letting go*.

S. has done fieldwork in clinics for people with long-lasting constipation. They have trouble excreting because they find it too demeaning an activity; do not want to do it anywhere but at home; fear that others might smell their feces; or are so busy that they keep missing the occasion. At some point, excreting may have been hurtful for them, and now that the feces have hardened, they expect it will hurt even more. They are tense. S. comes back from the field with stories about doctors who have drugs on offer that loosen up the anal musculature. These assure quick relief, but a few days later the constipation tends to recur. The hypnotherapist works differently. She does not overrule anal contractions with medication, but instead fosters people's imaginations. In the hope of evoking bowel movements, she encourages a businessman who travels internationally to dream up an airport where the check in, the border control, and the baggage control are all easy to clear. To a young boy she suggests that the contents of his bowels resemble fast-moving race cars.[29]

Letting go may be difficult to *do*. One cannot train it in the gym, but it is still a skill that may be acquired. The hypnotherapist encourages her clients to inhabit their bodies differently, less forcefully, with *less* control, more flowingly. Far more relaxed than the 'free men' on whose aspirations (says Kuriyama) the Western 'actor' has been modeled. These men maintained their strength for good reasons: if a Greek city-state lost a war, the inhabitants were in trouble. The 'women and slaves' would be handed over to new masters; the 'free men,' in their turn, would no longer be free. If not killed, they would be enslaved by the winners. By training their musculature, 'free men' hoped to avoid this fate. They did not want to be enslaved and thus sought to defend their independence. When *letting go*, however, one is off guard, if only partially and just for a moment. Such vulnerability is scary and not just for 'free men'. Liberating imaginations may help bodies to relax their sphincters, and so, too, may *letting go* jointly.

In a seminar on the complexities of bodily movements, S. (another S.) gives a beautiful analysis of the training of ballet dancers.[30] *In the discussion, H. talks about something that usually remains backstage: urinating. During their performances, dancers have to keep the muscles of their pelvic floor firmly contracted; afterward, it is difficult for them to quickly relax these same muscles enough to pee. To let go. H. says that the dancing classes in which she participated were marked by long, hard work and rare, short breaks. In those breaks, those seeking to empty their bladders would sit each on their own separate toilet. The walls of the stalls were open at the top and the bottom. For quite a while, total silence would reign: no peeing. None. Nobody could do it; nobody could let go. This was disconcerting, as class would resume soon. And then, finally, loud splattering sounds would announce that at least one person was relaxing. This liberating noise would be quickly followed by splattering sounds all around. Relief.*

Dancing may be understood as moving in a skillfully coordinated way. This sion. For a start, this has to do with the messiness of numbers. In one moment, people learn that their BMI is too high; in the next, they are being warned about their body weight. Professions call out the numbers, but BMI and body weight are different numbers. Body weight, in turn, is sometimes expressed in US pounds and sometimes in Spanish kilograms, depending on the country that has donated the scales. Even if scales use the same units, they say different things, as they are poorly calibrated. What makes things more confusing still is that, locally, the very idea of weighing a body and linking the result to individual food intake just does not make sense. It is a strange and uncomfortable new practice. "For them [elderly K'ichi women] the dieting body of a weight-regulating self was un-*familiar*, in the sense that this was not how their families operated. I suggest that when it came to eating, their bodies were not bounded bodies (individual, social or otherwise). Food was historically communal, servings regulated by both circumstances and food preparation practices. People no more controlled their individual patterns of consumption than they did their size. Clothing mattered, as did hair and other bodily presentations. But possession of one's flesh and a sense of ownership that gives rise to a statement of 'my weight' (*mi peso*) would make little sense as it did not have the broader implication of self-worth and self-control" (102–3).

Locally, fatness used to be a sign of health, and many people still experience it that way. But if the elder women saw

story suggests that *letting go* has its own choreography and that it may be easier to *do* when it is shared.[31] In most settings, urinating and defecating are done individually, while people tend to gather together for meals.[32] But half open toilet stalls help to reveal that *doing* is not caught in a brain-muscle dyad, but takes all kinds of forms and may be shared among collectives.

Over the last few decades, *thinking*, which Merleau-Ponty brought down to earth and located within 'the body,' has spread out from there. One text that lays out that *cognition* is not individual but *distributed* is Alva Noë's *Out of Our Heads*.[33] Noë's subtitle clearly summarizes his purposes: *Why You Are Not Your Brain, and Other Lessons from the Biology of Consciousness*. His argument is with neuroscientists who take thinking to be an achievement of the human brain. No, asserts Noë, the cerebral activities registered by EEGs and the color-coded shades made visible by brain scans should not be mistaken for the ultimate signs of consciousness at work. Thinking involves a lot more. It depends just as much on language repertoires that precede individual speakers, on external requirements and challenges, and on material circumstances and their affordances. And then it comes. To underscore what he is after, Noë urges us to give up on "what we can think of as a kind of 'gastric juices' conception of consciousness—that is, the idea that consciousness happens in the head the way digestion happens in the stomach."[34] Hence, when Noë insists that thinking is spread out, digestion forms his didactic counterpoint: "If we are to understand consciousness—the fact that we think and feel and that a world shows up for us—we need to turn our backs on the orthodox assumption that consciousness is something that happens inside us, like digestion. It is now clear, as it has not been before, that consciousness, like a work of improvisational music, is achieved in action, by us, thanks to our situation in and access to a world we know around us. We are in the world and of it."[35]

But if thinking is spread out, is digestion indeed "something that happens inside us"? Physiology textbooks and their popularized offshoots indeed present pictures in which digestion is located underneath the skin. These result from research into the digestive enzymes at work in the mouth, the stomach, and the bowels. This research was partly performed by surgically opening up dogs and partly with the aid of a man who, due to a war wound, had a lasting fistula between his stomach and his body-surface, which allowed researchers to directly access what went on in his gastrointestinal tract.[36] More recently, tiny tubes inserted through the nose or anus have made it possible to gain more fine-grained knowledge. It appears that even beneath my skin 'I' am not alone: a grand microbial feast is going on inside me. The tiny organisms that inhabit my bowels eat what I ate, leaving for me their end products that I may then either absorb or excrete. However, when Noë, eager to convince his readers of the distributed character of thinking, uses digestion as a counterpoint, he allows himself to be too quickly seduced by physiological imaginations. Had he stopped for a moment to think about it, he would have realized that when it comes to their location, thinking and digesting are quite similar. For yes, there is digestion going on underneath the skin, but not *just* there. Quite like thinking, digestion happens elsewhere, too. *Out of our bowels.*

Take my frittata again. Its digestion started long before I swallowed it. As I chopped the spinach, my knife turned its leaves into smaller bits, which made these more accessible to both my own digestive enzymes and those of the microbes residing inside me. The heat under the frying pan did yet more to digest the ingredients that went into my dish. Raw potatoes are bad food: human bowels (microbes and all) are not able to break them down and absorb the nutrients they contain. Spinach I might have eaten raw—but the 200 grams per person that I put in my frittata looked quite intimidating before being shrunk by cooking. Moreover, they would have offered less nourishment raw than cooked. Slurping up raw eggs, once again, can be done, but is not as nourishing as eating them coagulated in a frittata. Cooking,

nothing of value in guidelines suggesting what each individual should eat, this seemed to be changing for their daughters, "who were taught that their bodies were theirs and their weight their responsibility" (103). But it was not easy for the daughters to take the responsibility for 'their body' on board. In clinics and classes, they were offered knowledge about 'nutrition' in a simplified form. The simplifications, meant to be helpful, appeared to be rather bewildering. For instance, children were taught that fruits and vegetables are good 'because they make you grow.' From this, one of the mothers, who had been told to lose weight, had concluded that she should avoid eating vegetables 'that make you grow.' In a consultation room, Yates-Doerr noted (using N for the nutritionist and P for the person whom professionals called patient), "N: We're going to avoid beets and carrots. P: These I can't eat? N: No, because they're very sweet. No beets and carrots. They're bad. P: Potato also? N: No potato. No pasta either" (74). Living with such lists of prohibitions is difficult, and doing so does not alleviate the dizziness or prickling in their feet that had prompted people to seek help in the clinic. At the same time, the nutritionists, hoping to encourage people into compliance, offered grandiose promises. "N: So what we are going to want to drink—we're going to have two tablespoons of dry oatmeal. P: Very well. N: It's very good this way, and it will take away all the fat you have in your body. P: Very well, doctor" (74). Or, more ambi-

then, as cookbooks happily relate, is a form of extracorporeal digestion.[37] What is done outside an eating body affects what, later on, will happen inside it. Even adding cumin is a case in point: this is widely appreciated as a digestive adjuvant.

It is a simple story, banal really, but the point is consequential.[38] The work that physiology calls 'digestion' is partly done inside 'my bowels,' but partly elsewhere, too. Just as human consciousness is spread out beyond the head, human digestion is spread beyond the gastrointestinal tract. *We are in the world and of it*, as Noë nicely puts it. And if digestion is going on in my kitchen, where I cut and cook, it is being done in other sites and situations too.

On a summer Saturday, L. and I attend a workshop on old grains. It is not quite fieldwork, since we only hear stories and do not see our informants at work. But we learn plenty even so. Mainly we learn it from R., the baker in charge of the workshop. Supermarket bread, he tells the audience, is baked fast; the yeast is granted no more than an hour to ferment the grains. But in his bakery, he grants his sourdough a full night to work on the dough. This makes the bread easier to digest, as it allows the microbes more time for their digestive work. His bread also spends more time in the oven, where, as it transforms from a viscous, inedible mass into crunchy, airy bread, it becomes both tastier and more nourishing. Rye, R. tells us, is relatively heavy in the stomach; wheat is lighter. "And there are also serious differences between wheat variants," he adds. "Some are a lot easier to digest than others."

As R. talks, he mentions various sites pertinent to the digestion, not of all humans 'naturally,' but of the particular humans who eat his bread. Their digestion takes place in the pot where the sourdough microbes ferment the dough for their bread, and in the oven where it is baked. But their digestion also occurs in the fields and sheds of generations of farmers who have sowed grains easier to digest rather than grains hard on the stomach. Hence, the *doing* involved in digestion is spread out in space, over helpful organisms and kitchen implements; and it also stretches out in time, reaching back to earlier centuries when farmers adapted crops so as to make life easier on *my* bowels.

Eating, so we learned earlier, offers a model of *being* in which *I am* not sharply bounded. I incorporate substances that used to be part of my surroundings, while I excorporate excesses until they are no longer a part of me. Now, we learn that *eating* also offers a model of *doing* that stretches out beyond my skin. For the *doings* involved in my digestion are shared. See that flame under my pan? It is digesting for me. And my digestive tasks have also been facilitated by generations of farmers who selected the crops that feed me.[39]

Here is the lesson for theory. *Doing* is not necessarily centered in an embodied individual. It may as well be distributed over a stretched-out, historically dispersed, socio-material collective.

There is a digression I would like to make at this point. If distributed digestive efforts make *me*, they may also have made *humans*. This is the argument Richard Wrangham makes. He claims that by cooking, early hominids externalized significant amounts of digestive work from their bodies to their cooking fires. This, he says, allowed their bowels to shorten and their brains to grow. Human brains kept growing as cooking techniques improved—from laying food in hot ashes, to roasting, to burying food in sand inside a pile of hot coals, to using earth ovens, first packing food in leaves and following on from that using containers, first of plant materials, then of earthenware, and finally of metal. "Although the breakthrough of using fire at all would have been the biggest culinary leap, the subsequent discovery of better ways to prepare food would have led to continual increases in digestive efficiency, leaving more energy for brain growth."[40] Noë, we just saw, argues that human consciousness is spread out be-

tious still: "If we eat well, we won't get sick" (75).

All kinds of locally relevant concerns disappear behind short-cut categorizations of food as either *good* or *bad*. In the clinic, women are not asked how they find the time to shop for meals and cook them; how they manage the costs; what their skills are; who they cook for; which recipes the family cherishes most. There is no room for the problems of commuters who, now that the city has sprawled, cannot make it home to eat during their lunch break. If the restaurants close to their workplace are remotely affordable, they only offer meals that are invariably full of fat and heavy on sugar. There are further painful paradoxes. For instance, the nutritionists tell their patients that it is healthy to eat fruit and vegetables. But calories are not the only threat to health. "Vegetable export markets in the communities surrounding Xela, having expanded to meet international demand for healthy produce, depend on the importation of both seeds and synthetic pesticides used to grow them. Women, afraid of these pesticides, would commonly purchase packaged chips and candies for their children when they were out shopping. They spoke to me about 'chemicals of the dead' that had entered their food and cautioned me to avoid purchasing from women whose headscarves marked them as being from Almolonga, a regional center for export just a few kilometers from Xela's city center. Vegetables were not to be trusted" (44). Global public health experts are concerned about

yond the brain. Wrangham, in his turn, asserts that, over the course of millennia, cooking techniques have provided humans with added brain power. Taken together, these two authors may be read as suggesting that, in cooking fires, digestion and thinking intertwine. See that flame under my pan, that flame transforming my frittata from ingredients into food? It is both a thinking and an eating part of *me*.

Here is the lesson for *doing*. Eating offers a model according to which *doing* eludes the control of a willful center and is spread out through space and in time. The acting *I* does not act alone and is spread out beyond the skin lining of a single body. She is here and there, then and now, this and that. And as an *I* who radically abstains from eating is, after a while, no longer able to act, this particular *doing* also feeds into its own conditions of possibility.

Ways of Living and Dying

The contrast between *willful choices* and *natural processes* may have haunted 'the Western tradition,' but when considered as a task, eating escapes it. Philosophical anthropologist Hans Jonas did not use the term *task*, but he too presented eating as an activity, as something that living organisms engage in, that they *do*. In his book *The Phenomenon of Life. Towards a Philosophical Biology,* published in 1966, Jonas attended to three groups of organisms: plants, animals, and humans. Plants, lowest in the hierarchy, were able to engage in metabolic activity, something that in Jonas insisted was indeed an *activity*. It was not caught up in causal processes, as the natural sciences mistakenly seemed to presume. Metabolism was not a fact, but an act. Eating required organisms to muster their energy and abilities; it was something they might either *do* or leave *undone*. However, abstaining from metabolic activities, Jonas asserted, comes at a cost. "It [the organism] can, but it cannot cease to do what it can without ceasing to be."[41]

In Jonas's rendering, eating is not just *done* actively; it also turns the organism outward, to its surroundings: "In order to change matter, the living form must have matter at its disposal, and it finds this outside itself, in the foreign 'world.' Thereby life is turned outward and toward the world in a peculiar relatedness of dependence and possibility."[42] No independent individuals here: whoever eats depends on what is being eaten. At the same time, Jonas insists that eating entails something different for different kinds of organisms. Plants derive carbon and oxygen from the air, catch and store energy from sunlight, and soak up minerals from the ground in which they are rooted. Animals also breathe, but depend for both their energy and building blocks on other living beings, that is, on plants or other animals. "The animal, feeding on existing life, continually destroys its mortal supply and has to seek elsewhere for more."[43] Because animals destroy their food in the process of eating it, they have to move about to find new food. To help them move about, animals have sense organs. They perceive their surroundings, and this allows them to orient themselves in space and to locate sources of food. In addition, Jonas writes, animals also have emotions; they can, for instance, empathize with the suffering of others. This allows them to collaborate. All of which places animals *above* plants: "Three characteristics distinguish animal from plant life: motility, perception, emotion."[44] Since 1966, when the book was published, these distinctions have all been amended, but Jonas presented them as if they were obvious.[45] They were, he contended, tied to the differences between the ways in which plants and animals metabolize.

the increase in overweight, obesity, and metabolic syndrome for good reasons. But Yates-Doerr lays bare that there are tensions between the professional guidelines inspired by their expertise and the complexities of local food practices. Due to these tensions the guidelines have tragic unforeseen detrimental effects.

Then, finally there was 'the human,' the apex of evolution. In Jonas's philosophical biology, humans resemble plants in their eating; animals (he did *not* write 'other animals') in that they move about, perceive the world around them, and empathize with others. On top of this, 'man' has further characteristics: "Supremely concerned with what he is, how he lives, what he makes out of himself, and viewing himself from the distance of his wishes, aspirations and approvals, man and man alone is open to despair."[46] 'Man' has normative concerns that reach beyond life and death, beyond bodily pleasures and miseries, but also beyond empathy. They have to do with right and wrong. Jonas, writing in the 1960s, was painfully aware that the world does not readily bend itself to man's 'wishes, aspirations, and approvals.' In the 1930s, he had fled Nazi Germany, and when he returned there later as a member of the Jewish Brigade of the British army, he discovered that his mother had been killed in Auschwitz.[47] I do not want to suggest that my two-sentence summary of utterly complex lived realities directly translates into philosophical conclusions. But Jonas's historical context was crucial to his writing. It informed his urge to evade cynicism and his tenacious hope that evil might be countered. It gave depth to his assurance that *man,* beyond just living, has higher goals. Or, as Lawrence Vogel summarizes Jonas's philosophy of biology in the preface to the 2001 English edition of *The Phenomenon of Life*: "The evolution of the human species marks the transition within nature from vital goodness to the capacity for moral rightness: from desire to responsibility."[48]

In the present historical moment, however, this evolutionary layering no longer makes similar sense. For if in the death camps that haunted Jonas, the lives of millions of people were abruptly ended, now we face the possible eradication of all life on earth. It is not 'man' who is under threat, so much as 'metabolism.' Sadly, elevating the status of *eating* in theory will not do much to avert this. However, in seeking to avoid cynicism (a call by Jonas to hold on to!), it may help to adapt our terms to our times.[49] It is in this context that I care to underscore that when *I* eat, this is not an activity of the 'plant within the human.' My eating is not a natural, life-affirming endeavor on top of which further ethical commitments may be layered. Instead, my eating is always already technically and socially mediated. It involves agriculture, distribution networks, skills, equipment, shops, and money: in short, the efforts of a socio-material distributed collective. Moreover, while eating may contribute to my 'vital goodness,' it may also undermine it.

A bit of excorporeal digestion may leave me properly nourished after a cooked meal. Too much of it, however, can be detrimental. Or, in the words of an expert: "It is now generally acknowledged that the current pandemic of obesity and related chronic diseases has as one of its important causes increased consumption of convenience including pre-prepared foods. However, the issue of food processing is largely ignored or minimized in education and information about food, nutrition and health, and also in public health policies."[50]

If cooking a spinach frittata or baking bread partly digest my food for me, too much processing makes it too easy for the human bowels to absorb nutrients across their bowel linings. Hence, it may contribute to the "current pandemic of obesity and related chronic diseases." There are no simple causal links here; it all depends. In some situations, ultraprocessed foods may be a blessing, or at least better than foods poisoned by formaldehyde or pesticides, or than staying hungry.[51] Besides, if ultraprocessed foods contribute to overweight and obesity, this is not just because they are ultraprocessed. They also tend to take the form of added snacks rather than meals; and they are pushed on people by being heavily advertised, or by containing addictive excesses of sugars. One way or the other, the point for now is that my *eating* is not a natural activity, but a cultivated one. It does not necessarily serve my life, and may as well precipitate my death.[52]

What is more, life and death, health and disease, are not the only salient norms to do with eating. In the stretched-out networks in which my eating is suspended, many more *goods* and *bads* come into play. These may be in tension. To illustrate this with examples that are relatively trivial, but suitably emblematic, I return to the workshop on grains.

At some point, we are invited to taste. Small pieces of bread baked from the various grains that R. just talked about are passed around. In explorative mode, I try them all. R. has told us that many people who avoid gluten (the protein, prominently present in wheat, that is suspected of making bellies hurt) have no problems with his breads. This, he says, is due to the long time the microbes in his sourdough spend breaking gluten down. What is more, R. uses older wheat variants. The more recent ones were selected to have a high gluten content because gluten is a glue that helpfully holds the ingredients in dishes together. This selection, R. asserts, may have contributed to the recent increase in gluten sensitivity.

Here, then, we hit on a clash. It may be framed as a clash between interests: for *you*, gluten may be fine, but for *me*, it is not. However, it may also be framed as a clash between goods: for *binding*, gluten is grand, but for *digestion* (particularly for some people's digestion), it is not. If *goods* are foregrounded and compared, they often appear to be in tension.

We get to taste bread baked from spelt and bread baked from emmer, two wheat predecessors. The spelt piece is okay—but it cannot begin to compete with the emmer. Wow, what a wonderful taste! I ask how it is that spelt recently became popular in the Netherlands, while emmer is nowhere to be found. It tastes so much better! R. smiles about my enthusiasm and explains that emmer may taste better, but that it has a small and uncertain yield. Under the best of conditions, it gives a modest harvest, and if the weather does not cooperate, there may be no harvest at all. Growing emmer is hazardous.

Here the good of food *pleasure* clashes with that of food *security*. Emmer may provide me with surprising sensory gratification, but growing it in more than an experimental patch or two is too big a risk for farmers and also for me. It is as well that my life does not depend on it. All of which illustrates that 'my eating' is not quite the metabolic activity of a plantlike layer within 'the human,' but a complex socio-material achievement. It is not a matter of *life* and *death*, but of different *ways of living*. Living with hunger or with excessive weight. Cooking with ease, but then suffering from hurting bowels. Missing out on sensorial pleasures, but enjoying food security. *Eating* does not just form a precondition for the 'wishes, aspirations, and approvals' that are 'man's' destination. It is always already located in a complex normative force field.

Here is the lesson for theory. *Doing* is not simply good or bad. It may be good for some and bad for others or good in some ways and bad in others. Words like *pragmatic* and *effective* always have to be qualified: In relation to which goals? Even eating is not simply life giving, but involves complex negotiations between contrasting *goods* and *bads*.

These navigations are made all the more complex by a nagging lack of overview. It is often not very clear what eating activities achieve. Even the relativity simply 'vital goodness' of health is not straightforward. Take the spinach frittata: Does that serve us well, my guest and me?

When I try to look this up on the website of The Dutch Nutrition Center, proudly dealing in 'scientifically grounded information,' I hit up against insecurities. A few years ago, the center warned against eating spinach too often, as human bodies were said to transform the nitrate it contains into nitrosamine, which is carcinogenic. As I write this text, the site relates that there is no problem with eating spinach, as the quantities of nitrosamine involved are below the threshold of danger.[53] What about the eggs? A few years ago, their cholesterol was associated with an increased risk of vascular disease. Now this fear has waned. However, the website warns against eating eggs from chickens kept in backyards. They will peck their feed from the ground, but all over the Netherlands, the ground is polluted with dioxin, another carcinogenic substance, that sadly gets concentrated in eggs.[54] Potatoes are fine, if eaten in modest quantities, and I may fry them. But just a bit. If they get too dark, too much acrylamide is formed in the process, and this, once again, increases an eater's statistical chances of developing cancer.

If it is difficult to know which foods serve my 'vital goodness,' the 'moral rightness' that Jonas hoped I would strive after, is even more elusive. How can you do the right thing if you do not know what you are doing? There are ample food practices that are clearly *not* right. They are vile, demeaning, exploitative, as a rich and urgent body of literature points out.[55] Most of them deserve structural responses that have been postponed for far too long. But if, as the 'consumer' that advisory notices address, I seek to eat in an ethically sound way, I get quickly confused. All too easily, my well-intended *doings* have—invisible or unforeseen—adverse effects.

The shops I frequent offer organic, fair trade coffee. As I can afford them, it is easy for me to buy them. But is it good? When we get to talk, V., who studies coffee growing, tells that in the regions where he works, carrying heavy organic fertilizer up the steep mountains slopes on which coffee is grown is often too difficult for the farmers to do. In their attempts to hold on to the 'organic' label, some farmers therefore do not fertilize their land at all. In the short term, this provides them with the higher price traders pay for coffee that is organic. In the long term, however, and this may not be all that long, it is bad for their soil. This means that it is bad for their coffee plants and therefore for their income, too. The 'fair trade' label comes with its own problems. For instance, the labeling process is highly demanding. Moreover, while fair trade coffee farmers tend to have a better income than other farmers, the laborers who pick the coffee beans do not. If they were to receive better pay, fair trade farmers would get in trouble with their neighbors.[56]

I do not give these examples (from an endless list of possibilities) to promote cynicism. They are rather meant to illustrate that 'moral rightness' is an elusive ideal. You may do what you can, but the networks over which food care is suspended are often so complex and extended that you do not know what you are doing.[57] That is no excuse for feeding chickens dioxins, or exploiting farm laborers, or killing the insects on coffee plants with pesticides, or spraying fruit with formaldehyde: *those* are obviously bad things to do. Sadly, the list of things that are obviously bad, but nevertheless shamelessly done, is shockingly long. But that should not keep us imprisoned in a 'moral rightness' version of ethics. For if cynicism is dangerous, moral righteousness is delusional. Situations in which complexity stands out call instead for a genre of *doing* where good intentions are always combined with attentive inquiries into potential adverse effects.

Here is the lesson for theory. Some exemplary situations come with a clearcut division between good and evil. Nazi atrocities are a case in point. These prompted Jonas to overcome despair, be courageous, and call for moral rightness. However, in the context of present-day urban eating, ethics becomes something different. It is not a matter of deeds ostensibly done well, but requires recursive attentiveness to what happens as an unintended consequence of one's *doings*. In the absence of control, care is called for: the preparedness to *do* one's very best, acknowledge failure, take a step back, and begin again.

Jonas took eating to be a life-affirming act, but maintained that it was truly human to rise above concerns with one's bodily survival and have aspirations beyond that. Certainly, there is more to life than staying alive. But what I argue here is that 'staying alive' already always entails that *more*. The eating on which survival depends is not 'natural' but 'cultivated.' It is suspended between diverse socio-material configurations and may be done in different ways. There is an ethics to it, but this ethics is not clear-cut. Even if despair is best kept at bay, moral rightness is too much to hope for. As the networks on which 'my' eating depends are endlessly complex and elude a comprehensive overview, eating *well* involves trying, facing defeat, and trying again.

Here is the lesson for *doing*. No longer downgrading eating to a lowly precondition for life, but exploring how it is *done*, here and there, as a part of diverse socio-material practices, suggests a model of *doing* torn between countless tense conundrums. This means that *doing good* becomes a task to take on stubbornly, even if—or precisely because—it is tantalizingly elusive.

What Doing Becomes

Public health campaigns encourage people to make healthy food choices, while research laboratories investigate eating as if it were a natural process. In the clinic and the kitchen, by contrast, eating is a *task*. This suggest another type of *doing*: one that is more easily decided on than performed; one that is physical but not confined to the body of the actor; one that involves other people and a myriad of things. Tools, when adapted to the eater, may contribute to the taming of the task. But if, when modeled on *my* eating, *doing* is caring, it is also transformative. Enzymes—human and microbial—break down foods into particles small enough to transport across my bowel linings. So, too, do cooking fires. They transform indigestibles like raw potatoes into pleasant ingredients of a meal. Generations of farmers have changed cultivars so as to adapt them to the palates and the bowels of the people bound to eat their produce. The actor pertinent to this model of *doing*, the actor taking on the task of eating, is a stretched-out, historically dispersed, socio-material collective.

This complex aggregate is not quite predictable. Cultivation and care do not offer control. At any point, things may go this way or that; the result may turn out to be welcome or disappointing. Or, still more complex, when eating is being *done,* what is being *done* along with it is bound to be *good* for some and *bad* for others; *good* in one respect and *bad* in another. In the Chinese tradition, Kuriyama tells us, humans were taken to resemble plants, especially with respect to their moral growth and unfolding. Western philosophers, by contrast, elevated humans above plants. They asserted that plants only seek to ensure their survival, while humans are moral beings, with higher goals. In line with this, human eating was cast as a plantlike endeavor: a natural desire, a physical need, a precondition for attending to those higher goals. But this description does not fit *my eating,* for this is not just a matter of life and death. Instead, it helps to orchestrate different ways of living and different ways dying. I may want to do the right thing, I may want to eat well, but, one way or another, what I do may turn out to be bad. This lack of control, however, is no excuse for cynicism. Rather, it calls for another kind of ethics. An ethics without reassuring handholds, an ethics that does not envision this or that goal in isolation but realizes that deeds inevitably have diverse effects. An ethics that imagines worthy *doing* as caring, self-reflective, curious, attentive, adaptive. And tenacious.

5 Relating

THE PREVIOUS CHAPTERS SUGGESTED THAT *being*, *knowing*, and *doing* take on different meanings if they are no longer modeled on *the* human, who is able to think, but on *this or that* human who is eating. This chapter extends the investigation to *relating*.[1] The twentieth-century philosophical anthropologists recalled here thought to address a range of concerns, but what stood out for them was the havoc that twentieth-century totalitarian regimes wrought in Europe. Turning against Nazi and Soviet camps, they submitted that humans 'should not be treated as beasts.' Relations between people had to be based on equality and on the acknowledgment of a shared humanity. The philosophical anthropologist who most explicitly thematized human *relating* was Emmanuel Levinas. That is why in this chapter I recall his work and use it as a counterpoint to think away from. Eating played an important part in Levinas's theorizing of *relating*. In contrast to the authors discussed so far, he did not take it to be 'merely' a prerequisite for staying alive. Instead, and interestingly, Levinas celebrated eating as a joy. But while it was 'truly human,' a decent person might want to forgo this joy so as to afford it to an Other. Offering one's food to a stranger became Levinas's icon for ethical *relating*. When someone knocked on his door, the *I* was to open it, look the Other in the eyes, and recognize him as a fellow human. Moved by the similarity between them, the *I* should not rob the Other of his life, but offer him the precious gift of food. The *I* should not eat, but feed the stranger.

Levinas called on his fellow humans to recognize the *similarity* between themselves and Others. This call did not quite have the desired effect in the European context where it was proposed. In the rest of the world, likewise, inequality, exploitation, and violence have not stopped, but are ongoing. Even so, in this chapter I address another concern. What happens when we let go of human exceptionalism and consider *my relating* to nonhuman creatures?[2] The *I* may want to look in their eyes, too, or perceive their similarities with humans in another way. These similarities may or may not be taken as an appeal to forgo eating them. But wherever the demarcation, in the end I *do* eat, ingesting some bits and pieces of some creatures. What is there to learn from how I relate to those from whom I eat? Levinas suggests that eaters annihilate the creatures on which they feed. And as long as *eating* is understood on the individual level of *me* ingesting (a part of) an edible other, this makes eminent sense. But things change when we extend our scope to agricultural labor. For then it appears that most of the creatures on whom I feed have been fostered with an eye to their edibility. This suggests that *taking* is not only destructive, while *giving* is not simply generous. The quality of the relations between eaters and foods-to-be depends, again and again, on a myriad of further specificities.

When Levinas took similarity as a reason for respect, he drew on a long theoretical tradition of celebrating relations with kin. In Western philosophy, the bond between brothers has enduringly figured as an ideal type affiliation. Brotherhood formed the preferred model for friendship, which, as if this were self-evident, was tantamount to friendship between men. In Levinas's family picture, however, a woman is prominently present, more particularly the mother who lovingly nourished 'the subject' before he managed to disentangle himself. The subject, then, is a son. Theories of the relations between humans and other creatures have drawn on other images of the family. Evolutionary theory imported the family trees of the English gentry. These family trees suggest that the more recent the ancestor that two species have in common,

FEEDING RELATIONS

The *eating* with which I seek to think in this book comes in various forms. It can consist of swallowing a mouthful, ingesting nutrients, stocking up on calories, stilling hunger, enjoying tasty dishes, sharing a meal, devouring other creatures, and so on. Rather than remaining the same from one site to the next, it is multiple, more than one and less then many, since all these different varieties of eating encounter and interfere with each other. Traveling elsewhere, to sites farther afield, adds further variations to eating. In her article "Eating (and Feeding)," Marilyn Strathern

the closer their family ties. But if in kinship terms, I am close to chimpanzees, when it comes to eating, I am closer to apples. My relation with apples does not hinge on familial proximity; instead, apples *agree* with me. The agreement between eater and food may be physical, social, cultural, financial, but it is not symmetrical. Yet the question deserves to be asked: What is *agreeable* to creatures being eaten? Is it possible, in relation to feeding mothers as well as other foods-to-be, to straddle *violence* and *love*?

The English gentry was held together by blood ties, but later the term *kinship* was expanded to other relations and came to connote forms of *togetherness* that have little to do with similarity. What matters for nonfilial *kinship* is not shared traits, but shared activities. Among humans, these may include growing up together, working together, eating at the same table, and gathering for festivities and funerals. With nonhuman creatures, humans may engage in kin-making activities as well. A person may hang out with dogs, foster pigeons, walk over grassy paths, or enjoy the shade of trees. But is *eating* others also a way of making kin? Maybe this mode of relating asks for other terms. And so does my relating with creatures which I do *not* eat but which are nevertheless implicated by my eating. They had hoped to eat what I eat; they were expelled from the areas where my food was grown; or they were never born. Are they my competitors? It is possible to say that our relations boil down to a fight. But here is the problem: I may win and win again. But taking without giving is erosive to all life. Hence, if at first the loss is only theirs, in the end it is also mine.

Giving and Taking

Like other philosophical anthropologists, Levinas was suspicious of sociological schemes that explained individuality away. The human subject, he wrote, "is not defined by its references to a whole, by its place within a system, but by starting from itself."[3] However, the subject whom Levinas considered did not emerge from nowhere. Levinas paid explicit attention to how 'the self' came into being. "The fact of starting from oneself is equivalent to separation" (300). One became a subject by disentangling oneself from one's mother. She had first carried and given birth to her infant and then gone on to breastfeed him. Hence, all faces that the subject encountered later in his life had a reassuring shine to them, but especially those of women, as they reminded the subject of his mother. "The welcoming of the face is peaceable . . . primordially in the gentleness of the feminine face, in which the separated being can recollect itself" (150). Before the subject separated himself from his mother, their relation had been of a nonverbal, nourishing kind. Or, in Levinas's terms, the first "interhuman relationship is the relation, not with the interlocutor but with feminine alterity. This alterity is situated on another plane than language and nowise represents a truncated, stammering, still elementary language" (155). The mother, feeding her child, offers nourishment that assures his growth and is at the same time pleasurable. "To enjoy without utility, in pure loss, gratuitously, without referring to anything else, in pure expenditure—this is the human" (133).

Arendt considered eating to be a distraction from more worthwhile endeavors; for Merleau-Ponty, it was a banal precondition for cognition; Jonas took it to be a life-affirming activity on which nobler pursuits could be grounded. Levinas, by contrast, cherished eating. For him, it was something humans were able to enjoy 'without utility' and 'without referring to anything else.' However, the story did not end there, for the ultimate ethical deed was to forgo this joy and offer one's food to a stranger. This is the scene at the heart of Levinas's ethics: the *I* sits at the table, a needy stranger knocks on the door, and the *I*, opening the door, looks the stranger in the eyes. In this *face to face*, the I recognizes the other as both Other to the self and similarly human. This should then prompt the ethical subject to invite the stranger in and feed him. "To recognize the Other is to recognize a hunger. To recognize the other is to give" (75).[4] In

argues that the Hagen, specifically Northern Melpa speakers, make their own specific cuts around the term and its diverse meanings. "Eating/being eaten refers to a spectrum of actions, from killing someone in warfare, or as an ally causing someone to be killed, to being consumed by abstract afflictions such as poverty ('trubbishness'), or being devoured by the hot sun or by pain in childbirth. It can be used in a denigratory way . . . when men and women alike accuse others of being consumers of their efforts. It can also point to the pleasures and dangers of food and, for both sexes, of sexual relations—licit or otherwise" (7). Hence, the Hagen term that English-speakers translate into 'eating' evokes all kinds of activities that the English term *eating* does not. The stakes, Strathern adds, are also different. "Hageners lay no great culinary emphasis on the combination of tastes at a meal, but they do associate the eating of (safe, proper) food with pleasure, and pork above all. Explicitly, feeding someone pork can turn their hearts, make them feel good" (7). The good feelings result from the *pork* as well as from the *feeding*. These things are intertwined. Among Hagen, pork evokes a feeder, a person who offered it as a gift.

To further elucidate this, Strathern describes the gift of pork that (at least in the past) the mother of the bride would receive at her daughter's wedding. This pork came from a pig that had been raised by the mother of the groom. The mother of the bride would *eat* from it twice. First, when the pig was handed over to her. In English, one might say that

the background, once again, loom the harsh realities of the Holocaust. The Nazis did not remotely 'recognize the Other' but killed millions of people, while treating millions more appallingly. Those who managed to flee all too often knocked in vain on the doors of nation-states and private houses. These atrocities do not explain Levinas's thinking, but they informed it and gave it its urgency. They were the ultimate evil to avoid. Humans, he contended, should not be dehumanized. The Other, he insisted, should not be annihilated, but recognized instead as both similar enough to be respected and different enough to not assimilate. The exemplary situation on which Levinas modeled how one should *not* treat fellow humans was that of eating. Eating destroys otherness. "In the satisfaction of need the alienness of the world that founds me loses its alterity: in satiety the real I sank my teeth into is assimilated, the forces that were in the other become *my* forces, become me" (129). Here, by equating annihilation and eating, cannibalism was evoked (as it had been often before in the Western philosophical tradition) as an icon for the worst possible way of relating.[5]

Levinas, then, draws a contrast between two modes of relating: eating, which comes at the cost of another; and feeding, which comes at one's own cost. This is obviously an ultrashort summary of a rich intellectual project to which I do not begin to do justice here. Even so, I will take the liberty to ask a few questions at this point. Why, for a start, is ethical relating situated within the confines of a family home, skipping the question why some people have a home, while others roam around as hungry, wandering strangers? And how is it that 'the home' is so readily taken to be a safe place? Why, finally, is 'the subject' without any further ado equated with the grateful son, not the depleted mother?[6] In the next section, I will come back to this homely imagination. But first, I would like to focus on the implied humanism. Levinas was concerned about 'dehumanization.' He called on the *selves* he addressed to feed *others* who were similarly human, even if this came at their own cost. The costs to the creatures being eaten were recognized—'in satiety the real I sank my teeth into is assimilated'—but accepted as a matter of course. But are the creatures being eaten so very different from humans? Recognition may also strike when one finds oneself face to face with dished-up animals.

In 2015, after a spirited day at a conference discussing agriculture and food with a group of colleagues, we assemble for dinner in a Thai restaurant in Queenstown, New Zealand. When a waiter appears at our table, we order all kinds of dishes, planning to share. Most are vegetable dishes. There is, however, one with shrimp and another that the menu describes as 'a whole fish.' It will be fried and served with red pepper, garlic, ginger, lemon, and coriander. After a few minutes a second waiter comes to our table with a question. Do we want the fish with its head attached—or not? We ask how he would serve it in a Thai setting. Obviously, he shrugs, with the head attached. Then why did he ask us this question? Often, he says, at a table with mostly Westerners (his word) at least one guest is horrified by the sight of a head on a plate. Or, as he puts it in another sentence: "In my experience you people don't like eating things with heads."

To some people ('you people'), an animal face makes an appeal. It says 'do not eat me,' accept me as an Other, as being similar enough not to be assimilated. At our table of conference-goers, we readily agreed that this appeal should not be silenced with a kitchen knife. Seeking to achieve peace of mind by asking for a head to be cut off before a fish reaches the dinner table we took to be hypocritical. Either you abstain from eating animals (as some of us do) or you are prepared to face them (as is the case for others, with this or that caveat).[7]

Stretching Levinas's humanism beyond humans, it makes sense to forgo eating all creatures similar to humans. Respect them, do not eat them, they are like us, they are members of the same extended family. At this point, not just recognizable faces, but also vivid intelligence or remarkable sensibility are often

she 'received' the pig as a gift, but locally the word used is the one that translates as 'eating.' Receiving-eating would offer a woman pleasure, as it meant that she was granted recognition for having raised a daughter. Then, once the animal had been cooked, the mother would eat of it once again, this time savoring it, ingesting it, at a festive marriage meal. This particular eating meant recognition once again and, this time round, also the pleasure provided by the meat. The festive meal was a high point that the mother had looked forward to for years when feeding her daughter. Eating decomposed not just the meat being eaten but also the mother herself. Afterward, she no longer was 'the mother' in the same way, because her daughter, once married, would no longer live with her but move to the house of another family. All of this means that the crucial *relation* at stake in eating a bridal meal is not the relation between the eater and food—or the creature being eaten. It is instead the relation between two human mothers. The mother of the bride eats the pig that is gifted to her by the mother of the groom: "The relational operator in Hagen is social origin: entities become defined in terms of (relations with) who has given/received them and thus of their origins and destinations" (9).

Strathern contrasts Hagen eating-as-giving-receiving with Vilaça's descriptions of eating among the Wari' in Amazonia. The analysis is in the past tense as it involves the eating of dead people, which is no longer done. By tradition, Wari' eating would shape the identities both of eat-

evoked as impediments to eating.[8] But which creatures to recognize as intelligent and sensible? Monkeys—but then why not pigs? Dogs—but then why not octopuses?[9] Instead of reviewing these debates here, I wish to invoke another puzzle, which is that, beyond faces, wit, and awareness, similarities between species may take yet further forms. Here is a story of a long-gone but never-forgotten ethnographic moment.

In 1976, I was a student of medicine. In our anatomy class we learned about bodily structures by dissecting them. A corpse that had soaked in formaldehyde for at least six months was laid out on a metal table with holes in it. First, we had to free it from a plastic cover and a huge, wet, orange towel. Then, using tweezers and scalpels, we had to find the bodily components stipulated in our instruction manual. I volunteered to work close to the face, on the left side of the neck. Two other students tackled the right arm, two more the left leg. On alternate days, the other side was dissected by another group of five. It wasn't easy. We had to lift the skin with the tweezers, cut through it with the scalpel, and then scrape it free of the underlying fat and connective tissue to gradually lay bare the arteries, nerves, and muscles we were meant to see. I accidently severed one of the arteries that I was seeking. Gradually, dull-colored muscles became visible. They resembled the muscles of any other mammal. They looked like meat. Or, the other way around, meat suddenly came to look like the muscles of a human. After anatomy classes, H. and I made it a habit to eat vegetarian fare in the Green Aquarius. *There, without talking very much, we sat next to each other on floor cushions, using chopsticks to lift our meals from bowls: rice, chickpeas or lentils, cabbage, mushrooms. The atmosphere was, to use a term from the time,* countercultural.

As long as human bodies remain covered by their skin, the similarity between their striped muscles and those of other mammals remains hidden. For H. and me, in our student days, the practice of dissecting made this similarity visible. But the possibility of recognizing similarities between the substance of humans and that of edible creatures does not end there.

In 2011, seven of us gathered in an apartment in Amsterdam for an ethnographic experiment. We were to eat a hot meal with our fingers. Four of us were finger-eating experts; three of us had grown up using utensils. First, we cooked. Then we ate. Lifting one bite after the other, our fingers allowed us to sense the food, while the food made us attend to the sensations of our fingers. But how to call these sensations? Were they feelings, resulting from our sense of touch, or was it possible to say that our fingers were tasting our food? As I was feeling and tasting, it suddenly struck me how similar they were, my fingers and my food. As the finger-eating experts had just taught me, I pressed my food in little balls. The food pressed back. It was plant-based food. No meat around. But even so. Rice with dal, eggplant in sauce, as my hands appreciated their particular combination of solidity and viscosity, adaptability and firmness, they felt, they tasted, quite like mine.[10]

The seeds, fruits, and leaves I picked up from my plate with my fingers and then lifted to my mouth were enriched with herbs and spices. They had been cooked, but that did not erase the similarities between us. We were strikingly alike, my food and me. But this particular similarity did not invite my abstention. Yes, we were all living creatures, belonging to one big family, indeed. We shared a lot of traits. But why would that foreclose eating? I did not feel I had to forgo this meal of rice, lentils, eggplant. Instead, realizing in my fingers, on my tongue, that I resemble the plants I eat from, made me appreciate our shared vitality. I was grateful.

Here is my concern: inspired by Levinas, one may ponder what/who to eat and from whom/what to abstain.[11] But however relevant it is, this pondering hides another question, that of *my* relation to the creatures that, in the end, I *do* eat. And the problem with this relation is not that in the past we had common ancestors, but that I destroy their future. Or is it?

ers and of creatures being eaten: it turned the eater into a *person* and the creature being eaten into *food*. Eating deceased people was therefore a way to create distance from them as it treated the dead body not as a person, but as food. Eating the dead was done by neighbors who were not kin and who, in respect for the sadness of the occasion, ate with ostensive displeasure. At the end of the mourning period, the neighbors would visit again, now to share a meal in which the dead person's kin also participated. All those gathered would eat meat from an animal that stood in for the deceased. "Both ate the 'corpse,' kin weeping afresh while non-kin ate voraciously and with relish" (4). It was acceptable to take pleasure from eating the meat of animals that represented a deceased human. After a war, it was likewise acceptable to take pleasure from eating human flesh: "The same emphatic relish accompanied the devouring of fresh enemy bodies" (4). Eating the body of an enemy allowed a fighter to incorporate the enemy's spirit. Hence, it was not just pleasurable, but also fortifying. The identities of both eater (fortified) and enemy (food) were both transformed due to their eating/feeding relation.

Strathern draws a further contrast, this time with what she calls Euro-American or, more particularly, Dutch eating. To exemplify this, she uses a piece I wrote for the journal *Subjectivities*, a preliminary exploration of some of the themes that recur in the present book. "Mol's premise is that eating an apple provides a case through which to think about subjectiv-

Levinas asserts that in eating I destroy the other. So I do, as long as 'eating' is confined to what happens indoors, around the dinner table. I squeeze rice and dal into a ball, pick it up, lift it to my mouth, open my lips, insert the food between them, chew, swallow. Rice and lentils disappear from the scene. I live to tell the story. But if 'eating' is widened out to include what happens elsewhere, beyond the home in which I find myself, beyond the time span of a meal, things change. For, lucky me, in some future moment, I may eat a meal of rice and dal again, since right now someone whom I do not know, in a faraway field, is growing the ingredients for me. That my ancestors left offspring is due to the fact that they did not just devour the creatures they ate, but also grew others. With my food I do not just have kinship relations, but agri/cultural relations as well.

One of my favorite apples is the Belle de Boskoop. This is a Dutch delicacy which has a coarse skin, is fairly sour, and works really well in hot dishes, say with leek, sweet pepper, and red beans, or in an apple crumble. Because of its coarse skin and sourness many people do not like these apples raw, and at some point their popularity declined. There were still Belle de Boskoop on offer, but mostly in organic food stores and only in season. The supermarkets concentrated on sweeter apples. More recently, for some reason, Belle de Boskoop have risen in popularity again; they are easier to find. Most Dutch supermarkets have them on offer, while warehouse storage has considerably lengthened the time they are 'in season.'

This individual apple gets annihilated as I eat it. However, this *variety* of apple thrives when enough potential eaters appreciate its traits. It is a virtuous cycle: a propensity to eat contributes to the cultivation of the variety; the easy availability of the variety increases the likelihood that more people will acquire a taste for it. Hence, while *my* eating this *particular* apple destroys what I bite off, chew, and swallow, *our* eating this *kind* of apple is generative. It helps to care for the trees that bear the fruits we covet.[12]

Levinas, like other philosophical anthropologists, sought to disentangle individuals from the explanatory schemes of nascent sociology. When it comes to understanding eating, however, there are good reasons to widen one's scope beyond the individual. Doing so does not necessarily yield explanations, but it places the relations between eaters and the creatures whose fruits, or other parts, they eat in another light. For when pursued beyond the dinner table, it appears that my eating does not just annihilate my food, but also allows for the growth of the creatures on which I feed. Eating and feeding are entangled.

My friend G. has a small allotment at the northern edge of the city where she lives. She bikes there at the end of winter to prune trees and clear the ground. She prepares plant beds and then, when spring is in the air, she sows them with seeds or puts in plants that she has first grown in small seeding pots. G. also plants potatoes (of different colors) and sometimes buys small bushes (like raspberry canes) from the garden center. Throughout the spring, she spends her Saturdays tying up climbers, watering, and weeding. Especially weeding. The killing of undesirable plants, G. insists, forms a substantial part of growing food. Then, at some festive moment in early summer, harvesting starts. From that moment onward, G. tends to have plenty of vegetables and fruits she may eat, offer to her guests, or preserve for the coming winter.[13]

Before digging them up, G. plants her potatoes in well-prepared beds. She protects her raspberries against plants that might smother them. She gives to her garden before she takes from it. Eating, then, is not just destructive. But there is a corollary to that. Which is that, in gardens, giving does not present itself as an ethical thing to do. For G. may well care for her potatoes and raspberries, and she may even do so with dedication. But their edibility is always the horizon. Well

ities" (2–3). An eater, after all, is not a classic, well-rounded, self-sufficient subject. As an eater *I am* thanks to *the apple* I eat, while in the process of eating the boundary between us blurs and *I* come to consist, at least in part, of *apple*. But the apples that I eat are not just material, they are semiotic objects, too. *My* apples taste of the biblical stories of paradise, in which they figured as forbidden fruit. They are colored by the Dutch expression that translates as "saving an apple for when one is thirsty," which encourages thriftiness. Or they come with stains, like the Granny Smith from Chile in the late 1970s, which smelled of the dictatorship of Pinochet and therefore deserved to be boycotted. Hence, while Strathern insists that the Hagen word for 'eating' includes a lot more activities than the English one, I hint at the fact that in my Dutch fieldsites, other things are occurring simultaneously with eating, caught within it. Vilaça writes that Wari' personhood is lost at the moment that a person (animal or human) is eaten. I mention that, in my field, personhood may in theory have to do with autonomy, but in practice depends on food. Overall, I was—and am—analyzing eating practices in search of theoretical inspiration. And while in this book I *contrast* thinking and eating, I like Strathern's observation, when describing how academics relate, that thinking may be *modeled on* eating, too: "We consume one another's insights, feed each other with thoughts, recognizing their origin where we can" (12).

cared for, potatoes are satisfying food. Raspberry bushes reward proper protection with delicious raspberries. In G.'s allotment, then, feeding and eating, giving and taking, are intertwined. It makes no sense to disentangle the moralities involved. Rather than feeding being good and eating being bad, feeding and eating both presume and implicate each other.

G. only grows plants on her allotment. But the feeding and eating of animals may intertwine in similar ways. It does so in Hans Harbers's rendering. He wrote about the Dutch farm where he grew up in the 1950s and 1960s.[14]

"I remember the farm primarily as an economic system; as a source of income in an indirect sense, and of our own food supply in a direct sense—beef and pork from our own animals, eggs from the chickens, fresh milk from the cows, and vegetables from our own garden. . . . The economic character of the activities should not be limited to the strict sense of the market, only competition and profit making—although these did play a role, of course. Above all, it was a style of life—of survival."[15] For their survival, farming families depend on their farms and hence on all the creatures that live on it. They also depend on a lot of things, on the contexts in which farms operate. Hence, there is a lot to care for.

RELATING THROUGH DIFFERENCE

In the Western philosophical tradition, entities have characteristics that are intrinsic to them. They are 'themselves' before they relate. Paying attention to eating interferes with this to a certain extent, as it suggests that *I* can only ever be *me* thanks to the apple (buckwheat pancake, spinach frittata) I eat. A lot follows from that. But still, the apple (pancake, frittata) and I hold on to our names irrespective of our relations. I am I, the apple is an apple. I remain me, even if I eat something else. The apple remains an apple, whether eaten by me or by a horse. The wind is the wind; a fish is a fish. In the perspectivist world that Viveiros de Castro presents in his writings, this is different. There, what an entity *is*, follows from its relations. In the article "Exchanging Perspectives: The Transformation of Objects into Subjects in Amerindian Ontologies," Viveiros de Castro explain that in 'our' world, "you are a father only because there is another person

"Being a good farmer was a question of endless care, in various modes and degrees—care relating to the animals, the plants, the crops, the buildings, the tools, the drainage, etc. Taking care of was always coupled with having to care about diverse factors—the health of a particular cow, the next day's weather if the harvest was going to be brought in, the price of pigfeed, the risks involved in that essential new investment. And there was always concern about our school results, with an eye to a future without the farm. Caring for and caring about always materialised in the context of self-preservation, the preservation of that network, that way of life."[16]

What we have here is an acute awareness that sustaining one's life, one's way of living, depends on labor, on care.[17] Such care may be loving, but the love involved is definitely unsentimental. When they no longer contribute to the collective, the animals on the farm are killed. The favorite dog, having become ill and in pain, is euthanized and buried. The much-appreciated horse, replaced by a tractor, goes to the slaughterhouse. Chickens that no longer provide the family with eggs are eaten.

Chickens were fed and watered, Harbers tells. Their beaks were clipped so that they could not peck each other. However: "As soon as they stopped laying, even this limited care came to an abrupt end. They were slaughtered and we would enjoy a weekend of chicken soup and drumsticks, fighting about who would get the heart—a delicacy."[18]

On the farm, then, like in the allotment, feeding is not simply generous. Chickens are cared for because they lay eggs and with an eye on their future as drumsticks. But if eating were merely destructive, farming would quickly come to an end. The possibility of eating eggs and drumsticks next year, and the year after that, depends on enduringly caring for the chickens. Farm ethics is not suspended between giving and taking. The crucial question, rather, is how to care.

"On hot summer days, we removed a couple of planks at the back of the chicken sheds to give the chickens a little more fresh air. That's how the stoat could get in. She attacked the chickens like a pedigreed vampire, biting their throats and drinking their blood. We couldn't catch, kill or poison her. It was impossible among all those chickens. The only solution was to put the planks back, to keep her literally outside the system—even if the heat stunned the chickens. That was at least better (i.e., less bad) than being savaged by the stoat. Caring was also a matter of permanent consideration of the pros and cons of a certain situation."[19]

Harbers does not regret slurping up chicken soup or enjoying the chicken's heart when he won the fight with his siblings. But that the shed was allowed to get hot because a stoat found out about the plank loosened for fresh air—that he relates with retrospective apprehension. If he had chickens now, he would invent a better way to let cool air come into their shelter. He does not, however, offer retrospective judgments. Instead, he insists on the ethical style implied in caring for those on which one feeds. It was a "permanent consideration of the pros and cons of a certain situation."[20]

whose father you are. Fatherhood is a relation, while fishiness is an intrinsic property of fish. In Amerindian perspectivism, however, something is a fish only by virtue of someone else whose fish it is" (473). In *perspectivist* ways of apprehending, then, not just fatherhood, but fish-ness, too, is relational. This is not an epistemological point, as it would be in Western *perspectivalism*, where different spectators see different things as they each observe an object from different point of view. Instead, it is an ontological point; it regards the object. Variation is not in the eye (ear, nose, tongue) of the beholder, but in what relations make of reality. For example, if *we* like manioc beer, this means that what *we* like to drink *is* manioc beer. It is manioc beer if *we* are humans, and if *we* are jaguars, it is still *manioc beer*. Or, and here I quote from "Perspectival Anthropology and the Method of Controlled Equivocation," "When the jaguar says 'manioc beer' he is referring to the same thing as us (i.e., a tasty, nutritious and heady brew)" (6). However, were *humans* to taste the stuff that jaguars call manioc beer, they would quickly spit it out—as they would not want to drink what *for humans* is not manioc beer at all, but blood. They would spit it out for fear of turning into a jaguar.

In Viveiros de Castro's rendering, Amerindian ontology is relational. The properties of entities always emerge from their relations with other entities. At the same time, relating itself is specific. For Westerners, Viveiros de Castro writes, *relating* hinges on something shared. In

Levinas asked his fellow humans to forgo cannibalism and engage in feeding relations instead. Once separated from his mother, an ethical human subject was meant to feed the Other, not to eat him, to give to him, not to take from him. It is possible to broaden this humanist call and wonder which other creatures might be included in the taboo on cannibalism. Here I ask another question. What might we learn about *relating* from analyzing *my* relation to the creatures from whose flesh (eggs, milk, leaves, fruits, seeds, roots) I *do* eat? For physically separating oneself from one's mother does not equal autonomy. When infants are weaned, they may stop drinking their mother's milk, but that does not mean they become independent. Instead, they shift their dependence to cow milk, soy milk, oat milk, and/or other foods. This raises questions about how, as an eater, to best care back for those who, in their entirety or in parts, figure as one's food. These questions are acutely pertinent in a world where, as it is, in all too many sites and situations, the 'caring back' leaves a lot to be desired. This lack of care is unkind. It is immoral. And since I depend on what I eat, it is also dangerous.

Here is the lesson for *relating*. While, as an individual human, I absorb bits and pieces of the creatures on whom I feed, agricultural collectives orchestrate care that goes in two directions. There is an intertwinement between eating and feeding. This suggests a model of *relat-*

ing in which taking is not necessarily bad, while giving is not simply good. What makes a particular feeding/eating relation either good or bad cannot be sketched in broad strokes. It resides, again and again, in the specificities of the situation.

Violence and Love

The humanist *I* was an individual. Levinas did not start his theorizing from the moment this individual was fully formed. Instead, he insisted that the subject had grown inside his mother's womb and fed on her breast milk. Once separated from his mother, he would recognize her loving face in the faces of strangers. In this iconic story, nourishment is central to the mother-son family dyad. This is exceptional in the Western theoretical tradition. The bond between brothers has been far more widely used as a model for relations.[21] So have genealogical imaginations that prioritize the father. Highly influential were the genealogies of English gentry, which started out with a founding father whose name the family would carry, and his wife, whose name got lost. Several generations of their offspring would be depicted as the branches of an ever-widening, upside-down family tree. In such trees, assets—possessions or traits—were passed on from one generation to the next. This is the image that was imported into evolutionary theories of how species relate. In the eighteenth century, Linnaeus had classified plants and animals in nosological tables in accordance with their degree of similarity. For instance, animals with a spine, hair, and striped muscles found themselves grouped together under the label 'mammals.' Potatoes, eggplants, and peppers were all classified as 'nightshades.' In the nineteenth century, Darwin added time to these tables. He suggested that different species descended from common ancestors. The more recent their common ancestors, the more striking their similarities. This was the point at which family trees of the English gentry were imported as a model to illustrate kinship relations between species. This sparked a scandal: How could it be that chimpanzees were 'our cousins'? But kinship terms proved very helpful for making sense of the striking similarities between apes and humans.

However, if genealogical trees visualize ancestral relations, they hide nourishment. Evolutionary theory puts sexual procreation and the blood ties that follow from it in the center of biology's attention. Eating and being eaten are studied in another branch of biology, one that for a long time gained less philosophical attention: ecology. Ecology focuses not on similarity, but on sustenance. Its pivotal image is not a tree, but a cycle. This cycle draws together

the Western philosophical tradition, the foundational relation is that between two brothers sharing the same parents. Here is "Perspectival Anthropology" again: "All men are brothers to some extent, since brotherhood is in itself the general form of the relation. Two partners in any relation are defined as connected in so far as they can be conceived to *have something in common*, that is, as being in the *same* relation to a third term. To relate is to assimilate, to unify, and to identify" (18). The corresponding, contrasting Amerindian model of relating is that between a man and his brother-in-law. "My relation with my brother-in-law is based on my being in *another* kind of relation to his relating with my sister or my wife. The Amerindian relation is a difference of perspective. While we tend to conceive the action of relating as a discarding of differences in favor of similarities, indigenous thought sees the process from another angle: the opposite of difference is not identity but *indifference*" (19). Here, relating is not sharing a commonality, but negotiating a difference. Contrast is not something to be effaced, but something to which attention should be paid. Indifference is the thing to avoid.

Could *we* perhaps eat that? Viveiros de Castro suggests that we—and this time the term evokes 'Western' scholars—might. Not in a simple way, as again and again he makes a sharp contrast between *us* and *them*. This is how he phrases that contrast in "Exchanging Perspectives": "Our traditional problem in the West is how to connect and universalize: individ-

creatures who feed on each other's remnants. Grass is eaten by grazers; grazers are eaten by predators; everyone's excrement and corpses are eaten by worms, fungi, and microbes, whose metabolic products feed the grass. And if this cycle seems static, there are other images that stipulate how the numbers of those who eat and feed fluctuate in time: a lot of grass allows for the thriving of a lot of grass eaters. But if the grass eaters eat too much, they deplete the grass and no longer have enough to live on, which means that many of them starve. Add one or two predators and one or two extra food sources into the equation, and the possibilities of population growth and decline become astoundingly complex. Or add humans: then the complexities get out of hand. Ecology tout court changes into social, political, and cultural ecology as *my* eating-feeding relations still involve eaters and foods, but also tools and technologies, markets, traditions—you name it.[22]

Late in the summer, G. and I bike to her allotment. We park our bikes, carry our bags into the shed, take out two chairs, and put them on a grassy patch. Then we start harvesting. G. opens a gate in the fence meant to keep out rabbits and hares. To our left, small spots of orange peek up above the soil: carrots. We push aside a protective nylon net and pull up a few. A bit farther along, we push another net to one side and each gather a handful of beans, half hidden among the bean plants' green stalks and leaves. While I

wash our harvest, G. heats water in a cooking pot. By the time G. spoons car-
rots and beans onto our plates, they are done but still crisp. G. also serves boiled
potatoes of different colors that she dug up earlier that week. We sprinkle salt
on the potatoes and nutmeg on the beans and round off our meal with a piece
of store-bought cheese.

Carrots and beans are both similar to and different from us; they are distant kin. But G. and I eat them because they *agree* with us. Our human bodies (equipped with a versatile microbiome) are able to digest carrots (raw and cooked) and beans (cooked). What is more, having eaten carrots and beans from an early age onward, we have learned to appreciate them. Unadorned, or with a bit of nutmeg, but we can do without a sauce. It also helps that carrots and beans grow fairly easily on G.'s allotment, especially if they exchange places from one year to the next. The fungi that live on the roots of the bean plants spread nitrogen in the soil which, the next year, allows the carrots thrive. During the Dutch summer, G. does not need to protect either from the cold by using a greenhouse, nor from the heat by providing shade. There is some work to do; there are other plants to weed out and rabbits and hares to keep at bay with gates and meshes. But in the given setting, these are re-warding crops.[23]

Like rats, humans are able to thrive on a wide range of other living beings. But not everything I might hope to eat agrees with me. How to differenti-ate between what suits me and what does not? Rats who, in laboratory cages, were provided with foods they did not know appeared to test them. The rats took tiny bites to sense if these would make them sick or give them a good feeling. Maybe I should do the same.[24]

For years, I have avoided wheat because eating foods like bread or pasta made
my bowels hurt. In the terms available to me, I took my digestive system to be
oversensitive to gluten. Just recently, I learned that maybe it is not gluten, the
protein in the wheat, but fructans, a long-chain carbohydrate, that does not
agree with me.[25] This would fit my stubborn avoidance of onion soup ever since
eating some hurt so much that it kept me awake for a night, and my reluctance
to eat cabbage, even if cabbage is among the rare vegetables that grows locally
in northern winters. Like wheat, onions and cabbage contain ample amounts
of fructans. However, I am fine with asparagus, and asparagus contain fruc-
tans, too. The amounts are maybe small enough to deal with, or maybe other
relevant variables come into play. I do not know. I try to sense what is bad
for me. But this only goes so far. Beyond this, making sense of what might be

ual substances are given, while relations have to be made. The Amerindian problem is how to separate and particularize: relations are given, while substances must be defined" (476). That said, however, Viveiros de Castro goes on to argue for an anthropology that, inspired by Amerindian thinking, begins from difference. Instead of seeking to know *man*, an alleged universal, anthropology should respect that different groups of people are profoundly different. They do not just *look* differently at the *same* reality; they *live different* realities. Their ontologies are different. Rather than embarking on an inquiry into what humankind has in common, Viveiros de Castro argues, we would do well to sincerely attend to *equivocations*, to nonequivalence. This means that translation should not be oriented toward the erasure of differences, with the goal of ending up with a language we all share. Quite the contrary. In the anthropology that Viveiros de Castro envisions, difference is to be fostered. Or, as he puts it in "Perspectival Anthropology": "Translation becomes an operation of differentiation—a production of difference—that connects the two discourses to the precise extent to which they are *not* saying the same thing, in so far as they point to discordant exteriorities between the equivocal homonyms between them" (20). Rather than submitting *otherness* to common categories, often all too easily *English-language* categories, attending to differences all around can produce a more respectful, inspirational way of relating.

going on is done collectively. It involves research subjects and researchers who jointly investigate what, for some bowels, some of the time, is not advantageous but irritating.

I hope to eat what agrees with me, but what agrees with human eaters may differ from one person to the next and, for any single one of them, vary over time. While in my sensing I use collective understandings, practical sorting precedes me, too. Generations of growers and eaters in the past have figured out for 'me' that while potatoes are edible, their leaves and berries are poisonous. They learned to cultivate sweet lupines, even though bitter varieties may be lethal. In the present, institutional arrangements seek to protect me against bad foods. There are rules stipulating that restaurant kitchens should not host mice, that milk has to be kept free of microbes, that packages must display clear sell-by and eat-by dates. In practice, rules and regulations are not always implemented. Nor are they always obvious. Mice droppings are unlikely to be beneficial, but maybe the microbes in cheese made from raw milk are actually good for my bowels, and expired chocolate is bound to be perfectly safe beyond its eat-by date, only its flavor suffers.[26] In the present context, that of theory, the details do not count for most. My point for now is that between foods and eaters, there are individual as well as collective relations of agreement.

S. and I studied Hawaiian pizza to sketch out the complex topology of simple dishes.²⁷ In short: pizza traveled to North America along with Italian migrants. The Hawaiian variety may have been invented by a restaurant owner in Canada who also served Chinese fare, which encouraged him to combine sweet and savory, pineapple and bacon. At the time, most pineapple on the market was grown in Hawaii. It had reached there from South America via a detour through France and England, where it had been grown in greenhouses. These days, Costa Rica is the leading global seller of pineapple, but pineapple pizza is still called 'Hawaiian.' All in all, then, Italy, Canada, China, France, England, and Hawaii were folded together in this mundane dish. But where is it eaten? Not just in North America, where it was invented, or the Netherlands, where we started our investigation, but also, among other places, in Thailand. This began when, during the Vietnam War, US soldiers spent their leave time in Bangkok. By tradition, Thai kitchens did not have ovens, but local restaurants quickly picked up on market demand. When the soldiers left, backpackers became an eager clientele, while these days Thai youngsters covet pizza as an example of Western food. But if Hawaiian pizza is now eaten, not just in Thailand, but also in Vietnam and China, it has not reached Indonesia. The Muslim majority of that country considers pork haram. Nor is Hawaiian pizza 'Western,' if only because this dish never found its way back to Italy. For in Italy, pineapple, being sweet, is a dessert and should not be combined with savory bacon. In Italy, a flat bread topped with pineapple is not pizza at all.

Whether particular foods agree with particular eaters or not depends on a lot more than bodily responses alone. Many transformative histories mediate the relations between human eaters and the creatures of whom we eat. What agrees with you or me may have to do with soothing memories from home or with the appeal of the exotic; there may be religious taboos to consider or culinary rules.²⁸ But here is a question. What about the agreement of the creatures turned into food? Their pleasures and pains do not go hand in hand with mine. Eating/feeding relations are asymmetrical.

Levinas elevated nourishing into a model of relating. When the subject looks the Other in the eyes, he recognizes the mother from whose body he disentangled himself as a toddler. All his adult life he keeps seeing her face in the face of others. For the adult son, 'female alterity' epitomizes nourishing love. But what if we shift to the perspective of the mother? For Levinas's subject may fondly remember his mother's nurturing, but he forgets about his own devouring. For months on end, he depleted her.[29] Does gratitude compensate for sucking someone dry? What makes it possible to endure such consuming violence? And once we begin with 'the mother,' we may go on to wonder about the lives and times—the flourishing and suffering—of other creatures that provide nourishment.

Here is the lesson for theory. Eating relations turn not around degrees of similarity, but around agreement. If I am lucky, I love what I eat and I eat what I love. But eating is an asymmetrical relation. My love is of a violent kind. To compensate for that, to assuage it, I would do well to ask, again and again, what might agree with those of whom I eat. In theory, at least, eating offers a model of relating in which violence and love go together, intertwine.

This raises the question of how, in practice, I might show the creatures on whom I feed more of my deepfelt appreciation and my recompensing gratitude?

Companion or Implicated

Throughout the twentieth century, social and cultural anthropologists studied the kinship systems of diverse groups of people. For a long time, they employed a biological backdrop for understanding family relations. This is reflected in the terms they used in their work. In English, the word *father* is given to someone who combines the biological position of a progenitor with the social position of holding parental authority. If anthropologists came across a society where children fell under the parental authority of an uncle, they would not call this person 'father' (prioritizing social relations) but 'mother's brother' (terms that indicate bloodlines). At some point, however, anthropologists began to doubt their own obedience to biology and to historicize biological knowledge. They highlighted that evolutionary theory imported its images of ancestral relations between species from family trees of the English gentry. It is from their work that I learned that the 'inheritance' of traits and genes was modeled on the 'inheritance' of money and goods.[30] When asking open questions in the field, anthropologists found that 'kinship systems' did not necessarily align with blood ties. Even people in the English heartland did not necessarily associate 'kin' with shared traits or shared genes: shared lives counted for more. *Their* kinship had to do with growing up together, working the same land, lending each other money, or joining one another for meals.[31] Concurring with this view, anthropologists disentangled the term *kinship* from family trees and began to use it for the relations that were most important to the people in their fieldsites.

The kinship between human and nonhuman creatures has been similarly disentangled from evolutionary proximity and shifted to proximities salient in daily practices. Haraway did this when she proposed expanding formerly humanist notions of *togetherness* to other species: "To hold in regard, to respond, to look back reciprocally, to notice, to pay attention, to have courteous regard for, to esteem: all of that is tied to polite greeting, to constituting the polis, where and when species meet."[32] Haraway argued that we should acknowledge the many ways in which animals are implicated in human lives. She called (among many other critters) the *oncomouse* her kin. The oncomouse lives in laboratories and has been genetically tweaked so that she may be used to test experimental cancer treatments developed for humans. Hence, people who might someday develop cancer—and who does not?—are already related to the oncomouse. She is our sister even if we do not know her.[33] Another example of togetherness is that of Haraway's own living, working, and playing with two lively dogs. In this context, she calls dogs a 'companion species.' With this term, Haraway deliberately models human-dog relations on sharing food: "*Companion* comes from the Latin *cum panis*, 'with bread.' Messmates at table are companions."[34]

As Haraway uses tropes like 'holding in regard' and writes about eating together, she plays on the humanist imaginations of relating dreamed up by Levinas. She creatively expands these to other species. However, she also takes a further step. In her books, other creatures are not just 'messmates *at* table,' they may also find themselves *on* the table. They may be eaten by humans as food. Feeding relations, Haraway warns, are harsh. "There is no way to eat and not to kill, no way to eat and not to become with other mortal beings to whom we are accountable, no way to present innocence and transcendence or a final peace."[35] But even if it always involves killing, there are still better and worse ways of eating: "Because eating and killing cannot be hygienically sep-

THINKING AND EATING

In her article "Pleasures That Differentiate: Transformational Bodies among the Tupinambá of Olivença," De Matos Viegas recounts that the Tupinambá whom she got to know in her fieldwork link their own identity as Tupinambá not to what they think, but to what they eat. To find out whether or not another person is Tupinambá, they do not talk with them about traditions, epistemology, ontology, or other abstractions. They offer them *giroba*, a particular kind of manioc beer with a bitter taste. Outsiders who try it usually spit it out. What makes a person

arated does *not* mean that just any way of eating and killing is fine, merely a matter of taste and culture. Multispecies human and nonhuman ways of living and dying are at stake in practices of eating."[36] So they are. But here is a question: Is *kin* still the most suitable term for the togetherness implied? For as I eat, I do not continue to coexist with those of whom I eat; I incorporate them. Or, on an agricultural, collective level, my eating may make me coexist with the *species* from whose bodies I eat, but even so, the *specimen* being eaten disappears from the scene. Beyond *kin*, then, we may want other words for the relations with those of whom we eat. They are, after all, not our companions, but the *panis* itself. The act of eating turns them into *food*.

In the context of eating, there is a further problem with casting my relating to other species as a matter of kinship and togetherness. It is that in eating I do not just relate to the creatures whose flesh, seeds, roots, and so on I ingest. I also relate to creatures who do not constitute my food, but whom I rob of theirs.

Above I mentioned this in passing: G. states that a large part of her gardening work is weeding. She kills encroaching plants so that they do not crush her future crops. There are also animals to keep at bay. Before G. and I bike away from her garden, we carefully check the various gates and meshes. G. says that one evening, tired, she forgot to do this. When she came back after a few days, her plot had been plundered by hungry rabbits and hares. Since then she has never again forgotten to use her techno-tools to safeguard the plants from which she hopes to eat and from which she generously feeds her friends. Vandalizing humans are kept out of her garden as well. Only the members of the allotment society have keys to the gates around the terrain they share. Every evening they lock the gates to keep out unwelcome intruders.

Here, gates, meshes, and locks mediate a competition between eaters.[37] As it happens, the rabbits, hares, and humans excluded from the table should maybe not complain too much. It is, after all, only because of G.'s hard work that carrots and beans grow in the polder. If not for G.'s gardening, wetland grasses and marsh flowers (now eradicated as 'weeds') would have lived there, attracting different insects, coveted by different kinds of birds. Maybe these creatures—not even alive—are the true victims of our appetites. But then again, if not for the pumps that pump water out from the small ditches in the polder into larger canals outside it, and if not for the dikes around the polder, the terrain that now harbors G.'s allotment would be inundated with water.

In that case, underwater creatures would have had a chance to thrive where now there is polder. At whichever point in the range of possibilities we stop, there are always going to be others affected by my eating. I rob them of potential food or altogether prevent their living.[38]

J. had gathered a lot of materials about the 2001 outbreak of foot-and-mouth disease in Britain. Analyzing them, we come to talk about the trail that the virus took from regions in the world where it is endemic to regions that are usually kept 'disease free.' How are the borders being guarded? We also learn about cross-border eating. In the old days, pigs in Britain were household members who were mostly fed with household waste, like leftovers and potato peels. Acorns and other treats were added in to fatten them up in autumn, before they were slaughtered. As a vestige of this practice, in the late twentieth century, there were still a few farmers left who fed their pigs with catering waste, leftovers from restaurants and canteens. If these foods were cooked long enough, the bugs they might carry would be killed. The outbreak occurred when, plagued by illness and other woes, farmers on just a single farm failed to boil their catering waste. This allowed foot-and-mouth virus, most probably hidden in meat illegally imported from a region where it is endemic, to cross the border and reach a shed full of pigs. Due to the mass transportation of animals around the country, the infection spread quickly. To prevent another outbreak, European laws now forbid the use of food waste as pig feed.

It would be possible to solve the problem of foot-and-mouth disease in Europe by vaccinating pigs. But no. Instead, it is solved by importing yet more pig feed, which adds to the already massive imports of, for instance, soy from Brazil, where this is grown in large fields formed at the cost of rain forests being cleared away. This means that a person eating Hawaiian pizza in Britain or the Netherlands affects countless creatures in the Amazon region. They died when the trees on which they depended were felled. Their living space was transformed into a soy plantation.[39]

Tupinambá is the ability to drink *giroba* and, stronger still, to like it. How to handle this particular equivocation? Maybe this is where words reach their limits. For when savoring manioc beer counts for most, relating is neither a conversation, nor an exchange of stories. There is no equivocation to foster; there is no writing. There is manioc beer to savor or spit out. As far as Tupinambá are concerned, speaking *their* tongue, the tongue of *the whites*, is fine: it is not transformative. It does not undermine *our* Tupinamba distinctiveness. It is forgetting *giroba* and eating the foods of whites that risks to unduly turn one of us, an Amerindian, into one of them, a white person. An idea that painfully resonates with the bygone *You are what you eat* of the colonizers.

Are they my kin, the Amazonian frogs, parrots, and bromeliads whose lands have been turned into plantations? They might have been. But we cannot learn to live together if *my eating* means that they are never even born. The point is not that they figure as food individually, but that they are under pressure collectively: their habitats are being destroyed. Neither my companions nor my competitors, they are my might-have-beens. They are sore absences wiped out by my eating. They are ghosts. I relate to them, but they are no longer on the scene.[40]

Oncomouse is my sister, dogs are table companions, carrots and beans form our sustenance. But what about marsh plants and bromeliads? Where do they fit in? To the creatures that, partially, I eat, I may seek to show my gratitude better. It is possible to contribute to improving their lives. This is more difficult to envision for the creatures that are not on my table but excluded from it. We fight over food and I win. However, if I keep winning, and winning again, in the end I am left alone. For my winning does not just harm those who are defeated. It also harms those that depend on the defeated, as well as those that depend on them, and so forth. Hence, if the human eating *I* keeps taking without giving, receiving without caring in return, then, via the detour of all kinds of cycles, mediations, and spirals, at some point, it will be game over. There will be no more sisters to respect, no more companions with which to play. And no more vital others to eat.

Here is the lesson for theory. Eating suggests a model of relating in which fighting is not just detrimental for those who lose, but also for those who win. For if the *I* destroys the conditions of possibility on which countless others depend for their life, this is inevitably self-destructive, too.

Eating and Feeding

As Levinas called on his readers to look others in the face and recognize their common humanity, he flagged giving as good and taking as immoral. This makes eminent sense in many settings. But when it comes to my relations with the creatures of whom I eat, it does not. Here, giving and taking intertwine, eating and feeding go together. Neither is therefore good or bad in and of itself. Instead, the qualities of eating/feeding relations depend on the specificities of their organization. Specificities are also crucial when it comes to further evaluations. For, however asymmetrical our relation may be, if I eat what agrees with me, the violence of my eating and the love for my food may go together. This means that dreams of purity, of living without sin, are not helpful. They do not lead to utopia but, rather, hide downsides and backsides; that is to say, they deny devouring and depleting. Beyond guiltily fasting and carelessly feasting, then, we encounter the conundrum of wondering, again and again, individually and collectively, under which specific conditions eating might be okay, or not okay, and how, when it is done, to give shape to one's apposite gratitude. Gratitude might not be sufficient when it comes to relating to those who do not get to eat what I eat. For if in hungry moments, eradicating other forms of life is tempting, it is also self-defeating. Via cyclical and spiraling detours, eradicating competitors means eradicating the creatures who might have figured as my, your, food.

Here is the lesson for theory. If we let go of the family tree and instead model *relating* on eating, being generative is not about having offspring, but about cultivating crops. If we do not focus on the companions with whom we sit around to table, but on to the foods that are on the table, we find that our love for them harbors violence, while our devouring may go together with gratitude. There is something complicated to do with how, in eating, individuals and collectives relate. For while my eating destroys the single apple being eaten, it contributes to the survival of its kind. Hence, in eating, taking is not necessarily destructive. But giving loses its shine of generosity, as there is a self-serving side to caring for creatures with an eye to their edibility. Eating relations also stretch out to those who do not get to eat what I eat. But these are not simply my competitors, for we are part of each other's conditions of possibility. Outcompeting them ends up being self-defeating. Hence, the model of relating that eating inspires does not clearly divide between good and bad. Instead, it is marked by ambiguities and ambivalences, multivalences and incongruities. Reassuring distinctions give way to idiosyncratic specificities. Or, as Haraway puts it, "the devil is in the details, and so is the deity."[41]

6   Intellectual Ingredients

'THE HUMAN' WHOM, in the twentieth century, philosophical anthropologists sought to protect from domination, dehumanization, and violence, was an individual. His *being* was located within surroundings through which he moved. His *knowing* was done from a distance. His *doing* was steered from a center and afforded him control. If only he would acknowledge his similarity to other humans, their *relating* would be on an equal footing. He towered over other earthly beings, at least in part. For only his *thinking* elevated 'the human' over 'nature,' his *eating* did not. Eating brought humans down to earth and entangled them with other creatures. This is precisely why, seeking to escape the arrogance of humanism, I have sought inspiration in eating. In each of the preceding chapters, I have revisited a text from the canon of philosophical anthropology, pointed at the empirical realities it sought to address, and then contrasted it with stories about eating. By using situations of eating as exemplary situations with which to think, I have dreamed up alternative ways of understanding *being, doing, knowing*, and *relating*. The result is not a Theory with a capital T, nor a collection of concepts firmly outlined. Instead, this book offers transformative models, imaginaries with which to think. These are informed not by an updated version of 'the human,' but by specific stories about situated people, dependent on each other, on other creatures, and on a forgiving, but frightfully fragile earth.

A question left unresolved, to which I turn in this final chapter, is where all this attention to *eating* leaves *politics*. In *The Human Condition*, Arendt stated that caring for bodily survival was akin to subjugating oneself to the *laws of nature*, while engaging in politics meant that 'man' could set *his own laws*. She argued that humans should aspire to more than simply *living*: it was their call to choose between different *ways of living*. By participating in political arenas, citizens were to make joint decisions about how to order their societies. For her description of politics, Arendt sought inspiration in the democratic city-states of ancient Greece. In Athens and Sparta, political power was not held by a few authoritarian rulers, but shared among all 'free men.' They gathered together in the agora to engage in *action*, which meant that, instead of weapons, they used their rhetorical skills to convince each other. Arendt celebrated this as an achievement. So, too, did other political philosophers who, in the second half of the twentieth century, made normative blueprints of *politics*. However, as the century went on, the concern arose that a model of politics inspired by a gathering of 'free men' no longer sufficed. For what about the present-day incarnations of those whom in ancient Greece were classified as 'craftsmen' or 'women and slaves'? That is to say: What about artisans, workers, farmers, cooks, cleaners—and those active in all the other jobs, paid or unpaid—that did not yet exist in ancient Greece? They, too, had to be welcomed into the meetings of democracy. In the twenty-first century, it was subsequently proposed that politics should also take heed of nonhuman creatures: animals, plants, fungi, microbes, rocks, air, oceans. This raises the question as to whether engaging in *conversation* is still a fitting model for what *politics* entails.

In the section to follow I will expand on this to suggest that in seeking to rekindle *politics*, it may be helpful to descend in Arendt's hierarchy of pursuits. For she took the artisanal *work* of 'craftsmen' and the menial *labor* of 'women and slaves' to be *nonpolitical,* but are they? In ancient Greece, *work* and *labor* were associated with practice, not theory, with material life, not language, with routines, not decisions. But all these contrasts reiterate the hierarchical separation between 'culture,' high, and 'nature,' low, that is blurred in recent intellectual explorations, including those assembled in this book. If we do not take politics to hinge on decisions about how to order society, but on the alterity among *ways of living*, then *work* and *labor* have politics, too. As the stories told throughout this book amply demonstrate, there are many ways to *do* (shape, perform, enact) *eating*. It is not singularly natural, but variously cultivated. Below, I will present a few additional examples to illustrate that the *labor* involved in caring for food is not caught in a single, selfsame routine, but may follow different courses. Time and again, one possibility, one mode of ordering, contrasts with another. That it may be cultivated in ever so many ways means that *eating* does not obey preordained laws of nature. However, that does not imply that eating can be made to obey 'man-made' laws. For making decisions is one thing; the feasibility of projects is another. All the elements relevant to a situation may cede, resist, or otherwise respond to being pushed or pulled in one direction or another. From which it is possible to conclude that *labor* is not so much alien to politics, but rather has a politics of its own. The *politics of labor* is a matter of ongoing, practical, simultaneously social and material negotiations.

Perhaps the term *negotiations* sounds too conversational; perhaps it is difficult to bend it in a socio-material direction. But please give it a try: the negotiations to which I allude may take the form of barking, biting, failing to thrive, or refusing to be digestible. But while the negotiations that go into shaping socio-material worlds are not necessarily conducted verbally, language is still important to them. For the terms, models, and metaphors that we use to speak and write allow some things to be remarked on, some questions to be asked, some suggestions to be formulated, while hiding or foreclosing others. They play a part in ordering reality. They foster some ways of life and smother others. Words are crucial ingredients in the worlds in which humans participate. They allow for and help to shape what, in a fine oxymoron, may be called *intellectual labor*. This is what makes it worthwhile to carefully attend to them, to write and read articles and books, to spend effort on tweaking such big words as *being, knowing, doing*, and *relating*. If 'theory' is not elevated above 'practice,' neither it is superfluous. If 'thinking' is not 'the human's' unique destiny, it still informs other activities and is, in its turn, informed by them. There is intertwinement, entanglement, coexistence, transformation, tension, complexity, mutual incorporation. Such complex coconstitutions may, in their turn, be modeled on eating—and being eaten.

OTHERNESS

As it seeks to rekindle *being, knowing, doing*, and *relating*, this book interferes in 'the Western philosophical tradition.' If I hold on here to the term *Western* as a designator, this is because, if philosophers situate their work at all, this is the term they use. It signals a difference from categories such as *Chinese* or *Eastern* philosophy. These indicators may seem regional, but in theoretical practice they point to ways of thinking, to *styles*. In cultural anthropology, *Euro-American* authors tend to use the term *Euro-American* when they write about *we*. In doing this, they adjust the pertinent regionality, while, at the same time, they shift the location in which they look for *styles* from canonical texts to daily practices. In both cases, however, as *we* are being differentiated from so-called *others*, the differences among *us* (whether singled out as Western or as Euro-American) shift to the background. Or rather, *we* are homoge-

The Politics of Labor

At the end of the twentieth century, an issue among political philosophers arose, namely that in their ideal type democratic configuration, that of ancient Greece, the right to speak up in the agora was restricted to 'free men.' How could one retheorize democratic politics in such a way that it would accommodate everyone, including people with little wealth and small incomes, scant education, bad living circumstances, low social status, in short, people so far readily discarded or discriminated? Large differences between the power held by political agents easily introduced the possibility of domination.[1] Some philosophers argued that in order to keep powerplays at bay, social differences should be left at the door of political gatherings. In political meeting rooms, a 'free speech situation' had to be created so that everyone could speak their mind and rationality would rule. In response to this, the format of argumentative debates was questioned. These were not as inclusive as propagated to be, if only because 'free men' get more training in debating than others. Narrative formats should therefore likewise be welcomed. The format of the debate was also amended in other ways, for instance, with the proposition that when gathered in political arenas, people should deliberately ignore how the decisions they made then and there would affect their own lives. If everyone's personal situation were hidden behind a 'veil of ignorance,' it would become possible to come to conclusions bound to serve the 'common good,' even if these were more favorable to some than to others. The retort was that social differences should not be hidden at all, but overtly acknowledged. Only this would make it possible to formulate solutions that everyone might be willing to accept in real life, beyond the confines of artificially sheltered meeting rooms.[2] The discussions in political theory were lively. But whatever positions were taken, throughout, engaging in *conversation* figured as exemplary of political *action*.

Modeling politics on conversations is not self-evident. It most clearly became problematic once nonhumans were invited into the agora, since the ability to talk was supposed to be distinctively human. What to do? Some suggested that humans had to learn to attune better to the particular communication styles of other species. For nonhumans have ways of expressing themselves in their own, diverse, nonhuman ways. These radically diverse forms of semiosis might be telling enough, if only they were met with more openness and curiosity.[3] Another idea was that, in political settings, nonhumans could be represented by dedicated spokespeople: scientists, activists, amateurs, farmers, neighbors: volunteers enough. But which of them to

nized at the cost of some of *us* who are not taken into account. In the early 1980s, I spent a few days analyzing discourses in 'Western'—that is Dutch, German, English, and French—texts to find that the term *we* almost exclusively alluded to *men*. These days, the question of where to locate migrants, or international jetsets, when *we* and *they* are differentiated, is readily evaded. Differences between local *styles* are shifted to the background, too, be they the differences between anatomy and physiology, morality and aesthetics, or eating and buying. Plus *we* speak many languages: English may resemble French, German, and Dutch, but it still frames things significantly differently from these adjacent tongues. Beyond this, as differences *within* are hidden, code-switching, creolization, and other modes of coordination are understudied, too.

If I call the philosophical tradition that I hope to interfere with *Western*, I do not use this term for my field. For Western eating exists, but not in the Netherlands. When traveling as a tourist, I came across a pizzeria in Beijing that organized children's parties centered around Western eating. All the little guests would prepare their own pizza and then learn how to eat this: not with chopsticks, but with a fork and knife. Ironically, in New York or Amsterdam, pizzerias cut their fare in the kitchen and serve them in small triangles, so that 'Western' children tend to eat pizza *not* with fork and knife, but with bare hands. If pizza is Western food in Beijing, it is American or Italian in New

prioritize? Smallholders or large-scale farmers; evolutionary theorists or ecologists; physicists or biochemists; inhabitants of Amsterdam or Brittany? Those professing to speak on behalf of nonhumans were all saying different things. Hence, if, earlier, the question had been how to accommodate social differences between humans, now the question was how to coordinate between diverse representations of reality. In the parliaments of liberal democracies, only values had been up for discussion; facts were imported from outside. In a 'parliament of nature,' by contrast, facts about dogs and trees, forests and rivers, air and climate, could all be contested.[4]

These days, the facts pertaining to nonhumans are debated in parliaments, even if these are not equipped with the extra tools, rules, and procedural arrangements 'a parliament of nature' would require. The sophisticated methods that scientists, farmers, activists, and others cultivating nature have developed in order to get intimately acquainted with those they represent are manifestly absent. Belief and hearsay are introduced in their place. This sadly makes dreaming up parliaments of nature lose a lot of its attractiveness. But inviting political subjects into the agora for the action of making decisions is not the only way to go. Another method to reshape politics is to look for it in the sites where, according to Arendt, it does not exist: that is to say, in the work of 'craftsmen' whom she cast as constructing durable goods so as protect humans against 'nature' and in the labor of 'women and slaves' which, because it served physical survival, she considered as being in submission to 'nature'. It is possible to look for politics in those places, if we equate politics not with making decisions, but with exploring alternatives.

In 2011, I attend a food conference for health care professionals. One of the experts says that human health is served by eating lots of proteins and that most people, even in an affluent country such as the Netherlands, should eat more of it. You may want to tell that to your patients, he admonishes the audience, while pointing to images of broiled beef and roasted chicken. In the question-and-answer session afterward, he gets challenged. "If ever I were to accept what you say about individual health: What about feeding humanity? If every person on earth ate meat in the amounts you just recommended, we would need a few earths to make it happen." There is irritation in the speaker's voice as he responds. No, sorry, he does not know about humanity. That is a political issue, he says. He is not equipped to handle that. All he can do is report on his research, which has focused on the health of individuals. The outcome of this is the fact that we serve our health by eating lots of protein.

Here the speaker tries to keep politics at bay from his facts. However, the question from the audience suggests that this is not so easy, as there may be politics in the very setup of research practices. The research on which the speaker reported singled out 'the individual' as deserving of health and took this individual to be able and willing to eat beef or chicken. It did not ask questions about feeding humanity, the fate of farm animals, or the endurance of the earth. Hence, in the research the speaker presented alternative operationalizations of what it is to eat were moved to the background, out of sight. The 'health' under investigation in that research is not a *natural* phenomenon. Rather it emerges from a complex socio-material configuration. It depends on a particular research question, research subjects willing to participate, ample supplies of food with identifiable protein content, lab technicians who register the food intake of the research subjects, a few easy-to-measure parameters that stand in for 'health,' and so on. In other research projects, different realities are singled out as worthy of attention.

The same conference. The next speaker does not cast aside the question of 'feeding humanity' as unduly political, but takes it to be a concern that science should urgently address.[5] In line with this, his team of insect scientists has stopped fighting insect plagues and turned to strengthening the case for eating insects. He

York and Amsterdam. In food courts in Singapore, there are stalls branded as Indian, Szechuan, Cantonese, Malay, and Indonesian. Among them, there is one selling 'Western food' that offers large chunks of meat accompanied by deep-fried potato fingers, called 'french fries' in the US, even if they would be looked down on in France. French cuisine, in turn, is not uniform: there are serious differences between the food served in Bretagne and Paris. If I wrote that my fieldsites were mostly situated in *the Netherlands*, that, too, is just rough approximation. The professional institutions in which I observed food-related care were all located in just one among the twelve Dutch provinces. In the city where I live, there are plenty of shops that offer more than fifty kinds of organically grown tea, but this is not so in the average Dutch village. Specificity is fractal.

My field took the shape of a trail rather than a region. But that is fine. I do not seek to play out its 'Dutchness' against the 'Western' provenance of the philosophers whose work I recall. They wrote in French, German, or Dutch, and their work was (in most cases) translated into English. But what matters is not so much that particular situatedness, as the way that body of work informs present-day theoretical repertoires. My concern is with how to frame *being, knowing, doing*, and *relating*. If I proposed eating-inspired models with which to think, their *otherness* is not tied to 'elsewhere.' It is, rather, an otherness *within*. I play out *my* eating against *our* philosophical tradition.

relates that, in many parts of the world, insects are appreciated as a delicacy. In total, nearly 2000 species are eaten. But Western food is gaining in popularity all over the world and Westerners, he says, consider eating insects to be scary, backward, or both. This erodes the practice of eating insects all over the globe. That is a pity, he continues, because insects taste good, and, being cold-blooded, need far fewer resources to grow protein-rich flesh than the animals currently being farmed. Cows convert just over 10 percent of the mass they are fed with into meat; chickens convert nearly 50 percent, while crickets convert well over 60 percent of the mass they eat into edible flesh. Once again, a question from the audience. Why the detour through crickets? Isn't it yet more efficient if humans eat plants? The speaker answers that insects indeed form a detour if they are fed with foods that humans eat, say, rice and lentils, or carrots. But what makes insects so interesting is that many of them thrive on food waste or even manure. They transform materials unsuitable for human consumption into a delicacy.

If we take 'politics' to be a term for the *alterity*, not primarily between people, but between different ways of organizing socio-material realities, this setting is full of politics. For a start, in contrast with the previous research, rather than the health of individual humans, the sustenance of humanity is singled out as a research goal. Then, there are contrasts within what is presented as real. *Eating,* for one, is first configured as a way of using up resources, but then also as something more or less pleasurable to diverse eaters.[6] This is a difference not just in understanding but also in practice. If eating is a matter of using up resources, then insects are good food and the primary problem the research team must solve is how to best farm them. If, by contrast, eating has to do with food pleasure, there is an added problem to solve, which is how to convince 'consumers,' or more particularly the alleged 'Westerners,' that insects taste great.

The three of us—F., Y., and I—visit an open day organized by insect researchers to foster love for insects. There are talks given in lecture halls, illuminated by PowerPoint presentations. One of these reiterates the impressive numbers to do with efficiency that I had already heard at the conference mentioned above. Farming insects, the speaker insists, has the further advantage that it raises no animal rights issues. Contrary to, for instance, chickens, most insects like to live close together, in large numbers, in dark, confined spaces. In the large, open entrance hall, we see demonstrations of crawling creatures in boxes made partially transparent for instructive purposes. We learn that the species on show can be fed with food waste, even if, for simplicity's sake, here they are supplied with carrots. Outdoors, on the lawn, there is a large tent where a cooking teacher from a nearby vocational school oversees the preparation of a few dishes that, he tells us when we ask, he specially designed for the day. His pride is a minced meat sauce—part pork, part mealworm—served over spaghetti. He is convinced that this dish will make the transition to eating insects, preferably mealworms, attractive to the 'wider public.' This is a major target, as mealworms are easy to farm, we have just been told. However, when we sample his mealworm dish we do not find it appealing. The crickets, by contrast, are great: roasted, they have a pleasant texture and a nutty taste.[7]

In the lecture hall, *eating* is once again configured as a matter of using resources with greater of lesser efficiency. This time round, another concern is added, which is whether the creatures to be eaten appreciate the agricultural settings in which they are obliged to live. Chickens do not like to be packed together, but insects are totally fine with living in large groups in cramped quarters. This, or such is the idea, speaks in favor of eating insects, as it means they are fine with the circumstances under which they are farmed. In the demonstration downstairs in the entrance hall, we are invited to see their happiness for ourselves. Whether this display actually helps to attune 'consumers' to eating insects is questionable. For while the sight of all these small creatures crawling over and under each other may not raise concerns about

To highlight that both are equally provincial, I have presented you with a few stories about *eating* farther afield, borrowed from the writings of other authors. As insisting on *difference within* is part of my plot, I did not want to introduce the lessons they provide in the main text. But neither did I want to hide that *eating* takes on quite different shapes beyond my field—wherever this begins or ends. Twentieth-century philosophical anthropologists dreamed that their humanism was universal. The work presented here in asides expertly shatters that dream. It shows that, over time and between traditions, people do not just eat different foods in different ways. They also bestow different shapes to *being, knowing, doing,* and *relating.* They are embedded in different ontologies: what eating *is* differs from one setting to the next.

As people around the globe have become ever more tightly connected, universality has lost a lot of its former shine. Most so-called *others,* when speaking for themselves, insist that they prefer to live on their own terms. Here food figures as both a practical concern in its own right and as an interesting model for what 'their own terms' might mean. Take the concerns of groups of people who, due to this or that onslaught, are collectively left hungry. International organizations propose that they deserve *food security,* that is, access to *enough* food as proposed by nutrition science. However, the people concerned tend to insist that in

animal rights, all around us we hear visitors exclaim that watching this teeming liveliness is scary. On to the tent. There, *eating* is performed as a potential pleasure. To convince those gathered of the pleasure of eating insects, once more, two different strategies are deployed side by side. When the ground mealworms are mixed with ground pork, they are hidden. The hope is that the trusted appearance and taste will assure 'a wider public' that nothing offensive is occurring. The other strategy is that of serving crunchy treats fully recognizable as crickets. This might appeal more to what marketers call 'daring eaters,' eager to be surprised. We oblige them by dutifully conforming to this consumer category.

Here is the lesson for theory. Politics does not need to be verbal. It can also take the shape of cooking things up one way or another. Of *laboring* to order reality in this way or that.[8] Of enacting *eating* as boosting individual health or as amenable to feeding humanity. Of orchestrating *eating* as 'using up resources' or as 'taking pleasure from tasty food.' Of attending to the plight of creatures to be eaten or instead overlooking this. Of serving up dishes that are soothingly familiar or excitingly novel. What *is,* what is good, what is relevant: these may all be *done* in one way or another.

In the *labor* that goes into eating, evaluation is always implied. The question of what eating *is* flows over into the question what it means to *eat well*, what to make of this, and how to shape it.[9] The answers are not necessarily articulated in words, they may be provided in stealth, by doing things one way or another way, or by doing them in two or three ways in parallel. In a single conference, this speaker may talk about individuals, that other about humanity. In a single lecture, one PowerPoint slide may display the efficiency of resource conversion, while the next addresses animal preferences. On a single open day, insects may be visually admired in the hall and offered up as food in an adjacent tent. The tent's buffet invites visitors to sample mealworms-mixed-into-minced-meat or crunchy crickets, or both. The *politics of labor* does not necessarily result in univocal resolutions that fit within a single set of coordinates. It may also take on the shape of sliding coexistences and shifting balances.[10]

Whether or not the contrasts between such different modes of ordering deserve to be called *political* is a matter of conceptual strategy. Some scholars argue that in this way the word 'political' is stretched too far beyond its traditional usage. They prefer to reserve 'political' for contestations and debates, for decisions made at various levels of government, which, in one way or another, involve discretionary meetings. They are concerned that if, without further ado, we call contrasting modes of ordering the world 'political,' as I do here, this hides the work involved in articulating and politicizing the contrasts involved. Things only *become* 'political,' they say, if they are turned into an *issue* and gain public attention.[11] This is a fair point. Indeed, turning unspoken, idiosyncratic contrasts into articulated, shared concerns involves considerable amounts of effort.

However, directly calling contrasting ways of ordering reality 'political' also has a lot going for it. There is one particular advantage I would like to flag in the present context: it supports the ambition of expanding the constituency of the polity to include nonhumans. If we call facilitating or impeding this or that mode of ordering *political*, then all creatures involved in the situation participate in 'politics.' The humans may talk, but other creatures may push and pull reality in one way or the other without the use of a human tongue. They may, without needing words, still 'have a say' in how practices unfold. Cows use resources inefficiently, but diligently turn grass, otherwise inedible for humans, into milk and meat. Chickens, by getting aggressive, actively display their lack of agreement with inhabiting cramped living spaces. Crickets, in their turn, take a stance by happily eating most, but not all, food waste. It is to such propositions that humans respond. Farmers who find

the long run they prefer *food sovereignty*: they want to eat foods that fit their traditions, or their own creative adaptations thereof. Instead of having strangers stipulating their needs, they hope to live in ways that are in tune with their desires. Strange foods risk causing them to become estranged from themselves. This resonates with the fear of early colonial Spaniards, who warned each other that eating what they called 'Indian' food would rob them of their European characteristics, while suggesting that 'Indians' eating Spanish food might well acquire the vitality that allegedly marked Europeans. It resonates, likewise, with the way in which, these days, Amerindians in South America express the worry that eating the food of *whites* might unduly transform *us* into *white* persons. Present-day Orokaiva, likewise, suggest that by eating what *whitemen* eat, that is to say *light food*, a formerly Orokaiva person may transform into a *whiteman*. Accordingly, eating strange food may both *be* and *symbolize* an erasure of a distinctiveness that various groups of people wish to maintain.

That universality has lost its shine in theory has a lot to do with how globalization operates in practice. The assertion that all humans are to be treated equally sounds promising. However, while this was meant to counter a prior sense of 'Western' superiority, it has turned sour, if only because the alleged universalities were framed in Spanish, Portuguese, French, German, Dutch, or English. Awkward mixtures ensued. Take the way in which the individualist nutrition advice

themselves in a Dutch polder too wet to grow anything but grass may invite cows to graze there; or they may at some point start to worry about the methane that cow microbiomes produce. Citizens who love eggs but also care about chickens may vote in support of laws that oblige farmers to enlarge the size of chicken coops. Researchers seeking to contribute to feeding humanity may patiently attempt to discover on which forms of food waste crickets happen to thrive. But if they urgently need a successful demonstration, they may also, for the duration of an open day, supply their crickets with carrots.

Arendt wrote (as I quoted above): "The human body, its activity notwithstanding, is thrown back upon itself, concentrates upon nothing but its own being alive, and remains imprisoned in its metabolism of nature without ever transcending or freeing itself from the recurring cycle of its own functioning."[12] By calling up a *cycle* and suggesting that it recurs all by itself, Arendt unwittingly hid the very *labor*, on which, as she knew all too well, human 'metabolism' depends.[13] If we analyze this labor in detail, it appears that it is not subject to the laws of nature. Instead, it may take different shapes. However, that *eating* may be done in this way or that does not mean, that as they labor, humans set their own laws. In laboring, we are not 'free men.' There may be different ways of ordering practices, but these practices are populated by many more figures than humans alone. Hence, the *politics of labor* is matter of cultivation. It involves ongoing negotiations: among humans, with other creatures, converting materials—obdurate or fragile things—and the earth we share.

These negotiations do not hinge on arguments; they are a matter of fine-tuning practices. Try. Some things work out as hoped for; others do not. Some things agree with me, but not with you, and vice versa. Some things are good in one way but not in another.[14] Try again. Explore different ways of living, contrast them, and seek compromises that, for want of better options, will make do. For the time being. Soon enough, new frictions will come to the fore. Begin again. There is no cycle to close, no ending in which to seek rest, no solution that suits all involved. There will always be further slippages, strains, surprises.

Practically, given the current state of eating, better ways of attuning to other creatures and the earth we share are direly needed. For as it is, the labor upholding the global 'food system' allows for the *sustenance* of impressive amounts of humans. But we inhabit only one earth, not four or five, and the *sustainability* of that single earth is at stake. The theoretical lesson at this point, more modest, is that (socio-material) *labor* is not lower than (discursive) *action*. It does not reside below politics in the humanist hierarchy of old, but has a politics of its own. This particular kind of politics does not depend on conversations; rather, it is a matter of doing things in one way or another. It hinges not on decisions and choices, but on trying and adjusting. Ideally, it takes the shape of adaptive and responsive tinkering, of ongoing cultivation and never-ending care.[15]

The Spirit of Practices

The politics of orchestrating eating practices—this much is clear—is shot through with many stakes. These have to do with fostering health, sharing resources, taking pleasure, the working conditions of those who care for our food, the pains and pleasures of the creatures to be eaten, soils that risk being depleted and eroded, and, of course, water, which, in most places, is ever scarcer. You know about these things: they are all over the newspapers, and if you want to learn more, there are ample venues to which to turn. What I would like to add here is that the ways in which eating is ordered has relevance for theory as well. It says something. In writing this book, I kept using situations of eating as models with which to think. This means that I learned to wonder about every situation I encounter: What does it say, what does it remind of, what does it make me think?

provided to people in highland Guatemala interferes with communal eating. Or take the huge billboards where multinational companies advertise soft drinks: they are a lot more visible and colorful than the warnings from healthcare professionals against consuming sugar. And while in highland Guatemala maize is celebrated and turned into tortillas that undergird every meal, this is not a universal good either. Present-day Samburu never longed for maize. They prefer milk and meat. Only because there is no longer enough of those foods, do they fall back on unadorned maize porridge, which tastes of dry stick. Distinctiveness sounds more appealing than dry stick. How to foster distinctiveness? In India, medical doctors have done this in a remarkable way. They have declared that 'the human body' is not 'human' after all: they insist on the specificity of *Indian* bodies. Lowering the salient cutoff points between normal weight, overweight, and obesity to fit local reality, they use the language of science to escape from science's universal hold.

Carefully attending to *equivocations*—terms that elude translation, realities enacted in different ways, appreciations that do not add up—disrupts dreams of global *equivalence*. The sidelines to this book are meant to flag that *my* eating is not *human* eating. The *otherness* they present underscores the provincial character of *my* field. But while recognizing one's situatedness is a direly needed form of modesty, what is 'other' does not have

Here, for a painful example. In this book I recall philosophical anthropology. At the same time, the disposal practices in which I am engaged give human exceptionalism a material shape. My remnants are kept out of the metabolic loops and spirals on which my eating depends. I eat, but I am not being eaten by those on whom I feed. Not even my urine and feces are used to fertilize agricultural fields.

Within biking distance from my house, I visit a huge expo in which techno firms present water treatment technologies. Wandering around, I see smooth photos of enticing water and beautiful people drinking it, of a sunny earth somehow suspended above its own blue seas, of a river flowing among glistering rocks with beautiful trees in the background. But the stuff for sale is mostly made out of sturdy metal (pipes and pumps) and colored plastics (forming surfaces to which microbes may attach). The halls are huge. Tucked away in a side room, I find a demo called Circular Economy. *It describes experiments that involve capturing toilet paper from wastewater so as to reuse the cellulose. The person in charge of the demo explains that there is a problem with selling that cellulose. There is a shyness in the market, he says. Factories targeted fear that, even as a resource for making diapers, 'recycled toilet paper' does not sound enticing. There is a similar shyness with struvite, an amalgam containing phosphorus retrieved from human urine and feces. Currently, a few wastewater treatment plants in the Netherlands make struvite, hoping to sell it to farmers as fertilizer. But so far, my informant says, 'the public' does not like the idea of 'their excrement' being used to grow plants that will form their food.*

His remarks spark my research curiosity. Is it indeed true that 'the public' shies away from having their metabolic residues put back into circulation? If so, what might be done about that? And why do people living along rivers downstream from treatment plants not have similar anxieties? Some of them even swim in these rivers. Questions abound. For now, however, due to the infrastructural arrangements in which I am caught, my remnants are expelled from the food webs on which my life depends. Practically, this adds to all the other losses of potentially edible stuff, to the squandering and the wasting. Surplus foods are incinerated, rather than being fed to pigs or insects. Fertilizers, first mined at great cost to local landscapes, flow from agricultural land out into the sea. It is excruciating. *I* would feel less imposing if my urine and feces were collected and (after some clever treatment) used to fertilize agricultural fields. But the problem is not just material. It is also theoretical. That my urine and feces are not put to use, but squandered, says something. It suggests that I am an exceptional kind of creature. Someone who may eat others, but who is not, in her turn, destined to be turned into food.

Not only are my urine and feces wasted. My corpse-to-be also risks being taken out of the loop.[16]

In a draft of a talk about 'nature' for a policy audience, I write that I would hope that my body, once dead, might be inserted back into the food webs that made my life possible. Why assemble corpses in graveyards? Why burn them? I would rather be eaten by worms, fungi, and microbes so that my remnants could enrich the soils of an apple orchard, a broccoli field, or a meadow. However, when we discuss the draft in my research team, my colleagues say that this passage does not fit the context. It would be better to remind my audience of the ecological problems related to such dire practices as fracking or the massive burning of fossil fuels. I might talk about the meltdown of nuclear plants or, if I want my examples to be food-related, mention the mess left by the mining of phosphorus, or, for that matter, the fallout of pesticides. All in all, practically speaking, the issue of my corpse is minor. There is a second problem with this as well. It may be fine for me to talk about my future corpse in terms of the materials that compose it, but this might be offensive to those who attach spiritual

to be closed off. Distinctions do not necessarily need to solidify. If, in philosophical anthropology, *eating* was *other* to thinking, it may yet be used as a source of theoretical inspiration. While it may stand out as a joy to forgo, it can also be configured as a task to share. And so on. Perhaps it is possible to not just *control* equivocations but to also *play* with them. Take the notion of 'efficacy.' Maybe it is possible to disentangle this from classic Chinese texts that provided advice to idealized ruler-sages. Maybe *we*, too, can learn from it. It might inspire *us*, whoever *we* are, to pay better attention to the flavor of things. Or it might encourage *us* to reconcile argumentation and pleasure; ethics and aesthetics; resoluteness and moderation. Maybe *we* may even learn to forgo rigid dreams of coherence and cherish patchworks and polyphonies instead. *Others* might yet inspire *us* to stop erasing *otherness*. The otherness of others—and the otherness within.

values to theirs. Seeing the pertinence of these points, I cut out the passage.[17] *But I cannot forget it. Granted, if my corpse, via the mediation of worms, fungi, and microbes, were transformed into an apple tree, broccoli, or tasty grass, this would do little to save the earth. But I wonder about the symbolic power of offering up my flesh as food for future creatures—its spiritual qualities, so to speak.*

Humans like me may harbor the odd parasite, but we tend to eradicate this with medication. Bacteria and virus we tend to survive. Large predators we mostly avoid. We do not get seriously eaten. Even our corpses will not be appreciated for the fine food that they might be. Instead, they are expelled from the loops in which they might, with some added labor, minus some losses, have continued to flow. Whatever has led to this squandering, it expresses, in a material form, the idea that humans do not live on the earth and off it, but somehow stand apart. That they, we, can freely eat—one earth or four of them, never mind—without, in our turn, being eaten. This reiterates a long overdue, hierarchical model in which humans are exceptional creatures. I would rather, with my body as with my text, say something else instead.

Thinking Revisited

That eating calls for more appreciation does not mean that thinking, in its turn, deserves scorn. As I hope to revalue labor, I am not out to sing the praises of preverbal, fleshy bodies. Human eating is not preverbal. At the dinner table, my daughter and I talk, in between mouthfuls. Her question 'Did you add ginger?' alters the soup that we taste and turns two eating bodies into a daughter and a mother sharing a meal. Or, another example, if researchers use the term *protein*, this has an impact on their practices, even though this impact may be spun in different directions. It may mean that 'protein' gets all the attention, while the fate of the animals who form the 'sources of protein' is obstructed from view. Then again, using the term 'protein' also allows researchers to argue that eating insects consumes fewer resources and is less wasteful than eating beef; or to stake out the claim that a vegetarian meal of rice and lentils provides human eaters with ample 'protein'. But if this term can push and pull eating practices in different directions, there are limits to its versality. Talking of 'protein' does not allow for arguments about who does the cooking. It never suggests that soothing or surprising tastes might offer pleasure. And if on a long walk I become hungry, I tend to long for a muesli bar or a cracker with cheese. I crave not 'protein', but food.

Words are part of practice: they help to shape what is being done. Hence, it is important to mind our words and explore the worlds they carry with them. If terms do not quite fit, if their baggage is unwelcome, there are various solutions. One is to distance oneself from them by putting them into single quotations marks—as I have done with 'free men' and 'women and slaves'. Arendt used these terms, salient in ancient Greece, as if they still made sense. As I revisited her book, *The Human Condition*, to take leave from it, I put them in single quotes to indicate that these are not *my* words. I distanced myself from them because they suggest a contrast between 'freedom'—a status marked by independence from others—and 'slavery'—in which one is forced into submission. The situations of eating I invoke in this book interfere with that contrast. For masters depend for their survival on others: Other people, who care for their food, and other creatures, forming that food. And neither these other people, nor the edible creatures, are fully under the alleged master's control. They have their own propensities, they resist. The human condition, then, is not so easily disaggregated but marked by interdependence as well as friction throughout. And what about the category 'women?' The 'men/women' divide is pretty stubborn. Indeed, it is crucial to family trees that depict genealogies, in which, time and again, a man and a woman jointly generate offspring. But is it all that relevant elsewhere? Seeking to escape from society's obsession with sex, I left it to one side as I considered eating and edibility. This involves all kinds of other divides and divisions. Hence, the single quotation marks around 'men' and 'women'.

But if terms may be cast into doubt, they may also be revised. That is what I have tried to do in this book with *being, knowing, doing*, and *relating*. Taking inspiration from situations of eating, I have sought to reimagine them. A summary? I hesitate to disentangle the results of my analyses from the stories out of which they emerged. But I will give it a try.

Being is not necessarily epitomized by an individual moving through his apartment or walking through a terrain that spreads out around him. If, instead, we take inspiration from eating, the *I* that *is* exchanges materials with her surroundings through semipermeable boundaries. In designated places, these boundaries are crossed so that what was outside travels inside, while what was other becomes self. At the same time, or a little later, what was self, may, in turn, be expelled and othered. The stuff that this unstable form of *being* folds into its insides may come from diverse sites, near and far. *My* remnants spread out there, too. This kind of *being* thrives on the energy of others. It maintains its form by changing its substance. Its limits are formed not by its skin, but by the finiteness of its lifetime.

Knowing is not necessarily done from a distance. In situations of eating, perceptions and sensations may flow over into each other, so that the perceived outside world and the body's sensed insides intertwine. The *knowing* that accompanies eating proceeds from being attentive and staying attuned. It involves facting as well as valuing: establishing facts goes together with appraising worth. The object that attract appreciative interest is fluid: from the stuff being eaten, it flows over into the people present, the moment, the world. Nothing stays the same. The *knowing* relevant to eating is transformative: I adapt the food to my taste and my taste to the food. As I savor it, the food becomes me. But the circle is not simply virtuous: my pleasure may also turn into disgust. I love you, I love you not. I covet you, you make me nauseous. The *knowing* that emerges from my eating transforms, in not entirely predictable ways, all the subjects and objects involved.

Doing is not necessarily as neatly under control as are voluntary muscles that have been subject to dedicated training. Eating situations help to highlight that doing may also take an iterative form. Start, stop, begin again, but in a different way. Such explorative *doing* is not just *mine*; it involves a lot of actors situated far beyond my skin. They are here and there, now and then. They act in the present, have acted in the past, come to act in the future. They do my deeds for me or respond to what I do. They allow some deeds to unfold and obstruct others. The *doing* modeled on my eating may work toward a goal, but if the goal is reached, this is likely to come at the cost of adverse effects. What is more, disentangling desirable effects from unwanted side effects is not always easy. *Doing* is often ambivalent. Bad, but not just bad; good, but not just good. Not good for everyone. Not good enough. Suspended within complex normative force fields, *doing* goes on and on. It never comes to rest.

Relating does not have to be modeled on family trees or, for that matter, family life. With those whose flesh I eat, I do not sit around a table. I ingest them, or at least a part of them. At the same time, my eating contributes, for better or worse, to the survival of their species. My taking is generative, but my giving is self-serving. My love comes with violence. Moreover, while I seek to eat what agrees with me, current agricultural arrangements are not all that agreeable for other creatures. Not for those who are being eaten, but even less so for those who do not get to eat what I get to eat, who do not get to live in the fields dedicated to the growing of my food. We compete and I win. And win again. But in the model of *relating* that takes its cues from eating, all this winning is self-defeating. Wiping out others has the effect of eroding the conditions of possibility on which my life depends.

The Western philosophical tradition is marked by hierarchies. First, theory is elevated above practice. Within theory, the abstract rises above the concrete, generality wins out over specific cases. Clarity and distinctness are virtues; seduction and evocation stand out as vices. Solidly defined concepts are better than fluid, adaptable terms. What counts most is the proposition, the argument. This book, along with other work currently done, takes leave from those hierarchies. It does so by focusing on the stuff out of which theory is made, by exploring some of the elements that make thinking possible: words, models, metaphors, and exemplary situations. The small summary I just gave may make it seem as if, in the end, what I am after is to provide new definitions for *being, knowing, doing*, and *relating*. That it is fine to abstract these terms from the stories from which they emerged. But this ending is not a conclusion, not a place at which this book comes to rest. It instead offers an opening. Please, reader, if you found anything inspiring here, run with it. There is no need to take on board all my attempts at reimagining *being, knowing, doing*, and *relating*. By all means, work with whatever it is that speaks to you and adapt it to your own cases and your own concerns. Am I allowed a food metaphor? The proof of this pudding will be in its eating.

ACKNOWLEDGMENTS

THE THINKING THAT WENT INTO THIS BOOK was done by a spread-out, collective brain. My heartfelt thanks to the Eating Bodies team, which joined me in exploring the ins and outs of *eating* over many years: Anna Mann, Sebastian Abrahamsson, Filippo Bertoni, Emily Yates-Doerr, Michalis Kontopodis, Else Vogel, Rebeca Ibañez Martín, and Cristobal Bonelli—and to remind us that *eating* is not all there is to life—Tjitske Holtrop, Carolina Dominguez, Hasan Ashraf, Jeltsje Stobbe, Oliver Human, and Annelieke Driessen. Thanks as well to Justine Laurent, Ulrike Scholtes, Ignace Schoot, Arseny Alenichev, Mariya Shchleglovitova, and Mandy de Wilde for taking the quest in further directions and to Menno Maris, Maurizia Mezza, and Mandy de Wilde again for their help with the references. On and off, Marianne de Laet was a welcome guest. And there were many others who came for months on end or just once or twice for seminars or workshops—far too many to name. Thanks to all of you for your inspiration.

Thanks to the other members of the Department of Anthropology of the University of Amsterdam, especially Anita Hardon, Amâde M'charek, Mattijs van de Port, Annelies Moors, and Jeannette Pols and the heart of the Department, Muriël Kiesel. Thanks to the MA students whose inquiries into things food-related I supervised, especially Frank Heuts; the PhD students who took an iteration of the Ethnographic Methods class; and the many on-and-off participants of the Walking Seminar.

Indispensable was, and is, the support of the AISSR bureau—especially José Komen, Yomi van der Veen, Janus Oomen, Karin Kraal, Lotte Batelaan, Joanne Oakes, Bea Krenn, Alix Nieuwenhuis, Nicole Schulp, Teun Bijvoet, and Hermance Metrop. For their sustained support I also thank my friends Mieke Aerts and Geertje Mak, both of whom were sparring partners all along and figured as early readers. Some version or other of the manuscript was also, entirely or partially, read by Erik Rietveld, Oliver Human, Else Vogel, Anna Mann, and Mandy de Wilde. Filippo Bertoni even commented on the entire text twice. Throughout, Simon Cohn offered spirited supervisions. John Law read and reread all the chapters when I wrote them, gave comments, and corrected my English. That is a lot to be grateful for. Helen Faller came in at the last moment for a final round of editing—a treat.

And where to put Trudy Dehue and Ad Prins? Thank you!

Earlier bits and pieces of this book I presented to diverse audiences of anthropologists, sociologists, geographers, philosophers, and accidental others in Amsterdam, Groningen, Wageningen, Maastricht, Mainz, Bochum, Mainz, Berlin, Copenhagen, Aarhus, Paris, Cambridge, Oxford, London, Lancaster, Edinburgh, Linköping, New York, Ann Arbor, Berkeley, Stanford, Davis, Claremont, Singapore, Tokyo, Sydney, Palmerston North, Dunedin, and Queenstown. Invariably, I received helpful comments. If I were to spell it out, the list of people to whom I am grateful in all these places would be long indeed. I hope, dear colleagues, that you can live with an unspecified thank-you note.

My Mol family, including the Heikens branch, I thank for their enduring support. My Van Lieshout family saw me struggling with this book from nearby. Peter was encouraging even when we were no longer partners. Our children endured my strange intellectual passions and pointed me to *materials* both at home and on our travels. Elisabeth gave me permission to analytically chop up a few of our joint meals. When this project started, Johannes inquisitively asked why anyone was prepared to pay me and the Eating Bodies team for our work. And, indeed, that is not self-evident.

Thanks, therefore, to the Dutch taxpayer for the NWO grant "Good Information, Good Food," which gave me the chance to dream up this project, and for the Spinoza Grant, which allowed me to extend it. Thanks to the European taxpayer for ERC Advanced Grant AdG09 no. 249397 awarded to a proposal to study "the eating body in Western practice and theory." And thanks to all those working for these funding bodies as staff, committee members, and reviewers.

Thanks as well to the publishers' two anonymous reviewers for their extensive comments and suggestions. And thanks to all those working at Duke University Press for beautifully packaging these words and making them transportable!

And finally, of course, I am grateful to all the people whose eating I was allowed to observe, who granted me an interview and/or who otherwise taught me about eating. This is another long list of people who remain anonymous here. It includes everyone with whom I shared a meal over the last ten years. They did not sign informed consent forms, which helped to keep interactions fluid and to assure their anonymity, but sometimes in the middle of our daily doings I would call out: "Beware, I am doing fieldwork!" That particular fieldwork is over now. But I continue to be grateful to the people who care for my food and to the many creatures from whose fruits, roots, leaves, seeds, eggs, milk, or flesh I eat.

NOTES

One. Empirical Philosophy

1. For just a few among very many examples, see Charis Thompson, "When Elephants Stand for Competing Philosophies of Nature: Amboseli National Parc, Kenya," in *Complexities*, ed. John Law and Annemarie Mol (Durham, NC: Duke University Press, 2002); Thom van Dooren, *Flight Ways: Life and Loss at the Edge of Extinction* (New York: Columbia University Press, 2014); Marianne Lien and John Law, "'Emergent Aliens': On Salmon, Nature, and Their Enactment," *Ethnos* 76, no. 1 (2011); Lesley Head, Jennifer Atchison, and Catherine Phillips, "The Distinctive Capacities of Plants: Re-thinking Difference via Invasive Species," *Transactions of the Institute of British Geographers* 40, no. 3 (2015); Hugh Raffles, "Twenty-Five Years Is a Long Time," *Cultural Anthropology* 27, no. 3 (2012).

2. On this topic, see the fabulous *Dictionary of Untranslatables*, which traces what happens to philosophical terms between languages: Barbara Cassin et al., *Dictionary of Untranslatables: A Philosophical Lexicon* (Princeton, NJ: Princeton University Press, 2014); the collection of essays assembled in Annemarie Mol and John Law, eds., *On Other Terms*, Sociological Review Monograph (2020); and the twin volume to the present one, *Eating Is an English Word*, still in the making, that addresses some linguistic particularities to do with food pleasures.

3. See, for instance, Annemarie Mol, "Care and Its Values: Good Food in the Nursing Home," in *Care in Practice: On Tinkering in Clinics, Homes and Farms*, ed. Annemarie Mol, Ingunn Moser, and Jeannette Pols (Bielefeld, Germany: Transcript Verlag, 2010), 215; and Else Vogel and Annemarie Mol, "Enjoy Your Food: On Losing Weight and Taking Pleasure," *Sociology of Health and Illness* 36, no. 2 (2014); Sebastian Abrahamsson et al., "Living with Omega-3: New Material-

ism and Enduring Concerns," *Environment and Planning D: Society and Space* 33, no. 1 (2015).

4. Hannah Arendt, *The Human Condition* (1958; repr., Chicago: University of Chicago Press, 2013).

5. In the Dutch university system, students do not go to a college and sample courses in diverse disciplines. Instead, after completing secondary school, we enroll in a single discipline. This does not require special admission; a diploma from a targeted preuniversity secondary school is all that is needed. I had started as a medical student in my first year but was eager to acquire more tools with which to think. Hence, in my second year I took up a second discipline, philosophy.

6. In more recent scholarship, whether in ancient Greece 'women and slaves' shared a single fate is contested. If religious practices are taken into account as relevant to citizenship, women (certainly in Athens) were in a better position than people who had been captured in wars and thereby had the status of slaves. See Josine Blok, *Citizenship in Classical Athens* (Cambridge: Cambridge University Press, 2017).

7. Other feminists read Arendt's work quite differently and, focusing on other elements, even take feminist inspiration from it. See, for example, the contributions to Bonnie Honig, ed., *Feminist Interpretations of Hannah Arendt* (University Park: Penn State University Press, 2010). This signals that there are problems with treating 'theories,' let alone 'theorists,' as if they were coherent wholes.

8. Arendt, *The Human Condition*, 246.

9. As in ancient Greek city-states, war captives were given the status of 'slaves' and 'free men' were haunted by the fear that, sooner or later, if they were to lose a war, they would no longer be 'free men,' but someone else's slave. For the argument that this fear left deep marks in Greek philosophy, see Tsjalling Swierstra, *De sofocratische verleiding: Het ondemocratische karakter van een aantal moderne rationaliteitsconcepties* (Kampen, Netherlands: Kok/Agora, 1998). Thus, being a slave was a social position that, with bad luck, every person might come to inhabit, and it was not tied to other—say, physical—categorizations. Even so, later systems of slavery that were accompanied by racialization inherited a lot from those earlier, Greek ones; on this, see Enrico Dal Lago and Constantina Katsari, eds., *Slave Systems: Ancient and Modern* (Cambridge: Cambridge University Press, 2008).

10. Arendt, *The Human Condition*, 312–13.

11. Here Arendt skips over the fact that there was also a vivid Christian tradition of starving one's body so as to purify oneself and attain holiness. See, for example, Caroline W. Bynum, *Holy Feast and Holy Fast: The Religious Significance of Food to Medieval Women* (Berkeley: University of California Press, 1988).

12. Arendt, *The Human Condition*, 115.

13. This was clearly signaled in scholarly literature and reached general audiences through such publications as the reports of the Club of Rome, beginning

with the first one: Donella Meadows et al., *The Limits to Growth: A Report to the Club of Rome* (New York: Universe Books, 1972).

14. For this and other details on Descartes's investment in diets, see Steven Shapin, "Descartes the Doctor: Rationalism and Its Therapies," *British Journal for the History of Science* 33, no. 2 (2000). For a series of marvelous studies on the ways in which their own bodies mattered to early modern scientists, see Christopher Lawrence and Steven Shapin, eds., *Science Incarnate: Historical Embodiments of Natural Knowledge* (Chicago: University of Chicago Press, 1998).

15. This book grew out of a lecture the author gave to an audience of women who were members of an active women's organization. See Frederik J. J. Buytendijk, *De vrouw. Haar natuur, verschijning en bestaan* (Utrecht: Het Spectrum, 1951).

16. Published in Dutch in 1971 and in English in 1974. For a later reprint, see Else M. Barth, *The Logic of the Articles in Traditional Philosophy: A Contribution to the Study of Conceptual Structures* (Dordrecht: Springer Netherlands, 2012).

17. In doing so, they built on an earlier tradition of differentiating between physical traits and of using anthropology to both legitimize and facilitate colonial rule. See, among many other works, Henrika Kuklick, *The Savage Within: The Social History of British Anthropology, 1885–1945* (Cambridge: Cambridge University Press, 1991); Robert J. Young, *Colonial Desire: Hybridity in Theory, Culture and Race* (London: Routledge, 2005); and contributions to Peter Pels and Oscar Salemink, eds., *Colonial Subjects: Essays on the Practical History of Anthropology* (Ann Arbor: University of Michigan Press, 2000).

18. This is a marked difference with other regions, notably the US or South Africa, which have histories of racial segregation and related deprivation, though not the systematic murdering on the scale that the Nazis had introduced. However, racism in Europe did not disappear along with the term *race*; it was simply hidden in other terms, while taking different shapes from one European country to the next. On this, see Amâde M'charek, Katharina Schramm, and David Skinner, "Topologies of Race: Doing Territory, Population and Identity in Europe," *Science, Technology, and Human Values* 39, no. 4 (2014); and Francio Guadeloupe, *So How Does It Feel to Be a Black Man Living in the Netherlands? An Anthropological Answer* (forthcoming).

19. For how this plays out in the particular case of the Netherlands, see Dvora Yanow, Marleen van der Haar, and Karlijn Völke, "Troubled Taxonomies and the Calculating State: Everyday Categorizing and 'Race-Ethnicity'—the Netherlands Case," *Journal of Race, Ethnicity and Politics* 1, no. 2 (2016); Amâde M'charek, "Fragile Differences, Relational Effects: Stories about the Materiality of Race and Sex," *European Journal of Women's Studies* 17, no. 4 (2010); and Amâde M'charek, "Beyond Fact or Fiction: On the Materiality of Race in Practice," *Cultural Anthropology* 28, no. 3 (2013).

20. See, for a comparison between the US and Japan, Margaret Lock, *Encounters with Aging: Mythologies of Menopause in Japan and North America* (Berke-

ley: University of California Press, 1994). For questions about how genetics and environments may relate, see Jörg Niewöhner and Margaret Lock, "Situating Local Biologies: Anthropological Perspectives on Environment/Human Entanglements," *BioSocieties* 13, no. 4 (2018). On how bodies may differ from one site to another, while the way 'bodies' are enacted likewise differs, see Emily Yates-Doerr, "Counting Bodies? On Future Engagements with Science Studies in Medical Anthropology," *Anthropology and Medicine* 24, no. 2 (2017).

21. Despite this all-too-quick division, actual studies often mix these styles. Anthropologists who studied food could readily shift between its alleged physical, social, and cultural significance, while also presenting the relevant local terms. For true classics, see Audrey I. Richards, *Hunger and Work in a Savage Tribe: A Functional Study of Nutrition among the Southern Bantu* (1932; repr., London: Routledge, 2013); and Mary Douglas, ed., *Food in the Social Order* (1973; repr., London: Routledge, 2014).

22. The timeline disentangling the sciences from philosophy is stretched out and far from linear. Roughly, the natural sciences gained independence in the eighteenth and nineteenth centuries, and the social sciences in the nineteenth and twentieth centuries. But in the Netherlands, for instance, psychology was still situated in philosophy departments up until the 1950s. For an interesting history of the sciences, see Chunglin Kwa, *Styles of Knowing: A New History of Science from Ancient Times to the Present* (Pittsburgh: University of Pittsburgh Press, 2011); and for a history of the humanities, all too often skipped in histories of 'science,' see Rens Bod, *A New History of the Humanities: The Search for Principles and Patterns from Antiquity to the Present* (Oxford: Oxford University Press, 2013).

23. On Nauta's use of this term, see Lolle W. Nauta, "De subcultuur van de wijsbegeerte: Een privé geschiedenis van de filosofie," *Krisis* 38 (2006). In a festschrift in his honor, I picked the term up and elaborated on it. See Annemarie Mol, "Ondertonen en boventonen: Over empirische filosofie," in *Burgers en Vreemdelingen*, ed. Dick Pels and Gerard de Vries (Amsterdam: Van Gennep, 1994). For a more extensive articulation, written on the occasion that the (at the time still entirely Dutch-language) journal *Krisis* was granted the subtitle "Journal for Empirical Philosophy" (which later it lost again), see Annemarie Mol, "Dit is geen programma: Over empirische filosofie," *Krisis* 1, no. 1 (2000).

24. For recent editions, see Ludwig Wittgenstein, *Philosophical Investigations* (1953; repr., Hoboken, NJ: John Wiley & Sons, 2009). For an interesting reading of the latter work (and of the lecture notes in the years preceding it) that argues that Wittgenstein opened up the possibility for a sociology of all kinds of knowledge, including scientific knowledge, see David Bloor, *Wittgenstein: A Social Theory of Knowledge* (New York: Columbia University Press, 1983).

25. For the method of writing history involved and the idea that over time particular discourses came and went along with their conditions of possibility, see Michel Foucault, *Archaeology of Knowledge* (1969; repr., London: Routledge, 2013); for an extensive inquiry into the 'normality' that emerged historically as a

counterpoint of 'madness,' see Michel Foucault, *Madness and Civilization* (1962; repr., London: Routledge, 2003); and for the connection to the modes of governing that normalization processes allowed for, Michel Foucault, *Discipline and Punish: The Birth of the Prison* (1975; repr., New York: Vintage Books, 2012). For an analysis of normalization in grammar and what this meant in France, see George Canguilhem, *The Normal and the Pathological* (1966; repr., Cambridge, MA: MIT Press, 1989) (this issue is dealt with in a chapter that was newly added to second edition of the French original, which came out in 1966).

26. See Thomas S. Kuhn, *The Structure of Scientific Revolutions* (Chicago: University of Chicago Press, 1962). In the philosophy of science, reflecting on materials was more widespread than in some other branches of philosophy. The moot point there was *which* materials counted for most: final theories and the arguments on which they were based, or the questions asked and the practices that were orchestrated to answer them?

27. On Locke and property, see Barbara Arneil, "Trade, Plantations, and Property: John Locke and the Economic Defense of Colonialism," *Journal of the History of Ideas* 55, no. 4 (1994).

28. George Lakoff and Mark Johnson, *Metaphors We Live By* (Chicago: University of Chicago Press, 1980).

29. For these stories, see Michel Serres, *Le Passage du Nord-Ouest* (Paris: Éditions du Minuit, 1980). For an interesting and accessible introduction into Serres's work, see Latour's book of interviews with him: Michel Serres and Bruno Latour, *Conversations on Science, Culture, and Time* (Ann Arbor: University of Michigan Press, 1995).

30. Here, for the sake of simplicity, I presented Serres's cloth, fluids, and fire models. In his expansive work, he uses many other evocative images as well. Among these is that of the parasite. The French term *parasite* encompasses a species eating a host from the inside, an uninvited human guest, and meaningless noise that accompanies messages. Serres uses these disturbers of equivalence and equity to critique social scientific and economic fantasies about the possibility of clear, fair, and friction-free exchange. See Michel Serres, *The Parasite* (Minneapolis: University of Minnesota Press, 2013).

31. On this, see Michel Foucault, *The History of Sexuality*, vol. 2: *The Use of Pleasure* (1985; repr., New York: Vintage Books, 2012). This book has been read as if Foucault were praising the particular self-care in which Greek men engaged. But he extensively comments on all kinds of implicit problems, for instance, for the boys, slaves, and women with whom the self-celebratory 'free men' had sex. Rather than the particulars of the ancient Greek circumstances, it was the very possibility of *otherness* in which Foucault was invested.

32. For more versions of 'woman' and for an English translation of the article (originally from 1985) on which I draw here, see Annemarie Mol, "Who Knows What a Woman Is . . . : On the Differences and the Relations between the Sciences," *Medicine, Anthropology, Theory* 2, no. 1 (2015).

33. Later work would insist that this does not just have different implications for women, men, and potential offspring, but also for other entities, such as the rubber trees on plantations that supply the materials for condom and diaphragm production, or the fish confronted with the hormonal effluent of women on the pill, and so on. On this, see Max Liboiron, Manuel Tironi, and Nerea Calvillo, "Toxic Politics: Acting in a Permanently Polluted World," *Social Studies of Science* 48, no. 3 (2018).

34. The term *multiple* is used here in differentiation from *plural*. In pluralism, different *entities* form a plurality, while each of them is individuated. Multiplicity, by contrast, suggests that different *versions* of an entity may clash *here* while *elsewhere* they overlap or are interdependent. On this, see Annemarie Mol, *The Body Multiple: Ontology in Medical Practice* (Durham, NC: Duke University Press, 2003).

35. In earlier work on multiplicity, I use the term *ontologies*—in the plural— to interfere with the idea that a single 'ontology' precedes diverse kinds of knowledge about it. Alternatively, I proposed *ontonorms* to insist that normativities and realities tend to be *done* together. As these technical terms lead (often confusing) lives of their own, in the present book I have mostly abstained from using them.

36. Food studies is a great interdisciplinary field and some of its richness will be apparent from the references in the chapters to follow. Pivotal studies have 'used' food facts to place other concerns in a new light, such as the seminal rewriting of the history of both modern slavery and capitalism in Sidney W. Mintz, *Sweetness and Power: The Place of Sugar in Modern History* (New York: Viking, 1985). The contributions to James Watson, ed., *Golden Arches East: McDonald's in East Asia* (Redwood City, CA: Stanford University Press, 2006), challenge the idea that globalization and homogenization necessarily go together. Food serves as an entrée into studying socioeconomic class in Jack Goody, *Cooking, Cuisine and Class: A Study in Comparative Sociology* (Cambridge: Cambridge University Press, 1982); or gender, as in Carole M. Counihan, *The Anthropology of Food and Body: Gender, Meaning, and Power* (Hove, UK: Psychology Press, 1999). For a more recent overview, that takes (English) words as stepping stones, see Peter Jackson, ed., *Food Words: Essays in Culinary Culture* (London: Bloomsbury, 2014). Even more recently, eating has been topicalized in a practice-theory theory mode, see Alan Warde, *The Practice of Eating* (Hoboken, NJ: John Wiley & Sons, 2016).

37. For the argument that in ethnographic research, the particularities of the performance of 'gender,' like that of 'sex,' deserve to be investigated time and again, rather than carried from one context to another, see Stefan Hirschauer and Annemarie Mol, "Shifting Sexes, Moving Stories: Feminist/Constructivist Dialogues," *Science, Technology, and Human Values* 20, no. 3 (1995). For a careful analysis of the way different categorizations may inform and transform one another as they intersect, see Ingunn Moser, "On Becoming Disabled and Articulating Alternatives: The Multiple Modes of Ordering Disability and Their Interferences," *Cultural Studies* 19, no. 6 (2005).

38. Obviously, this also comes with methodological limits and challenges. On this, see Marilyn Strathern, "The Limits of Auto-Ethnography," in *Anthropology at Home*, ed. Anthony Jackson (London: Tavistock, 1987); or, in a very different vein, Carolyn Ellis, *The Ethnographic I: A Methodological Novel about Autoethnography* (Walnut Creek, CA: Altamira Press, 2004). For the argument that method is always an issue of theory rather than just one of access, see Stefan Hirschauer, "Putting Things into Words: Ethnographic Description and the Silence of the Social," *Human Studies* 29, no. 4 (2006).

Two. Being

1. John Wylie, "A Single Day's Walking: Narrating Self and Landscape on the South West Coast Path," *Transactions of the Institute of British Geographers* 30, no. 2 (2005): 234.

2. Wylie, "A Single Day's Walking," 235.

3. Wylie, "A Single Day's Walking," 243.

4. Wylie, "A Single Day's Walking," 243.

5. Wylie, "A Single Day's Walking," 241.

6. Tim Ingold and Jo Lee Vergunst, eds., *Ways of Walking: Ethnography and Practice on Foot* (Aldershot, UK: Ashgate, 2008).

7. Ingold and Vergunst, *Ways of Walking*, 245. I added italics here and deleted internal author-date references to facilitate the reading.

8. This quote is from Maurice Merleau-Ponty, *The Phenomenology of Perception* (1958; repr., London: Routledge, 2005), 353.

9. Merleau-Ponty, *The Phenomenology of Perception*, 235.

10. For an introduction to Merleau-Ponty's work that is invested in its salience to present-day concerns to do with bodies, affect, animality, intersubjectivity, and so on, see Rosalyn Diprose and Jack Reynolds, *Merleau-Ponty: Key Concepts* (London: Routledge, 2014).

11. In the analysis in this chapter, I foreground 'my' relation with the food I eat, pushing to the background (to reduce complexity) those who cared for my food, from the cooks working in the restaurant kitchen (on their work, see Gary Alan Fine, *Kitchens: The Culture of Restaurant Work* [Berkeley: University of California Press, 2008]) to those who cultivated, harvested, and transported it (see Michael Carolan, *The Sociology of Food and Agriculture* [London: Routledge, 2016] and *The Real Cost of Cheap Food* [London: Routledge, 2018]). More on the theoretical salience of this follows in the chapter on *doing*.

12. For this history and more on Goldstein and the context in which he worked, see Anne Harrington, *Reenchanted Science: Holism in German Culture from Wilhelm II to Hitler* (Princeton, NJ: Princeton University Press, 1999).

13. Kurt Goldstein, *The Organism: A Holistic Approach to Biology Derived from Pathological Data in Man* (New York: Zone Books, 1995).

14. Merleau-Ponty, *The Phenomenology of Perception*, 146.

15. For a rich analysis of hunger strikes, see Patrick Anderson, *"So Much Wasted": Hunger, Performance, and the Morbidity of Resistance* (Durham, NC: Duke University Press, 2010). For an analysis of what 'global hunger' and 'malnutrition' mean beyond these numerical forms, see Emily Yates-Doerr, "Intervals of Confidence: Uncertain Accounts of Global Hunger," *BioSocieties* 10, no. 2 (2015).

16. I make remarks like these repeatedly as shortcuts. They may all be opened up for further differentiation. What I skip at this particular point is the variety of modes in which people may engage with foods that they prepare for swallowing, such as biting and chewing, or rather slurping. On this, see, for example, Mattijs Van de Port and Annemarie Mol, "Chupar Frutas in Salvador da Bahia: A Case of Practice-Specific Alterities," *Journal of the Royal Anthropological Institute* 21, no. 1 (2015).

17. For this particular field research, it greatly helped that earlier I had supervised, learned from, and coauthored with colleagues working on rehabilitation practices. See, inter alia, Ant Lettinga and Annemarie Mol, "Clinical Specificity and the Non-generalities of Science," *Theoretical Medicine and Bioethics* 20, no. 6 (1999); and Rita M. Struhkamp, Annemarie Mol, and Tjitske Swierstra, "Dealing with In/Dependence: Doctoring in Physical Rehabilitation Practice," *Science, Technology, and Human Values* 34, no. 1 (2009).

18. Throughout, I use terms like *client* or *patient*, forms of address such as *Mr.* or *Mrs.* or a first name pertinent to the sites studied. The names are invented. Professionals I either allude to with the titles of their professions or a first name (if this is how they presented themselves to me). But I have also altered their names.

19. Recent work confirms Goldstein's argument that this ability does not just depend on the physical ability to walk, but also requires abilities to do with recognizing the various objects and people in one's surroundings. See Christa Nanninga et al., "Unpacking Community Mobility: A Preliminary Study into the Embodied Experiences of Stroke Survivors," *Disability and Rehabilitation* 40, no. 17 (2018).

20. Historical studies reveal how recently it is that individual bodies are taken to be bounded. For the notion of enclosing membranes, see Laura Otis, *Membranes: Metaphors of Invasion in Nineteenth-Century Literature, Science, and Politics* (Baltimore: Johns Hopkins University Press, 2000). For work on the self/body open to alien stuff against which it must defend itself, see Ed Cohen, *A Body Worth Defending: Immunity, Biopolitics, and the Apotheosis of the Modern Body* (Durham, NC: Duke University Press, 2009).

21. For an extended analysis of what tube feeding may entail in practice, taking the case of ALS patients, see Jeannette Pols and Sarah Limburg, "A Matter of Taste? Quality of Life in Day-to-Day Living with ALS and a Feeding Tube," *Culture, Medicine, and Psychiatry* 40, no. 3 (2016).

22. For a more extensive analysis of eating in a nursing home, see Annemarie Mol, "Care and Its Values: Good Food in the Nursing Home," in *Care in Practice:*

On Tinkering in Clinics, Homes and Farms, ed. Annemarie Mol, Ingunn Moser, and Jeannette Pols (Bielefeld, Germany: Transcript Verlag, 2010).

23. If I write that 'the body' has two sets of boundaries, it is the human body that I mean, or rather the human body in as far as it is human. By now it is amply clear that the bowels of mammals like humans are inhabited by immensely large numbers of other, microbial, organisms. These are crucial to the functioning of the human-plus-microbiome assemblage. That this makes it possible to define 'the organism' as either excluding or including the many nonhumans living inside it, was already remarked on by Ludwig Fleck in the 1930s. See Ludwig Fleck, *Genesis and Development of a Scientific Fact* (1935; repr., Berkeley: University of California Press, 1981).

24. For a related analysis of bodily boundaries, see Sebastian Abrahamsson and Paul Simpson, "The Limits of the Body: Boundaries, Capacities, Thresholds," *Social and Cultural Geography* 12, no. 4 (2011).

25. I use here a snippet of fieldwork that I have analyzed more extensively elsewhere. See Annemarie Mol, "Mind Your Plate! The Ontonorms of Dutch Dieting," *Social Studies of Science* 43, no. 3 (2013).

26. For the argument that energy remains in the background and should not be, when social scientists write about materiality, see Andrew Barry, "Thermodynamics, Matter, Politics," *Distinktion* 16, no. 1 (2015).

27. On these complexities, see Else Vogel, "Metabolism and Movement: Calculating Food and Exercise or Activating Bodies in Dutch Weight Management," *BioSocieties* 13, no. 2 (2018).

28. For more on the care of people living with kidney disease, see Ciara Kierans, "The Intimate Uncertainties of Kidney Care: Moral Economy and Treatment Regimes in Comparative Perspective," *Anthropological Journal of European Cultures* 27, no. 2 (2018).

29. On the argument that flushing removes what people excrete so quickly that they experience their urine and feces not as belonging to their body, but as alien, see Rose George, *The Big Necessity: Adventures in the World of Human Waste* (London: Portobello Books, 2011).

30. Recent understandings of eating broaden from simply absorbing energy and assembling building blocks to changing one's genes in response to food that holds information about one's environment. This is another complexity I leave out here. See Hannah Landecker, "Food as Exposure: Nutritional Epigenetics and the New Metabolism," *BioSocieties* 6, no. 2 (2011); and Hannah Landecker and Aaron Panofsky, "From Social Structure to Gene Regulation, and Back: A Critical Introduction to Environmental Epigenetics for Sociology," *Annual Review of Sociology* 39 (2013).

31. Tim Ingold, "Footprints through the Weather-World: Walking, Breathing, Knowing," *Journal of the Royal Anthropological Institute* 16, no. 1 (2010). Hereafter page citations are given parenthetically in the text.

32. For a fine-grained critique of this mode of thinking, see the comparison

of TGV riding and jungle walking, presented similarly as events in a particular here and now in Bruno Latour, "Trains of Thought: Piaget, Formalism, and the Fifth Dimension," *Common Knowledge* 6 (1997). An added problem with the way Ingold discards technology is that he 'forgets' small technologies like shoes, and makes it seem as if only able-bodied people can lead authentic lives. On this, see Patrick Devlieger and Jori De Coster, "On Footwear and Disability: A Dance of Animacy?," *Societies* 7, no. 2 (2017).

33. For the invention of the imagination of the implied landscape, see Chunglin Kwa, "Alexander von Humboldt's Invention of the Natural Landscape," *European Legacy* 10, no. 2 (April 2005).

34. On that see Tim Lang and Michael Heasman, *Food Wars: The Global Battle for Mouths, Minds and Markets* (London: Routledge, 2015). And for history of 'my' eating foods from so many places around the globe, see David Inglis and Debra Gimlin, eds., *The Globalization of Food* (Oxford: Berg, 2009).

35. For the implied geography, see Ian Cook et al., "Food's Cultural Geographies: Texture, Creativity and Publics," in *The Wiley-Blackwell Companion to Cultural Geography*, ed. Nuala C. Johnson, Richard H. Schein, and Jamie Winders (Oxford: Wiley-Blackwell, 2013); and Sebastian Abrahamsson and Annemarie Mol, "Foods," in *The Routledge Handbook of Mobilities*, ed. Peter Adey et al. (London: Routledge, 2014).

36. On their history in the UK and the US, see Daniel Schneider, *Hybrid Nature: Sewage Treatment and the Contradictions of the Industrial Ecosystem* (Cambridge, MA: MIT Press, 2011). For the bacteria involved, see Andrew Balmer and Susan Molyneux-Hodgson, "Bacterial Cultures: Ontologies of Bacteria and Engineering Expertise at the Nexus of Synthetic Biology and Water Services," *Engineering Studies* 5, no. 1 (2013).

37. On such issues, see, for instance, Joshua Reno, "Waste and Waste Management," *Annual Review of Anthropology* 44 (2015).

Three. Knowing

1. Merleau-Ponty, *The Phenomenology of Perception*, 207.

2. Merleau-Ponty, *The Phenomenology of Perception*, 239.

3. Merleau-Ponty, *The Phenomenology of Perception*, 185.

4. For more on this topic, see Dick Willems, "Inhaling Drugs and Making Worlds: The Proliferation of Lungs and Asthmas," in *Differences in Medicine: Unravelling Practices, Techniques and Bodies*, ed. Marc Berg and Annemarie Mol (Durham, NC: Duke University Press, 1998); Timothy K. Choy, *Ecologies of Comparison: An Ethnography of Endangerment in Hong Kong* (Durham, NC: Duke University Press, 2011); and Erik Bigras and Kim Fortun, "Innovation in Asthma Research: Using Ethnography to Study a Global Health Problem," *Ethnography Matters*, October 27, 2012, http://ethnographymatters.net/blog/2012/10/27/the -asthma-files/.

5. Carolyn Korsmeyer, *Making Sense of Taste: Food and Philosophy* (Ithaca, NY: Cornell University Press, 1999), 24.

6. Korsmeyer, *Making Sense of Taste*, 25.

7. Korsmeyer, *Making Sense of Taste*, 37.

8. Korsmeyer, *Making Sense of Taste*, 25.

9. That said, social science research attending to more senses than just one or two, has resulted in interesting work. See, for instance, David Howes, *Sensual Relations: Engaging the Senses in Culture and Social Theory* (Ann Arbor: University of Michigan Press, 2010); and David Howes and Constance Classen, *Ways of Sensing: Understanding the Senses in Society* (London: Routledge, 2013).

10. Hearing has its own complexities that also stretch from a perceptual to a sensing engagement. Interesting work on that includes Veit Erlmann, ed., *Hearing Cultures: Essays on Sound, Listening and Modernity* (Oxford: Berg, 2004); Cyrus C. Mody, "The Sounds of Science: Listening to Laboratory Practice," *Science, Technology, and Human Values* 30, no. 2 (2005); Veit Erlmann, *Reason and Resonance: A History of Modern Aurality* (New York: Zone Books, 2010); Trevor Pinch and Karin Bijsterveld, eds., *The Oxford Handbook of Sound Studies* (Oxford: Oxford University Press, 2010).

11. Wylie, "A Single Day's Walking: Narrating Self and Landscape on the South West Coast Path." *Transactions of the Institute of British Geographers* 30, no. (2005): 243.," 243.

12. Wylie, "A Single Day's Walking," 243.

13. On the relevant Romantic tradition in England, see Jonathan Bate, *Romantic Ecology: Wordsworth and the Environmental Tradition* (London: Routledge, 1991). However, Romantic does not necessarily mean technology-averse; it also inspired particular versions of technology. On this see John Tresch, *The Romantic Machine: Utopian Science and Technology after Napoleon* (Chicago: University of Chicago Press, 2012).

14. Gry S. Jakobsen, "Tastes: Foods, Bodies and Places in Denmark" (PhD diss., University of Copenhagen, 2013). With many thanks to Gry for giving me permission to use her work here.

15. Jakobsen, "Tastes," 43.

16. Jakobsen, "Tastes," 43.

17. The idea that tasting may help to acquire knowledge also arose among ethnographers and inspired them to use their own sense of taste as much as their other senses. For an early, spirited encouragement to do so, see Paul Stoller, *The Taste of Ethnographic Things: The Senses in Anthropology* (Philadelphia: University of Pennsylvania Press, 1989). In science and technology studies, attention to the sense of taste came somewhat later. See Steven Shapin, "The Sciences of Subjectivity," *Social Studies of Science* 42, no. 2 (2012).

18. Gordon M. Shepherd, *Neurogastronomy: How the Brain Creates Flavor and Why It Matters* (New York: Columbia University Press, 2011).

19. Shepherd, *Neurogastronomy*, 65.

20. Shepherd, *Neurogastronomy*, 186.

21. That tasting can be left undone does not mean it is always possible to avoid it, as is clear from stories of ethnographers who had a hard time liking the foods available or offered to them in their fieldsites. See the contributions to Helen R. Haines and Clare A. Sammells, eds., *Adventures in Eating: Anthropological Experiences in Dining from around the World* (Boulder: University Press of Colorado, 2010).

22. My analysis here owes a great deal to the work of Else Vogel. For additional care practices in which sensing figures as something to learn, see Else Vogel, "Hungers That Need Feeding: On the Normativity of Mindful Nourishment," *Anthropology and Medicine* 24, no. 2 (2017).

23. Resulting in satisfaction is one among many things that tasting may do. It may also rekindle memories, provide people with a sense of belonging or a disappointment, and so on. See anthropological studies on tasting and eating such as David E. Sutton, *Remembrance of Repasts: An Anthropology of Food and Memory,* 2nd ed. (Oxford: Berg, 2001).

24. Of particular relevance in this context is the fascinating work of Paul Rozin and his colleagues. Rozin does most of his research in a laboratory, while he aims to gather general psycho-physiological insights. However, the perceptions and evaluations he describes are not confined to individualized 'bodies' but speak to wider concerns. See, for instance, Paul Rozin, Maureen Markwith, and Caryn Stoess, "Moralization and Becoming a Vegetarian: The Transformation of Preferences into Values and the Recruitment of Disgust," *Psychological Science* 8, no. 2 (1997).

25. The five senses are surrounded by single quotation marks because they are not the universal categories they are made out to be. For a good version of the argument that people belonging to different cultural and linguistic traditions may practice different sensoria, see Kathryn Geurts, *Culture and the Senses: Bodily Ways of Knowing in an African Community* (Berkeley: University of California Press, 2003).

26. This entire chapter owes a lot to Anna Mann's work, especially with regard to what I write about mundane valuing. On this, see our joint article: Anna Mann and Annemarie Mol, "Talking Pleasures, Writing Dialects: Outlining Research on Schmecka," *Ethnos* (2018).

27. This is different in other laboratories. See Anna Mann, "Sensory Science Research on Taste: An Ethnography of Two Laboratory Experiments in Western Europe," *Food and Foodways* 26, no. 1 (2018).

28. With cooking competitions being popular on TV, such a judgmental take may well be spreading. For the particularities involved, see Emma Casey, "From *Cookery in Colour* to *The Great British Bake Off*: Shifting Gendered Accounts of Home-Baking and Domesticity," *European Journal of Cultural Studies* 2, nos. 5–6 (2019).

29. My analysis here is indebted to work in psychology that uses discourse

analysis as a method. See, for instance, Sally Wiggins, "Talking with Your Mouth Full: Gustatory Mmms and the Embodiment of Pleasure," *Research on Language and Social Interaction* 35, no. 3 (2002); Sally Wiggins and Jonathan Potter, "Attitudes and Evaluative Practices: Category vs. Item and Subjective vs. Objective Constructions in Everyday Food Assessments," *British Journal of Social Psychology* 42, no. 4 (2003); and Petra Sneijder and Hedwig F. M. te Molder, "Disputing Taste: Food Pleasure as an Achievement in Interaction," *Appetite* 46, no. 1 (2006).

30. In situations of care, where people attempt to achieve a local good, seeking improvement is often taken to be more relevant than evaluating or judging. See Ingunn Moser, "Perhaps Tears Should Not Be Counted but Wiped Away: On Quality and Improvement in Dementia Care," in *Care in Practice: On Tinkering in Clinics, Homes and Farms,* ed. Annemarie Mol, Ingunn Moser, and Jeannette Pols (Bielefeld, Germany: Transcript Verlag, 2010).

31. In Dutch, tasty food is 'lekker,' a positive appreciation that has slipped in talk about sex, the weather, a shower, or other enjoyable things—even work when it goes well—so that food pleasure has come to color other pleasures. See Annemarie Mol, "Language Trails: 'Lekker' and Its Pleasures," *Theory, Culture and Society* 31, nos. 2–3 (2014).

32. If objects are comprehended together, the question arises: Together with *what*? For an analysis that brings to light the relevance of diverse forms of contextual togetherness, see Anna Mann, "Which Context Matters? Tasting in Everyday Life Practices and Social Science Theories," *Food, Culture and Society* 18, no. 3 (2015).

33. The interview I conducted jointly with Else Vogel and the food rating card also figure in our article: Else Vogel and Annemarie Mol, "Enjoy Your Food: On Losing Weight and Taking Pleasure," *Sociology of Health and Illness* 36, no. 2 (2014). About attempts to get children to eat vegetables, see also Michalis Kontopodis, "How and Why Should Children Eat Fruit and Vegetables? Ethnographic Insights into Diverse Body Pedagogies," *Social Science and Medicine* 143 (2015).

34. Korsmeyer, who (as mentioned) defended *tasting* against the heirs of Plato and Aristotle, has also a written fascinating book on *disgust*. See Carolyn Korsmeyer, *Savoring Disgust: The Foul and the Fair in Aesthetics* (Oxford: Oxford University Press, 2011).

35. About this situation, see also Annemarie Mol, "Bami Goreng for Mrs Klerks and Other Stories on Food and Culture," in *Debordements: Mélanges offerts à Michel Callon*, ed. Madeleine Akrich et al. (Paris: Presses Ecole de Mînes, 2010).

36. This was a relatively large group. Until the late nineteenth century, the colonial government allowed European men to settle in the colony but kept European women away. Hence, the European men overseeing plantations, working as clerks, and so on lived with (and sometimes married) local women. The offspring of these unions did well in the colonial status hierarchy—especially the girls, who were suitable marriage partners for subsequent waves of incoming

Dutch men. See Jean Gelman Taylor, *The Social World of Batavia: European and Eurasian in Dutch Asia* (Madison: University of Wisconsin Press, 1983).

37. For stories about foods elevated to the status of cultural icons, see the contributions to James Watson and Melissa Caldwell, eds., *The Cultural Politics of Food and Eating: A Reader* (Malden, MA: Blackwell, 2005). For a good inquiry into the relevance of food taste in everyday lives, on Bengali middle-class people and the servants cooking their meals, see Manpreet K. Janeja, *Transactions in Taste: The Collaborative Lives of Everyday Bengali Food* (New Delhi: Routledge, 2010).

38. On this particular kind of connoisseurship, modest rather than upper class, see Bodil Just Christensen and Line Hillersdal, "The Taste of Intervention," in *Making Taste Public: Ethnographies of Food and the Senses,* ed. Carole Counihan and Susanne Højlund (London: Bloomsbury Academic, 2018).

39. Most social scientists either concentrate on cultural belonging tied to formation of taste or training sensitivities. From empirical studies on traveling *cuisines*, however, we learn that these may first cater to those for whom they suggest belonging and then gradually spread as a treat for others. See, for instance, the contributions to Sidney Cheung and David Y. H. Wu, eds., *The Globalisation of Chinese Food* (London: Routledge, 2014).

40. Eating in a restaurant has its own specific practices, among them the peculiarity that (at least in a Parisian setting) people seated at the same table may eat different dishes but should be served at the same time, while the timing of adjacent tables is different. For a history of restaurant eating and the gastronomic culture tied to it, see Rebecca L. Spang, *The Invention of the Restaurant* (Cambridge, MA: Harvard University Press, 2001).

41. Acknowledging *fullness* would not be appreciated as a refined thing to do in a fine Parisian restaurant, even if it is seen as a sign of gratitude in other contexts. On this and related issues skipped over here see Margaret Visser, *The Rituals of Dinner: The Origins, Evolution, Eccentricities, and Meaning of Table Manners* (1991; repr., New York: Open Road Media, 2015).

42. Geneviève Teil and Antoine Hennion extensively argue that *taste* is not just a matter of relating to other people (as in *displaying* one's taste), but also involves relating to the food or drink being tasted and gradually attuning to it, "learning to be affected." However, they mostly wrote on wine, where, in order to stay sober enough to taste, the wine is expectorated. Here, I pursue the fact that swallowing affects taste. Geneviève Teil and Antoine Hennion, "Discovering Quality or Performing Taste? A Sociology of the Amateur," in *Qualities of Food: Alternative Theoretical and Empirical Approaches*, ed. Mark Harvey, Andrew McMeekin, and Alan Warde (Manchester: Manchester University Press, 2004). On the diverse ways in which eating may be relevant to tasting, see also Anna Mann, "Ordering Tasting in a Restaurant: Experiencing, Socializing, and Processing Food," *Senses and Society* 13, no. 2 (2018).

43. That a knowing subject may be affected by the object becoming known

is not specific to eating. My point is rather that eating offers a fine *model* of this. For a very different example of how subjects are altered as they are interpellated, by aircrafts, see John Law, "On the Subject of the Object: Narrative, Technology, and Interpellation," *Configurations* 8, no. 1 (2000).

Four. Doing

1. Shigehisa Kuriyama, *The Expressiveness of the Body and the Divergence of Greek and Chinese Medicine* (New York: Zone Books, 1999), 190.
2. Kuriyama, *The Expressiveness of the Body*, 190.
3. Kuriyama, *The Expressiveness of the Body*, 144.
4. Kuriyama, *The Expressiveness of the Body*, 149.
5. Kuriyama, *The Expressiveness of the Body*, 151.
6. In twentieth-century cultural anthropology, a difference was made between tinkering modes of doing, that were allegedly premodern, and engineering, modern modes of doing that were supposed to directly, and with control, work toward a goal. See Claude Lévi-Strauss, *The Savage Mind* (Chicago: University of Chicago Press, 1966). In science and technology studies, the idea was formulated that modern technology does not specifically offer the promised control, but itself depends on adaptive caring and tinkering. See, for example, Bruno Latour, *The Pasteurization of France* (Cambridge, MA: Harvard University Press, 1993). This chapter builds on the latter line of work. See also Annemarie Mol and John Law, "Regions, Networks and Fluids: Anaemia and Social Topology," *Social Studies of Science* 24, no. 4 (1994); and Marianne De Laet and Annemarie Mol, "The Zimbabwe Bush Pump: Mechanics of a Fluid Technology," *Social Studies of Science* 30, no. 2 (2000).
7. Hans Jonas, *The Phenomenon of Life: Toward a Philosophical Biology* (1966; repr., Evanston, IL: Northwestern University Press, 2001).
8. There are theorists who seek to formulate empirically grounded and normatively salient theories of *doing* based on what they take to be true facts about bodies. See Sharon R. Krause, "Bodies in Action: Corporeal Agency and Democratic Politics," *Political Theory* 39, no. 3 (2011). My style of theorizing is quite different. I do not mobilize what I take to be true facts about bodies, but take inspiration from some of the ways in which, in practices (including scientific practices), bodies are enacted.
9. This kind of public health emerged as 'new' in the 1970s and 1980s. See John Ashton and Howard Seymour, *The New Public Health* (Milton Keynes, UK: Open University Press, 1988). In the context of food and eating, there are different versions of information and choice that I do not expand on here: see Annemarie Mol, "Mind Your Plate! The Ontonorms of Dutch Dieting," *Social Studies of Science* 43, no. 3 (2013). Interpellations in the Netherlands are different from those in adjacent European countries. See, for instance, Bente Halkier et al., "Trusting, Complex, Quality Conscious or Unprotected? Constructing the Food

Consumer in Different European National Contexts," *Journal of Consumer Culture* 7, no. 3 (2007).

10. Voedingscentrum, "Missie en visie," accessed August 2016, http://www .voedingscentrum.nl/nl/service/over-ons/hoe-werkt-het-voedingscentrum -precies/missie-en-visie-voedingscentrum.aspx.

11. In an analysis of the term *consumption*, David Graeber remarks that it is strange that, with this term, *buying* has come to be modeled on *eating* (David Graeber, "Consumption," *Current Anthropology* 52, no. 4 [2011]). In the Eating Bodies team, we were equally surprised that the use of the term *consumer* hides eating behind being buying. Hence, in this book I have avoided both *consumption* and *consumer* and instead use *eating* and the neologism *eater*. I only fall back to *consumer* where this term is used—as a buyer-eater conglomerate—in my field.

12. Voedingscentrum, "Hoeveel en wat kan ik per dag eten?," accessed August 2016, http://www.voedingscentrum.nl/nl/schijf-van-vijf/eet-gevarieerd.aspx.

13. Voedingscentrum, "Schijf van Vijf," accessed August 2016, http://www .voedingscentrum.nl/nl/schijf-van-vijf/schijf.aspx.

14. Voedingscentrum, "Eiwitten," accessed August 2016, http://www.voedings centrum.nl/encyclopedie/eiwitten.aspx.

15. Here, my analysis is informed by fieldwork that both Anna Mann and Else Vogel conducted with this research group, as well as by an insightful interview I had with their research director. Thanks therefore to Kees de Graaf and his research team, who, as I use one of their articles, do not remain anonymous.

16. Sanne Griffioen-Roose et al., "Protein Status Elicits Compensatory Changes in Food Intake and Food Preferences," *American Journal of Clinical Nutrition* 95, no. 1 (2012).

17. In the field of science and technology studies, such work and its relevance have been brought to the foreground, from Bruno Latour and Steve Woolgar, *Laboratory Life: The Construction of Scientific Facts* (1979; repr., Princeton, NJ: Princeton University Press, 1986); through to Karin Knorr-Cetina, *Epistemic Cultures: How the Sciences Make Knowledge* (Cambridge, MA: Harvard University Press, 1999). In my research team, we revisited the relevance of the practicalities of research against the 'new materialists,' who suggest that it is possible to directly access the liveliness of materials. On this, see Sebastian Abrahamsson et al., "Living with Omega-3: New Materialism and Enduring Concerns," *Environment and Planning D: Society and Space* 33, no. 1 (2015).

18. Elsewhere, when it is not the causes but the effects that are at stake, it tends to be the work of 'users' (eaters, takers of drugs, etc.) that is hidden. On this, see Anita Hardon and Emilia Sanabria, "Fluid Drugs: Revisiting the Anthropology of Pharmaceuticals," *Annual Review of Anthropology* 46 (2017).

19. Here I draw on and quote from Rita M. Struhkamp, "Patient Autonomy: A View from the Kitchen," *Medicine, Health Care and Philosophy* 8, no. 1 (2005): 105.

20. Struhkamp, "Patient Autonomy," 110–11.

21. Quite like in individual cases like Fred's, in the case of 'cultures,' it is also

an all-too-rapid naturalization to give causal explanations for food patterns by pointing to natural needs. The latter is done (with admirable zeal) in Marvin Harris, *Good to Eat: Riddles of Food and Culture* (Long Grove, IL: Waveland Press, 1998). For a critique, see Sidney W. Mintz and Christine M. Du Bois, "The Anthropology of Food and Eating," *Annual Review of Anthropology* 31, no. 1 (2002).

22. Taking eating as a task foregrounds materialities that all too easily fade into the backgrounded, if it is configured as a choice or a psychological concern. On this, see regarding the case of undereaters who are diagnosed as having anorexia, Anne Lavis, "Food, Bodies, and the 'Stuff' of (Not) Eating in Anorexia," *Gastronomica* 16, no. 3 (2016).

23. There is an added complexity that I leave out here, which is that the 'information' in consideration tends to be about 'nutrients' and that this does not necessarily, or easily, translate into 'food'—such as pizza, apples, or spinach frittatas. On this issue, see Emily Yates-Doerr, "The Opacity of Reduction: Nutritional Black-Boxing and the Meanings of Nourishment," *Food, Culture and Society* 15, no. 2 (2012).

24. For one among many good studies on hunger and marginal eating in the global south, see Karen Coen Flynn, *Food, Culture, and Survival in an African City* (New York: Palgrave Macmillan, 2005). For an inquiry into shame related to the inability to afford good food (in the Netherlands), see Hilje Van der Horst, Stefano Pascucci, and Wilma Bol, "The 'Dark Side' of Food Banks? Exploring Emotional Responses of Food Bank Receivers in the Netherlands," *British Food Journal* 116, no. 9 (2014).

25. Pointing out the efforts that people, and this often means women, spend on daily care tasks has a long feminist tradition. See, as examples, Anne Murcott, "Cooking and the Cooked: A Note on the Domestic Preparation of Meals," in *The Sociology of Food and Eating*, ed. Anne Murcott (Farnham, UK: Gower, 1983); and the contributions to Pat Caplan, ed., *Food, Health and Identity* (Milton Park, UK: Routledge, 2013).

26. For a related analysis in the specific context of care for people who are overweight, where not-eating or eating-well become tasks, see Else Vogel, "Clinical Specificities in Obesity Care: The Transformations and Dissolution of 'Will' and 'Drives,'" *Health Care Analysis* 24, no. 4 (2016).

27. There are clear resonances here with how my colleagues and I describe caring ways of doing in contrast to making choices and/or having control. See Annemarie Mol, *The Logic of Care: Health and the Problem of Patient Choice* (London: Routledge, 2008); and Annemarie Mol, Ingunn Moser, and Jeannette Pols, "Care: Putting Practice into Theory," in *Care in Practice: On Tinkering in Clinics, Homes and Farms,* ed. Annemarie Mol, Ingunn Moser, and Jeannette Pols (Bielefeld, Germany: Transcript Verlag, 2010).

28. Instead of using eating-inspired models, it is also possible here to use *performative* models of action such as they were developed in some (notably Euro-

pean) branches of cybernetics. On that, see Andrew Pickering, *The Cybernetic Brain: Sketches of Another Future* (Chicago: University of Chicago Press, 2010).

29. Here I gratefully draw on the work of Sebastian Abrahamsson: "An Actor Network Analysis of Constipation and Agency: Shit Happens," *Subjectivity* 7, no. 2 (2014); and "Cooking, Eating and Digesting: Notes on the Emergent Normativities of Food and Speeds," *Time and Society* 23, no. 3 (2014).

30. For her work on how bodies may share movements, see Sophie M. Müller, "Ways of Relating," in *Moving Bodies in Interaction—Interacting Bodies in Motion: Intercorporeality, Interkinesthesia, and Enaction in Sports,* ed. Christian Meyer and Ulrich V. Wedelstaedt (Amsterdam: John Benjamins, 2017). For further analysis of ballet bodies, see Sophie M. Müller, "Distributed Corporeality: Anatomy, Knowledge and the Technological Reconfiguration of Bodies in Ballet," *Social Studies of Science* 48, no. 6 (2018).

31. It may be difficult to let go if control is overdone—but it may be even more difficult to lack control over the muscles of one's anal and urethral sphincters and leak in inappropriate times and places. I skip that complication here, but see Maartje Hoogsteyns and Hilje van der Horst, "How to Live with a Taboo Instead of 'Breaking It': Alternative Empowerment Strategies of People with Incontinence," *Health Sociology Review* 24, no. 1 (2015).

32. In Luis Buñuel's 1974 film *Fantome de la liberté* this was famously reversed. At some point, four people sat around a table on toilets, while individually and sneakily retreating to a small room with food when hungry.

33. Alva Noë, *Out of Our Heads: Why You Are Not Your Brain, and Other Lessons from the Biology of Consciousness* (New York: Hill and Wang, 2009). Noë builds on earlier work that argues that cognition is distributed as it is done in practice. See Jean Lave, *Cognition in Practice: Mind, Mathematics and Culture in Everyday Life* (Cambridge: Cambridge University Press, 1988); and Edwin Hutchins, *Cognition in the Wild* (Cambridge, MA: MIT Press, 1995).

34. Noë, *Out of Our Heads*, 6–7.

35. Noë, *Out of Our Heads*, 186.

36. See on this history Horace W. Davenport, *A History of Gastric Secretion and Digestion: Experimental Studies to 1975* (New York: Springer, 1992).

37. For a simultaneously culinary and biochemical explanation of cooking, see the Harold McGee's masterful *On Food and Cooking: The Science and Lore of the Kitchen* (New York: Scribner, 2004).

38. When I was in Berkeley, Alva Noë was so kind as to receive me in his office. He said, yes, sure, *of course,* when I confronted him with extracorporeal digestion. And he smiled. But his concerns were different. They were with cognition and its distributed character.

39. That said, *digestion* has not enduringly been the number one criterion in selecting what to grow. For wheat, for instance, high gluten content has taken precedence, and this serves a range of preparation techniques. See below.

40. Richard Wrangham, *Catching Fire: How Cooking Made Us Human* (New

York: Basic Books, 2009), 127. It is up for debate whether Wrangham's analysis makes (pre)historical sense. Here, however, I am not after facts, but after models. But see Gregory Schrempp, "Catching Wrangham: On the Mythology and the Science of Fire, Cooking, and Becoming Human," *Journal of Folklore Research* 48, no. 2 (2011).

41. Jonas, *The Phenomenon of Life*, 83. In a lot of other work on the philosophy of biology, the survival of the species and procreation, rather than eating, that have stood out. See, for example, John Dupré, *Processes of Life: Essays in the Philosophy of Biology* (Oxford: Oxford University Press, 2012).

42. Jonas, *The Phenomenon of Life*, 84.

43. Jonas, *The Phenomenon of Life*, 105.

44. Jonas, *The Phenomenon of Life*, 99.

45. For instance, what animals appear to *be* and *do* changes along with research methods. See Vincianne Despret, *What Would Animals Say If We Asked the Right Questions?* (Minneapolis: University of Minnesota Press, 2016). Beyond this, new research has found plants to also be far more sensitive and communicative than previously thought. See Daniel Chamovitz, *What a Plant Knows: A Field Guide to the Senses* (New York: Scientific American / Farrar, Straus and Giroux, 2012).

46. Jonas, *The Phenomenon of Life*, 186.

47. Jonas, *The Phenomenon of Life*.

48. Lawrence Vogel, preface to Jonas, *The Phenomenon of Life*, xvi.

49. Attempts to avoid cynicism while still 'staying with the trouble' are shared among a wide range of present-day scholars on whose work I build here. See Donna J. Haraway, *Staying with the Trouble: Making Kin in the Chthulucene* (Durham, NC: Duke University Press, 2016); Isabelle Stengers, *In Catastrophic Times: Resisting the Coming Barbarism* (London: Open Humanities Press, 2015); and the contributions to Anna L. Tsing et al., eds., *Arts of Living on a Damaged Planet: Ghosts and Monsters of the Anthropocene* (Minneapolis: University of Minnesota Press, 2017).

50. Carlos A. Monteiro, "Nutrition and Health: The Issue Is Not Food, nor Nutrients, So Much as Processing," *Public Health Nutrition* 12, no. 5 (2009): 729.

51. On the dire reality that eating is often detrimental to one's health and the uncertainties implied, see Emilia Sanabria and Emily Yates-Doerr, "Alimentary Uncertainties: From Contested Evidence to Policy," *BioSocieties* 10, no. 2 (2015).

52. This is not a matter of individual eaters and accidental foods, but structurally embedded in present-day food systems. See Julie Guthman, *Weighing In: Obesity, Food Justice, and the Limits of Capitalism* (Berkeley: University of California Press, 2011). Or, as one example among many about recent changes in 'food culture,' Shahaduz Zaman, Nasima Selim, and Taufiq Joarder, "McDonaldization without a McDonald's: Globalization and Food Culture as Social Determinants of Health in Urban Bangladesh," *Food, Culture and Society* 16, no. 4 (2013).

53. Voedingscentrum, "Nitraat," accessed August 2016, http://www

.voedingscentrum.nl/nl/nieuws/voedingscentrum-herziet-adviezen-voor
-nitraatinname.aspx.

54. Voedingscentrum, "Dioxines," accessed June 24, 2019, https://www
.voedingscentrum.nl/encyclopedie/dioxines.aspx.

55. See Marion Nestle, *Food Politics: How the Food Industry Influences Nutrition and Health* (Berkeley: University of California Press, 2013); Eric Holt-Giménez and Rai Patel, eds., *Food Rebellions: Crisis and the Hunger for Justice* (Oakland, CA: Food First Books; Oxford: Pambazooka Press, 2012); and Tim Lang and Michael Heasman, *Food Wars: The Global Battle for Mouths, Minds and Markets* (London: Routledge, 2015).

56. There are diverse, rich case studies of coffee growing in which tragic dilemmas abound. See Robert Rice, "Noble Goals and Challenging Terrain: Organic and Fair Trade Coffee Movements in the Global Marketplace," *Journal of Agricultural and Environmental Ethics* 14, no. 1 (2001); and Maria Elena Martinez-Torres, *Organic Coffee: Sustainable Development by Mayan Farmers* (Athens: Ohio University Press, 2006).

57. For the issue of how to think through such complex situations and how *doing* may be understood as a part of them, see also Angga Dwiartama and Christopher Rosin, "Exploring Agency beyond Humans: The Compatibility of Actor-Network Theory (ANT) and Resilience Thinking," *Ecology and Society* 19, no. 3 (2014); and Beth Greenhough and Emma Roe, "From Ethical Principles to Response-Able Practice," *Environment and Planning D: Society and Space* 28, no. 1 (2010).

Five. Relating

1. Once again, this chapter owes a lot to work of other members of the eating bodies team, this time especially that of Filippo Bertoni and Sebastian Abrahamsson. See Filippo Bertoni, "Charming Worms: Crawling between Natures," *Cambridge Journal of Anthropology* 30, no. 2 (2012); Filippo Bertoni, "Soil and Worm: On Eating as Relating," *Science as Culture* 22, no. 1 (2013); and Sebastian Abrahamsson and Filippo Bertoni, "Compost Politics: Experimenting with Togetherness in Vermicomposting," *Environmental Humanities* 4, no. 1 (2014).

2. In English, by tradition, humans are referred to by *who* and nonhumans by *that*. Recently, *that* is also used to indicate people. But then again, it is also possible to stretch up the use of *who* to nonhumans.

3. Quotes are from the second English edition: Emmanuel Levinas, *Totality and Infinity: An Essay on Exteriority* (Dordrecht: Martinus Nijhoff, 1979), here 300. Hereafter page citations are given parenthetically in the text.

4. For a more extensive analysis of the way eating formed a crucial model for Levinas, which I have drawn on here with gratitude, see David Goldstein, "Emmanuel Levinas and the Ontology of Eating," *Gastronomica* 10, no. 3 (2010).

5. On the way cannibalism figured in Western philosophy, see Cătălin Avra-

mescu, *An Intellectual History of Cannibalism*, trans. Alistair Ian Blyth (Princeton, NJ: Princeton University Press, 2009). See, for analyses of literal and metaphorical anthropophagy, the contributions to Francis Barker, Peter Hulme, and Margaret Iversen, eds., *Cannibalism and the Colonial World* (Cambridge: Cambridge University Press, 1998).

6. See on the enduring use of the home as a safe space even long after feminists had pointed out the smaller and larger tensions within it, Bonnie Honig, "Difference, Dilemmas, and the Politics of Home," in "Liberalism," special issue, *Social Research* 61, no. 3 (1994).

7. For some of the work presented at this conference, see the contributions to Richard Le Heron et al., eds., *Biological Economies: Experimentation and the Politics of Agri-Food Frontiers* (Abingdon, UK: Routledge, 2016). For an extensive exploration of what it entails to eat fish, see Elspeth Probyn, *Eating the Ocean* (Durham, NC: Duke University Press, 2016).

8. On vegetarianism grounded in an animal rights discourse, see Gary L. Francione and Robert Garner, *The Animal Rights Debate: Abolition or Regulation?* (New York: Columbia University Press, 2010).

9. For a compelling exploration of animal cognition extending to octopi, see the popular science/philosophy book by Peter Godfrey-Smith, *Other Minds: The Octopus, the Sea, and the Deep Origins of Consciousness* (New York: Farrar, Straus and Giroux, 2016).

10. For a more extensive analysis of this ethnographic experiment, see Anna Mann et al., "Mixing Methods, Tasting Fingers: Notes on an Ethnographic Experiment," *HAU: Journal of Ethnographic Theory* 1, no. 1 (2011).

11. This is done in a great many ways and registers. For an analysis, see Petra Sneijder and Hedwig F. M. te Molder, "Normalizing Ideological Food Choice and Eating Practices: Identity Work in Online Discussions on Veganism," *Appetite* 52, no. 3 (2009).

12. Inspired by this particular relation between apples and humans, Michael Pollan inventively turns around the agency and describes apples as tricking humans into propagating their growth and the expansion of their habitat—all the way from a small region in the Caucasus to anywhere on earth the climate suits them. See Michael Pollan, *The Botany of Desire: A Plant's-Eye View of the World* (New York: Random House, 2002).

13. Growing a considerable part of one's own food as a city dweller contrasts with the push toward ever-larger agricultural systems. About this, see also Annga Dwiartama and Cinzia Piatti, "Assembling Local, Assembling Food Security," *Agriculture and Human Values* 33, no. 1 (2016). One further complexity I leave out here is the origins of the seeds and bushes and so on that G. might use in her garden. But for concerns about this, see Catherine Phillips, *Saving More Than Seeds: Practices and Politics of Seed Saving* (London: Routledge, 2016).

14. In what follows, I not only use Hans Harbers's farm stories but also draw heavily on his analysis, for which I thank him.

15. Hans Harbers, "Animal Farm Love Stories," in *Care in Practice: On Tinkering in Clinics, Homes and Farms,* edited by Annemarie Mol, Ingunn Moser and Jeanette Pols (Bielefeld, Germany: Transcript Verlag, 2010), 147.

16. Harbers, "Animal Farm Love Stories," 148.

17. For a related, more extensive analysis of farming, and of the ways in which traditional patterns of rural living, of animals and people, depend on particular forms of eating that are squeezed out by more industrial means of food 'production,' see James Rebanks, *The Shepherd's Life: A Tale of the Lake District* (London: Penguin, 2015).

18. Harbers, "Animal Farm Love Stories," 152.

19. Harbers, "Animal Farm Love Stories," 154.

20. For an analysis of present-day approaches to weighing the pros and cons of raising and eating animals, see Henry Buller and Emma J. Roe, *Food and Animal Welfare* (London: Bloomsbury, 2018). There are resonances here with the 'use' of animals in laboratory research. See Gail Davies, "Caring for the Multiple and the Multitude: Assembling Animal Welfare and Enabling Ethical Critique," *Environment and Planning D: Society and Space* 30, no. 4 (2012). For the argument that even well-meaning animal care comes with its own kinds of violence, see John Law, "Care and Killing: Tensions in Veterinary Practice," in *Care in Practice: On Tinkering in Clinics, Homes and Farms*, ed. Annemarie Mol, Ingunn Moser, and Jeannette Pols (Bielefeld, Germany: Transcript Verlag, 2010).

21. For a further analysis of this investment in brotherly similarity, see the work of Eduardo Viveiros de Castro, who points out that, among Amerindians, the exemplary relation is instead that between brothers-in-law, who have something in common that is different to each of them: sister to one, wife to the other. See, for example, the fabulous book, highly relevant to the present in many other ways as well: Eduardo Viveiros de Castro, *Cannibal Metaphysics*, trans. P. Skafish (Minneapolis: University of Minnesota Press, 2015).

22. For a collection of excellent examples of the way present-day ecologies are socially and materially mediated that employs cases from the Global South, see Lesley Green, ed., *Contested Ecologies: Dialogues in the South on Nature and Knowledge* (Cape Town: HSRC Press, 2013).

23. What does and does not agree with eaters, what might become food and what not, is obviously complex and contested in a range of ways. For some of these, see Emma J. Roe, "Things Becoming Food and the Embodied, Material Practices of an Organic Food Consumer," *Sociologia Ruralis* 46, no. 2 (2006).

24. For more on rats and humans and the different ways in which tasting/testing foods may be relevant to them, see Annemarie Mol, "Layers or Versions? Human Bodies and the Love of Bitterness," in *The Routledge Handbook of Body Studies*, ed. Bryan S. Turner (Abingdon, UK: Routledge, 2012).

25. For the research behind this, see Gry I. Skodje et al., "Fructan, Rather Than Gluten, Induces Symptoms in Patients with Self-Reported Non-celiac Gluten Sensitivity," *Gastroenterology* 154, no. 3 (2018).

26. For the microbes, Heather Paxson, *The Life of Cheese: Crafting Food and Value in America* (Berkeley: University of California Press, 2012).

27. I cowrote with Sebastian Abrahamsson on the topology of Hawaiian pizza. Once again, I thank him for his inspiration. See Sebastian Abrahamsson and Annemarie Mol, "Foods," in *The Routledge Handbook of Mobilities*, ed. Peter Adey et al. (London: Routledge, 2014). For the complex topology of global 'things,' see also John Law, "And If the Global Were Small and Noncoherent? Method, Complexity, and the Baroque," *Environment and Planning D: Society and Space* 22, no. 1 (2004).

28. Such rules are famously topicalized by Mary Douglas, who, for instance, in her own brand of auto-ethnography, tells that her family would complain if she served them soup and dessert, 'leaving out' the main dish. Mary Douglas, "Deciphering a Meal," *Daedalus* 101, no. 1 (1972).

29. There is, at present, also unwitting violence flowing out with mother's milk—in the form of toxins amassed in her body that she feeds involuntarily to her babies. On this point, see Eva-Maria Simms, "Eating One's Mother: Female Embodiment in a Toxic World," *Environmental Ethics* 31, no. 3 (2009).

30. For a more extensive analysis, see Marilyn Strathern, *After Nature: English Kinship in the Late Twentieth Century* (New York: Cambridge University Press, 1992).

31. On this example, based on research done in northern England, see Jeanette Edwards and Marilyn Strathern, "Including Our Own," in *Cultures of Relatedness: New Directions in Kinship Studies,* ed. Janet Carsten (New York: Cambridge University Press, 2000).

32. Donna J. Haraway, *When Species Meet* (Minneapolis: University of Minnesota Press, 2013), 19.

33. The story about the oncomouse comes from Donna J. Haraway, *Modest _Witness@Second_Millennium.FemaleMan©_Meets_OncoMouse™: Feminism and Technoscience* (New York: Routledge, 1997). Other authors have stretched human-animal kinship beyond the evolutionary tree as well. See, for example, Nickie Charles and Charlotte A. Davies, "My Family and Other Animals: Pets as Kin," in *Human and Other Animals*, ed. Bob Carter and Nickie Charles (London: Palgrave Macmillan, 2011).

34. Haraway, *When Species Meet*, 17.

35. Haraway, *When Species Meet*, 295.

36. Haraway, *When Species Meet*, 295.

37. In political and social/cultural ecology, this has been variously theorized for quite some time already. See, among many others, Arturo Escobar, "After Nature: Steps to an Anti-essentialist Political Ecology," *Current Anthropology* 40, no. 1 (1999).

38. Again, empirically I recount nothing new here. I only seek to transport this fraught situation to our understanding of *relating*. For good examples of what is ecologically and politically at stake, see the contributions to Richard

Peet, Paul Robbins, and Michael Watts, eds., *Global Political Ecology* (Abingdon, UK: Routledge, 2011). For the argument that local vegetation has been erased all around in 'the colonies' so as to grow European crops, see Alfred W. Crosby, *Ecological Imperialism: The Biological Expansion of Europe, 900–1900* (Cambridge: Cambridge University Press, 1986).

39. For a longer version of this boundary story, see John Law and Annemarie Mol, "Globalisation in Practice: On the Politics of Boiling Pigswill," *Geoforum* 39, no. 1 (2008). For more on the disease, see John Law and Annemarie Mol, "Veterinary Realities: What Is Foot and Mouth Disease?," *Sociologia Ruralis* 51, no. 1 (2011).

40. For more about complex, often long-distance relations of growth and destruction, see Anna L. Tsing, *The Mushroom at the End of the World: On the Possibility of Life in Capitalist Ruins* (Princeton, NJ: Princeton University Press, 2015). For the topic of the ghosts that human interferences spread, see the contributions in Anna L. Tsing et al., eds., *Arts of Living on a Damaged Planet: Ghosts and Monsters of the Anthropocene* (Minneapolis: University of Minnesota Press, 2017).

41. This quote is taken from Haraway, *When Species Meet*, 21.

Six. Intellectual Ingredients

1. In this paragraph, I take inspiration from a memorable collection of essays on how to combine democracy and difference: Sheila Benhabib, ed., *Democracy and Difference: Contesting the Boundaries of the Political* (Princeton, NJ: Princeton University Press, 1996).

2. For the ideal of the 'free speech situation' see also Jürgen Habermas, *The Theory of Communicative Action: Lifeworld and Systems, a Critique of Functionalist Reason*, vol. 1, trans. Thomas McCarthy (Cambridge, UK: Polity, 1985). For storytelling as a political forum, see Francesca Polletta, *It Was Like a Fever: Storytelling in Protest and Politics* (Chicago: University of Chicago Press, 2006). For the 'veil of ignorance,' see John Rawls, *A Theory of Justice* (1971; repr., Cambridge, MA: Harvard University Press, 2009). On the acceptance of antagonism as a part of politics, see Chantal Mouffe, *The Return of the Political* (London: Verso, 2005); and Chantal Mouffe, *Agonistics: Thinking the World Politically* (London: Verso, 2013).

3. For the idea that animals are much cleverer than expected if researchers ask the right questions, see Vincianne Despret, *What Would Animals Say If We Asked the Right Questions?* (Minneapolis: University of Minnesota Press, 2016). For listening to plants, see Eduardo Kohn, *How Forests Think: Toward an Anthropology beyond the Human* (Berkeley: University of California Press, 2013); and Hannah Pitt, "An Apprenticeship in Plant Thinking," in *Participatory Research in More-Than-Human Worlds*, ed. Michelle Bastian et al. (London: Routledge, 2016).

4. On this and other inspiring ideas about how profoundly our understanding of politics has to shift if we want to take ecological concerns seriously, see Bruno Latour, *Politics of Nature*, trans. Catherine Porter (Cambridge, MA: Harvard University Press, 2004). For more recent and radical iterations, see Bruno Latour, *Facing Gaia: Eight Lectures on the New Climatic Regime*, trans. Catherine Porter (Cambridge, UK: Polity, 2017).

5. On the ambition to farm insects to feed the world, see Arnold Van Huis, Marcel Dicke, and Joop J. A. van Loon, "Insects to Feed the World," *Journal of Insects as Food and Feed* 1, no. 1 (2015).

6. Note that when eating is taken as a matter of using up resources, the immediate next question is which resources to include. For instance, do we prioritize calories (energy) or nutrients (and, if so, which ones: carbohydrates, fats, proteins?). Do the resources consumed include water or not? Do they also comprehend externalities, such as the manure and methane produced—and where this goes? Added to this comes the question of representation. Are 'resources' (nutrients here, water there) disentangled and counted separately? Or are the entanglements considered? On that latter complexity, see Carolina Domínguez Guzmán, Andres Verzijl, and Margreet Zwarteveen, "Water Footprints and 'Pozas': Conversations about Practices and Knowledges of Water Efficiency," *Water* 9, no. 1 (2017).

7. Thanks to Filippo Bertoni and Emily Yates-Doerr for a fine day of joint fieldwork. Emily has studied this field further, and here I gratefully take inspiration from her analyses. In her articles, among other things, she aptly shows how the category 'insects' rapidly breaks down in the propagation of 'eating insects.' See Emily Yates-Doerr, "The World in a Box? Food Security, Edible Insects, and 'One World, One Health' Collaboration," *Social Science and Medicine* 129 (2015). On the task of reframing insects as edible, see also Alexandra E. Sexton, "Eating for the Post-Anthropocene: Alternative Proteins and the Biopolitics of Edibility," *Transactions of the Institute of British Geographers* 43, no. 4 (2018).

8. Here, I pursue the *eating* of insects, but insects obviously also relate to diverse stakes that have little to do with eating. On this, see Hugh Raffles's magnificent *Insectopedia* (New York: Vintage Books, 2010).

9. Hence, the 'eating well' that I am concerned with here differs in many ways from the 'eating well' that figures as title and topic in a conversation between Jacques Derrida and Jean-Luc Nancy. There, 'the subject,' and what 'comes after it' are theorized in a philosophical, nonempirical mode; and 'eating' figures as a slipping symbol rather than a reality enacted in contrasting ways; while the 'well' (or, the more interesting, ambivalent, French *bien*) is a play on, and an attempt to go beyond, Levinas's ethics. See Jacques Derrida, "'Eating Well,' or the Calculation of the Subject: An Interview with Jacques Derrida," in *Who Comes after the Subject?*, ed. Eduardo Cadava, Peter Connor, and Jean-Luc Nancy (New York: Routledge, 1991). For a spirited analysis of this text, see Sara Guyer, "Albeit Eating: Towards an Ethics of Cannibalism," *Angelaki* 2, no. 1 (1997).

10. The different versions of reality at stake do not form a plurality; there may be both interdependence and frictions between them. See, on the former, Marilyn Strathern, *Partial Connections*, updated ed. (Savage, MD: Rowman & Littlefield, 2004), and on the latter, Anna L. Tsing, *Friction: An Ethnography of Global Connection* (Princeton, NJ: Princeton University Press, 2004).

11. On the work of articulating the politics embedded in practices and their materials, see Andrew Barry, *Political Machines: Governing a Technological Society* (London: A&C Black, 2001); Andrew Barry, *Material Politics: Disputes along the Pipeline* (Chichester, UK: John Wiley & Sons, 2013); and for added insights, Noortje Marres, "Why Political Ontology Must Be Experimentalized: On Eco-Show Homes as Devices of Participation," *Social Studies of Science* 43, no. 3 (2013); Noortje Marres, *Material Participation: Technology, the Environment and Everyday Publics* (New York: Springer, 2016).

12. Hannah Arendt, *The Human Condition* (1958; repr., Chicago: University of Chicago Press, 2013), 115.

13. An added complexity here is that the English word *cycle* does not necessarily equal a loop. The term *life cycle* is used, not for something that goes on and on, but for something, like a life, with a 'beginning, middle, end'—as if nothing happens after the end. See Angela M. O'Rand and Margaret L. Krecker, "Concepts of the Life Cycle: Their History, Meanings, and Uses in the Social Sciences," *Annual Review of Sociology* 16, no. 1 (1990).

14. 'Eating well' brings into play diverse registers of value that specify the 'well' and diverse techniques for (e)valu(at)ing, which do not just include *judging* but also *tinkering* and of ways of *improving* the entity being valued. See Frank Heuts and Annemarie Mol, "What Is a Good Tomato? A Case of Valuing in Practice," *Valuation Studies* 1, no. 2 (2013).

15. Once again, as in the chapter on *doing*, I admit the obvious resonance with the way my colleagues and I have sought to describe 'care' in the context of living with disease, disability, or while managing other complexities. See Annemarie Mol, *The Logic of Care: Health and the Problem of Patient Choice* (London: Routledge, 2008), and the contributions to Annemarie Mol, Ingunn Moser, and Jeannette Pols, ed., *Care in Practice: On Tinkering in Clinics, Homes and Farms* (Bielefeld, Germany: Transcript Verlag, 2010).

16. For an earlier and more extensive version of this argument, see two works by Valerie Plumwood: *Feminism and the Mastery of Nature* (London: Routledge, 1993) and *Environmental Culture: The Ecological Crisis of Reason* (London: Routledge, 2002). Recently, a concern has been introduced that however much 'I' might like to end up as food, I am maybe not such a good fertilizer after all. Due to years of eating, an elderly, well-fed human body has most likely amassed a lot of poisonous chemicals. Another complexity I leave out here: Jacqueline Elam and Chase Pielak, *Corpse Encounters: An Aesthetics of Death* (Lanham, MD: Lexington Books, 2018). For an inspiring experiment, see Jae R. Lee, "My Mushroom Burial Suit," TED Talk, July 2011, www.ted.com/talks/jae_rhim_lee.

17. For the final talk, see Annemarie Mol, "Natures in Tension," in *Natures in Modern Society, Now and in the Future*, ed. Ed Dammers (The Hague: Netherlands Environmental Assessment Agency, 2017), https://www.pbl.nl/en /publications/nature-in-modern-society.

BIBLIOGRAPHY

Abrahamsson, Sebastian. "An Actor Network Analysis of Constipation and Agency: Shit Happens." *Subjectivity* 7, no. 2 (2014): 111−30.

Abrahamsson, Sebastian. "Cooking, Eating and Digesting: Notes on the Emergent Normativities of Food and Speeds." *Time and Society* 23, no. 3 (2014): 287−308.

Abrahamsson, Sebastian, and Filippo Bertoni. "Compost Politics: Experimenting with Togetherness in Vermicomposting." *Environmental Humanities* 4, no. 1 (2014): 125−48.

Abrahamsson, Sebastian, Filippo Bertoni, Annemarie Mol, and Rebeca Ibañez Martín. "Living with Omega-3: New Materialism and Enduring Concerns." *Environment and Planning D: Society and Space* 33, no. 1 (2015): 4−19.

Abrahamsson, Sebastian, and Annemarie Mol. "Foods." In *The Routledge Handbook of Mobilities*, edited by Peter Adey, David Bisell, Kevin Hannam, Peter Merriman, and Mimi Sheller, 298−307. London: Routledge, 2014.

Abrahamsson, Sebastian, and Paul Simpson. "The Limits of the Body: Boundaries, Capacities, Thresholds." *Social and Cultural Geography* 12, no. 4 (2011): 331−38.

Anderson, Patrick. *"So Much Wasted": Hunger, Performance, and the Morbidity of Resistance*. Durham, NC: Duke University Press, 2010.

Arendt, Hannah. *The Human Condition*. 1958. Reprint, Chicago: University of Chicago Press, 2013.

Arneil, Barbara. "Trade, Plantations, and Property: John Locke and the Economic Defense of Colonialism." *Journal of the History of Ideas* 55, no. 4 (1994): 591−609.

Ashton, John, and Howard Seymour. *The New Public Health*. Milton Keynes, UK: Open University Press, 1988.

Avramescu, Cătălin. *An Intellectual History of Cannibalism*. Translated by Alistair Ian Blyth. Princeton, NJ: Princeton University Press, 2009.

Balmer, Andrew, and Susan Molyneux-Hodgson. "Bacterial Cultures: Ontologies of Bacteria and Engineering Expertise at the Nexus of Synthetic Biology and Water Services." *Engineering Studies* 5, no. 1 (2013): 59–73.

Barker, Francis, Peter Hulme, and Margaret Iversen, eds. *Cannibalism and the Colonial World*. Cambridge: Cambridge University Press, 1998.

Barry, Andrew. *Material Politics: Disputes along the Pipeline*. Chichester, UK: John Wiley & Sons, 2013.

Barry, Andrew. *Political Machines: Governing a Technological Society*. London: A&C Black, 2001.

Barry, Andrew. "Thermodynamics, Matter, Politics." *Distinktion* 16, no. 1 (2015): 110–25.

Barth, Else M. *The Logic of the Articles in Traditional Philosophy: A Contribution to the Study of Conceptual Structures*. Dordrecht: Springer Netherlands, 2012.

Bashkow, Ira. *The Meaning of Whitemen: Race and Modernity in the Orokaiva Cultural World*. Chicago: University of Chicago Press, 2006.

Bate, Jonathan. *Romantic Ecology: Wordsworth and the Environmental Tradition*. London: Routledge, 1991.

Benhabib, Sheila, ed. *Democracy and Difference: Contesting the Boundaries of the Political*. Princeton, NJ: Princeton University Press, 1996.

Bertoni, Filippo. "Charming Worms: Crawling between Natures." *Cambridge Journal of Anthropology* 30, no. 2 (2012): 65–81.

Bertoni, Filippo. "Soil and Worm: On Eating as Relating." *Science as Culture* 22, no. 1 (2013): 61–85.

Bigras, Erik, and Kim Fortun. "Innovation in Asthma Research: Using Ethnography to Study a Global Health Problem." *Ethnography Matters*, October 27, 2012. http://ethnographymatters.net/blog/2012/10/27/the-asthma-files/.

Blok, Josine. *Citizenship in Classical Athens*. Cambridge: Cambridge University Press, 2017.

Bloor, David. *Wittgenstein: A Social Theory of Knowledge*. New York: Columbia University Press, 1983.

Bod, Rens. *A New History of the Humanities: The Search for Principles and Patterns from Antiquity to the Present*. Oxford: Oxford University Press, 2013.

Buller, Henry, and Emma J. Roe. *Food and Animal Welfare*. London: Bloomsbury, 2018.

Buytendijk, Frederik J. J. *De vrouw: Haar natuur, verschijning en bestaan*. Utrecht: Het Spectrum, 1951.

Bynum, Caroline W. *Holy Feast and Holy Fast: The Religious Significance of Food to Medieval Women*. Berkeley: University of California Press, 1988.

Canguilhem, George. *The Normal and the Pathological.* 1966. Reprint, Cambridge, MA: MIT Press, 1989.

Caplan, Pat, ed. *Food, Health and Identity.* Milton Park, UK: Routledge, 2013.

Carolan, Michael. *The Real Cost of Cheap Food.* London: Routledge, 2018.

Carolan, Michael. *The Sociology of Food and Agriculture.* London: Routledge, 2016.

Casey, Emma. "From *Cookery in Colour* to *The Great British Bake Off*: Shifting Gendered Accounts of Home-Baking and Domesticity." *European Journal of Cultural Studies* 2, nos. 5–6 (2019): 579–94.

Cassin, Barbara, Emily Apter, Jacques Lezra, and Michael Wood. *Dictionary of Untranslatables: A Philosophical Lexicon.* Princeton, NJ: Princeton University Press, 2014. Originally published as *Vocabulaire européen des philosophies: Dictionaire des intraduisibles* (Paris: Le Seuil and Le Robert, 2004).

Chamovitz, Daniel. *What a Plant Knows: A Field Guide to the Senses.* New York: Scientific American / Farrar, Straus and Giroux, 2012.

Charles, Nickie, and Charlotte A. Davies. "My Family and Other Animals: Pets as Kin." In *Human and Other Animals*, edited by Bob Carter and Nickie Charles, 62–92. London: Palgrave Macmillan, 2011.

Cheung, Sidney, and David Y. H. Wu, eds. *The Globalisation of Chinese Food.* London: Routledge, 2014.

Choy, Timothy K. *Ecologies of Comparison: An Ethnography of Endangerment in Hong Kong.* Durham, NC: Duke University Press, 2011.

Christensen, Bodil Just, and Line Hillersdal. "The Taste of Intervention." In *Making Taste Public: Ethnographies of Food and the Senses,* edited by Carole Counihan and Susanne Højlund, 25–38. London: Bloomsbury Academic, 2018.

Cohen, Ed. *A Body Worth Defending: Immunity, Biopolitics, and the Apotheosis of the Modern Body.* Durham, NC: Duke University Press, 2009.

Cook, Ian, Peter Jackson, Allison Hayes-Conroy, Sebastian Abrahamsson, Rebecca Sandover, Mimi Sheller, Heike Henderson, Lucius Hallet, Shoko Imai, Damian Maye, and Ann Hill. "Food's Cultural Geographies: Texture, Creativity and Publics." In *The Wiley-Blackwell Companion to Cultural Geography,* edited by Nuala C. Johnson, Richard H. Schein, and Jamie Winders, 343–54. Oxford: Wiley-Blackwell, 2013.

Counihan, Carole M. *The Anthropology of Food and Body: Gender, Meaning, and Power.* Hove, UK: Psychology Press, 1999.

Crosby, Alfred W. *Ecological Imperialism: The Biological Expansion of Europe, 900–1900.* Cambridge: Cambridge University Press, 1986.

Dal Lago, Enrico, and Constantina Katsari, eds. *Slave Systems: Ancient and Modern.* Cambridge: Cambridge University Press, 2008.

Davenport, Horace W. *A History of Gastric Secretion and Digestion: Experimental Studies to 1975.* New York: Springer, 1992.

Davies, Gail. "Caring for the Multiple and the Multitude: Assembling Animal Welfare and Enabling Ethical Critique." *Environment and Planning D: Society and Space* 30, no. 4 (2012): 623–38.

De Laet, Marianne, and Annemarie Mol. "The Zimbabwe Bush Pump: Mechanics of a Fluid Technology." *Social Studies of Science* 30, no. 2 (2000): 225–63.

De Matos Viegas, Susana. "Pleasures That Differentiate: Transformational Bodies among the Tupinambá of Olivença (Atlantic Coast, Brazil)." *Journal of the Royal Anthropological Institute* 18, no. 3 (2012): 536–53.

Derrida, Jacques. "'Eating Well,' or the Calculation of the Subject: An Interview with Jacques Derrida." In *Who Comes after the Subject?*, edited by Eduardo Cadava, Peter Connor, and Jean-Luc Nancy, 96–119. New York: Routledge, 1991.

Despret, Vinciane. *What Would Animals Say If We Asked the Right Questions?* Minneapolis: University of Minnesota Press, 2016.

Devlieger, Patrick, and Jori De Coster. "On Footwear and Disability: A Dance of Animacy?" *Societies* 7, no. 2 (2017): 16.

Diprose, Rosalyn, and Jack Reynolds. *Merleau-Ponty: Key Concepts*. London: Routledge, 2014.

Domínguez Guzmán, Carolina, Andres Verzijl, and Margreet Zwarteveen. "Water Footprints and 'Pozas': Conversations about Practices and Knowledges of Water Efficiency." *Water* 9, no. 1 (2017): 16.

Douglas, Mary. "Deciphering a Meal." *Daedalus* 101, no. 1 (1972): 61–81.

Douglas, Mary, ed. *Food in the Social Order*. 1973. Reprint, London: Routledge, 2014.

Dupré, John. *Processes of Life: Essays in the Philosophy of Biology*. Oxford: Oxford University Press, 2012.

Dwiartama, Angga, and Cinzia Piatti. "Assembling Local, Assembling Food Security." *Agriculture and Human Values* 33, no. 1 (2016): 153–64.

Dwiartama, Angga, and Christopher Rosin. "Exploring Agency beyond Humans: The Compatibility of Actor-Network Theory (ANT) and Resilience Thinking." *Ecology and Society* 19, no. 3 (2014): 28.

Earle, Rebecca. *The Body of the Conquistador: Food, Race and the Colonial Experience in Spanish America, 1492–1700*. Cambridge: Cambridge University Press, 2012.

Edwards, Jeanette, and Marilyn Strathern. "Including Our Own." In *Cultures of Relatedness: New Directions in Kinship Studies*, edited by Janet Carsten, 149–66. New York: Cambridge University Press, 2000.

Elam, Jacqueline, and Chase Pielak. *Corpse Encounters: An Aesthetics of Death*. Lanham, MD: Lexington Books, 2018.

Ellis, Carolyn. *The Ethnographic I: A Methodological Novel about Autoethnography*. Walnut Creek, CA: Altamira Press, 2004.

Erlmann, Veit, ed. *Hearing Cultures: Essays on Sound, Listening and Modernity*. Oxford: Berg, 2004.

Erlmann, Veit. *Reason and Resonance: A History of Modern Aurality*. New York: Zone Books, 2010.

Escobar, Arturo. "After Nature: Steps to an Anti-essentialist Political Ecology." *Current Anthropology* 40, no. 1 (1999): 1–30.

Farquhar, Judith. *Appetites: Food and Sex in Post-socialist China*. Durham, NC: Duke University Press, 2002.

Fine, Gary Alan. *Kitchens: The Culture of Restaurant Work*. Berkeley: University of California Press, 2008.

Fleck, Ludwig. *Genesis and Development of a Scientific Fact*. 1935. Reprint, Berkeley: University of California Press, 1981.

Flynn, Karen Coen. *Food, Culture, and Survival in an African City*. New York: Palgrave Macmillan, 2005.

Foucault, Michel. *Archaeology of Knowledge*. 1969. Reprint, London: Routledge, 2013.

Foucault, Michel. *Discipline and Punish: The Birth of the Prison*. 1975. Reprint, New York: Vintage Books, 2012.

Foucault, Michel. *The History of Sexuality*, vol. 2: *The Use of Pleasure*. 1985. Reprint, New York: Vintage Books, 2012.

Foucault, Michel. *Madness and Civilization*. 1962. Reprint, London: Routledge, 2003.

Francione, Gary L., and Robert Garner. *The Animal Rights Debate: Abolition or Regulation?* New York: Columbia University Press, 2010.

George, Rose. *The Big Necessity: Adventures in the World of Human Waste*. London: Portobello Books, 2011.

Geurts, Kathryn. *Culture and the Senses: Bodily Ways of Knowing in an African Community*. Berkeley: University of California Press, 2003.

Godfrey-Smith, Peter. *Other Minds: The Octopus, the Sea, and the Deep Origins of Consciousness*. New York: Farrar, Straus and Giroux, 2016.

Goldstein, David. "Emmanuel Levinas and the Ontology of Eating." *Gastronomica* 10, no. 3 (2010): 34–44.

Goldstein, Kurt. *The Organism: A Holistic Approach to Biology Derived from Pathological Data in Man*. New York: Zone Books, 1995.

Goody, Jack. *Cooking, Cuisine and Class: A Study in Comparative Sociology*. Cambridge: Cambridge University Press, 1982.

Graeber, David. "Consumption." *Current Anthropology* 52, no. 4 (2011): 489–51.

Green, Lesley, ed. *Contested Ecologies: Dialogues in the South on Nature and Knowledge*. Cape Town: HSRC Press, 2013.

Greenhough, Beth, and Emma Roe. "From Ethical Principles to Response-Able Practice." *Environment and Planning D: Society and Space* 28, no. 1 (2010): 43–45.

Griffioen-Roose, Sanne, Monica Mars, Els Siebelink, Graham Finlayson, Daniel Tomé, and Cees de Graaf. "Protein Status Elicits Compensatory Changes in Food Intake and Food Preferences." *American Journal of Clinical Nutrition* 95, no. 1 (2012): 32–38.

Guadeloupe, Francio. *So How Does It Feel to Be a Black Man Living in the Nether-lands? An Anthropological Answer.* Forthcoming.

Guthman, Julie. *Weighing In: Obesity, Food Justice, and the Limits of Capitalism.* Berkeley: University of California Press, 2011.

Guyer, Sara. "Albeit Eating: Towards an Ethics of Cannibalism." *Angelaki* 2, no. 1 (1997): 63–80.

Habermas, Jürgen. *The Theory of Communicative Action: Lifeworld and Systems, a Critique of Functionalist Reason.* Vol. 1. Translated by Thomas McCarthy. Cambridge, UK: Polity, 1985.

Haines, Helen R., and Clare A. Sammells, eds. *Adventures in Eating: Anthropological Experiences in Dining from around the World.* Boulder: University Press of Colorado, 2010.

Halkier, Bente, Lotte Holm, Malfada Domingues, Paolog Magaudda, Annemette Nielsen, and Laura Terragni. "Trusting, Complex, Quality Conscious or Un-protected? Constructing the Food Consumer in Different European National Contexts." *Journal of Consumer Culture* 7, no. 3 (2007): 379–402.

Haraway, Donna J. *Modest_Witness@Second_Millennium.FemaleMan©_Meets _OncoMouse™: Feminism and Technoscience.* New York: Routledge, 1997.

Haraway, Donna J. *Staying with the Trouble: Making Kin in the Chthulucene.* Durham, NC: Duke University Press, 2016.

Haraway, Donna J. *When Species Meet.* Minneapolis: University of Minnesota Press, 2013.

Harbers, Hans. "Animal Farm Love Stories." In *Care in Practice.* Mol, Moser and Pols, 141-170

Hardon, Anita, and Emilia Sanabria. "Fluid Drugs: Revisiting the Anthropology of Pharmaceuticals." *Annual Review of Anthropology* 46 (2017): 117–32.

Harrington, Anne. *Reenchanted Science: Holism in German Culture from Wilhelm II to Hitler.* Princeton, NJ: Princeton University Press, 1999.

Harris, Marvin. *Good to Eat: Riddles of Food and Culture.* Long Grove, IL: Wave-land Press, 1998.

Head, Lesley, Jennifer Atchison, and Catherine Phillips. "The Distinctive Capaci-ties of Plants: Re-thinking Difference via Invasive Species." *Transactions of the Institute of British Geographers* 40, no. 3 (2015): 399–413.

Heuts, Frank, and Annemarie Mol. "What Is a Good Tomato? A Case of Valuing in Practice." *Valuation Studies* 1, no. 2 (2013): 125–46.

Hirschauer, Stefan. "Putting Things into Words: Ethnographic Description and the Silence of the Social." *Human Studies* 29, no. 4 (2006): 413–41.

Hirschauer, Stefan, and Annemarie Mol. "Shifting Sexes, Moving Stories: Feminist/Constructivist Dialogues." *Science, Technology, and Human Values* 20, no. 3 (1995): 368–85.

Holt-Giménez, Eric, and Rai Patel, eds. *Food Rebellions: Crisis and the Hunger for Justice.* Oakland, CA: Food First Books; Oxford: Pambazooka Press, 2012.

Holtzman, Jon. *Uncertain Tastes: Memory, Ambivalence, and the Politics of Eating in Samburu, Northern Kenya*. Berkeley: University of California Press, 2009.

Honig, Bonnie. "Difference, Dilemmas, and the Politics of Home." In "Liberalism," special issue, *Social Research* 61, no. 3 (1994): 563–97.

Honig, Bonnie, ed. *Feminist Interpretations of Hannah Arendt*. University Park: Penn State University Press, 2010.

Hoogsteyns, Maartje, and Hilje van der Horst. "How to Live with a Taboo Instead of 'Breaking It': Alternative Empowerment Strategies of People with Incontinence." *Health Sociology Review* 24, no. 1 (2015): 38–47.

Howes, David. *Sensual Relations: Engaging the Senses in Culture and Social Theory*. Ann Arbor: University of Michigan Press, 2010.

Howes, David, and Constance Classen. *Ways of Sensing: Understanding the Senses in Society*. London: Routledge, 2013.

Hutchins, Edwin. *Cognition in the Wild*. Cambridge, MA: MIT Press, 1995.

Inglis, David, and Debra Gimlin, eds. *The Globalization of Food*. Oxford: Berg, 2009.

Ingold, Tim. "Footprints through the Weather-World: Walking, Breathing, Knowing." *Journal of the Royal Anthropological Institute* 16, no. 1 (2010): S121–S139.

Ingold, Tim, and Jo Lee Vergunst, eds. *Ways of Walking: Ethnography and Practice on Foot*. Aldershot, UK: Ashgate, 2008.

Jackson, Peter, ed. *Food Words: Essays in Culinary Culture*. London: Bloomsbury, 2014.

Jakobsen, Gry S. "Tastes: Foods, Bodies and Places in Denmark." PhD diss., University of Copenhagen, 2013.

Janeja, Manpreet K. *Transactions in Taste: The Collaborative Lives of Everyday Bengali Food*. New Delhi: Routledge, 2010.

Jonas, Hans. *The Phenomenon of Life: Toward a Philosophical Biology*. 1966. Reprint, Evanston, IL: Northwestern University Press, 2001.

Kierans, Ciara. "The Intimate Uncertainties of Kidney Care: Moral Economy and Treatment Regimes in Comparative Perspective." *Anthropological Journal of European Cultures* 27, no. 2 (2018): 65–84.

Knorr-Cetina, Karin. *Epistemic Cultures: How the Sciences Make Knowledge*. Cambridge, MA: Harvard University Press, 1999.

Kohn, Eduardo. *How Forests Think: Toward an Anthropology beyond the Human*. Berkeley: University of California Press, 2013.

Kontopodis, Michalis. "How and Why Should Children Eat Fruit and Vegetables? Ethnographic Insights into Diverse Body Pedagogies." *Social Science and Medicine* 143 (2015): 297–303.

Korsmeyer, Carolyn. *Making Sense of Taste: Food and Philosophy*. Ithaca, NY: Cornell University Press, 1999.

Korsmeyer, Carolyn. *Savoring Disgust: The Foul and the Fair in Aesthetics*. Oxford: Oxford University Press, 2011.

Krause, Sharon R. "Bodies in Action: Corporeal Agency and Democratic Politics." *Political Theory* 39, no. 3 (2011): 299–324.

Kuhn, Thomas S. *The Structure of Scientific Revolutions.* Chicago: University of Chicago Press, 1962.

Kuklick, Henrika. *The Savage Within: The Social History of British Anthropology, 1885–1945.* Cambridge: Cambridge University Press, 1991.

Kuriyama, Shigehisa. *The Expressiveness of the Body and the Divergence of Greek and Chinese Medicine.* New York: Zone Books, 1999.

Kwa, Chunglin. "Alexander von Humboldt's Invention of the Natural Landscape." *European Legacy* 10, no. 2 (April 2005): 149–62.

Kwa, Chunglin. *Styles of Knowing: A New History of Science from Ancient Times to the Present.* Pittsburgh: University of Pittsburgh Press, 2011.

Lakoff, George, and Mark Johnson. *Metaphors We Live By.* Chicago: University of Chicago Press, 1980.

Landecker, Hannah. "Food as Exposure: Nutritional Epigenetics and the New Metabolism." *BioSocieties* 6, no. 2 (2011): 167–94.

Landecker, Hannah, and Aaron Panofsky. "From Social Structure to Gene Regulation, and Back: A Critical Introduction to Environmental Epigenetics for Sociology." *Annual Review of Sociology* 39 (2013): 333–57.

Lang, Tim, and Michael Heasman. *Food Wars: The Global Battle for Mouths, Minds and Markets.* London: Routledge, 2015.

Latour, Bruno. *Facing Gaia: Eight Lectures on the New Climatic Regime.* Translated by Catherine Porter. Cambridge, UK: Polity, 2017.

Latour, Bruno. *The Pasteurization of France.* Cambridge, MA: Harvard University Press, 1993.

Latour, Bruno. *Politics of Nature.* Translated by Catherine Porter. Cambridge, MA: Harvard University Press, 2004.

Latour, Bruno. "Trains of Thought: Piaget, Formalism, and the Fifth Dimension." *Common Knowledge* 6 (1997): 170–91.

Latour, Bruno, and Steve Woolgar. *Laboratory Life: The Construction of Scientific Facts.* 1979. Reprint, Princeton, NJ: Princeton University Press, 1986.

Lave, Jean. *Cognition in Practice: Mind, Mathematics and Culture in Everyday Life.* Cambridge: Cambridge University Press, 1988.

Lavis, Anne. "Food, Bodies, and the 'Stuff' of (Not) Eating in Anorexia." *Gastronomica* 16, no. 3 (2016): 56–65.

Law, John. "And If the Global Were Small and Noncoherent? Method, Complexity, and the Baroque." *Environment and Planning D: Society and Space* 22, no. 1 (2004): 13–26.

Law, John. "Care and Killing: Tensions in Veterinary Practice." In Mol, Moser, and Pols, *Care in Practice,* 57–72.

Law, John. "On the Subject of the Object: Narrative, Technology, and Interpellation." *Configurations* 8, no. 1 (2000): 1–29.

Law, John, and Annemarie Mol. "Globalisation in Practice: On the Politics of Boiling Pigswill." *Geoforum* 39, no. 1 (2008): 133–43.

Law, John, and Annemarie Mol. "Veterinary Realities: What Is Foot and Mouth Disease?" *Sociologia Ruralis* 51, no. 1 (2011): 1–16.

Lawrence, Christopher, and Steven Shapin, eds. *Science Incarnate: Historical Embodiments of Natural Knowledge*. Chicago: University of Chicago Press, 1998.

Lee, Jae R. "My Mushroom Burial Suit." TED Talk, July 2011. www.ted.com/talks /jae_rhim_lee.

Le Heron, Richard, Hugh Campbell, Nick Lewis, and Michael Carolan, eds. *Biological Economies: Experimentation and the Politics of Agri-Food Frontiers*. Abingdon, UK: Routledge, 2016.

Lettinga, Ant, and Annemarie Mol. "Clinical Specificity and the Non-generalities of Science." *Theoretical Medicine and Bioethics* 20, no. 6 (1999): 517–35.

Levinas, Emmanuel. *Totality and Infinity: An Essay on Exteriority*. Dordrecht: Martinus Nijhoff, 1979. Originally published as *Totalité et infini: Essai sur l'extériorité* (La Haye: Martinus Nijhoff, 1961).

Lévi-Strauss, Claude. *The Savage Mind*. Chicago: University of Chicago Press, 1966.

Liboiron, Max, Manuel Tironi, and Nerea Calvillo. "Toxic Politics: Acting in a Permanently Polluted World." *Social Studies of Science* 48, no. 3 (2018): 331–49.

Lien, Marianne, and J. Law. "'Emergent Aliens': On Salmon, Nature, and Their Enactment." *Ethnos* 76, no. 1 (2011): 65–87.

Lock, Margaret. *Encounters with Aging: Mythologies of Menopause in Japan and North America*. Berkeley: University of California Press, 1994.

Mann, Anna. "Ordering Tasting in a Restaurant: Experiencing, Socializing, and Processing Food." *Senses and Society* 13, no. 2 (2018): 135–46.

Mann, Anna. "Sensory Science Research on Taste: An Ethnography of Two Laboratory Experiments in Western Europe." *Food and Foodways* 26, no. 1 (January 2018): 23–39.

Mann, Anna. "Which Context Matters? Tasting in Everyday Life Practices and Social Science Theories." *Food, Culture and Society* 18, no. 3 (2015): 399–417.

Mann, Anna, and Annemarie Mol. "Talking Pleasures, Writing Dialects: Outlining Research on Schmecka." *Ethnos* (2018): 1–17.

Mann, Anna, Annemarie Mol, Pryia Satalkar, Amalinda Savirani, Nasima Selim, Malini Sur, and Emily Yates-Doerr. "Mixing Methods, Tasting Fingers: Notes on an Ethnographic Experiment." *HAU: Journal of Ethnographic Theory* 1, no. 1 (2011): 221–43.

Marres, Noortje. *Material Participation: Technology, the Environment and Everyday Publics*. New York: Springer, 2016.

Marres, Noortje. "Why Political Ontology Must Be Experimentalized: On Eco-Show Homes as Devices of Participation." *Social Studies of Science* 43, no. 3 (2013): 417–43.

Martinez-Torres, Maria Elena. *Organic Coffee: Sustainable Development by Mayan Farmers*. Athens: Ohio University Press, 2006.

McGee, Harold. *On Food and Cooking: The Science and Lore of the Kitchen*. New York: Scribner, 2004.

M'charek, Amâde. "Beyond Fact or Fiction: On the Materiality of Race in Practice." *Cultural Anthropology* 28, no. 3 (2013): 420−42.

M'charek, Amâde. "Fragile Differences, Relational Effects: Stories about the Materiality of Race and Sex." *European Journal of Women's Studies* 17, no. 4 (2010): 307−22.

M'charek, Amâde, Katharina Schramm, and David Skinner. "Topologies of Race: Doing Territory, Population and Identity in Europe." *Science, Technology, and Human Values* 39, no. 4 (2014): 468−87.

Meadows, Donella, Dennis Meadows, Jurgen Randers, and William Behrens III. *The Limits to Growth: A Report to the Club of Rome*. New York: Universe Books, 1972.

Merleau-Ponty, Maurice. *The Phenomenology of Perception*. 1958. Reprint, London: Routledge, 2005. Originally published as *La phénoménologie de la perception* (Paris: Editions Gallimard, 1945).

Mintz, Sidney W. *Sweetness and Power: The Place of Sugar in Modern History*. New York: Viking, 1985.

Mintz, Sidney W., and Christine M. Du Bois. "The Anthropology of Food and Eating." *Annual Review of Anthropology* 31, no. 1 (2002): 99−119.

Mody, Cyrus C. "The Sounds of Science: Listening to Laboratory Practice." *Science, Technology, and Human Values* 30, no. 2 (2005): 175−98.

Mol, Annemarie. "Bami Goreng for Mrs Klerks and Other Stories on Food and Culture." In *Debordements: Mélanges offerts à Michel Callon*, edited by Madeleine Akrich, Yannick Barthe, Fabian Muniesa, and Phelippe Mustar, 325−34. Paris: Presses Ecole de Mînes, 2010.

Mol, Annemarie. *The Body Multiple: Ontology in Medical Practice*. Durham, NC: Duke University Press, 2003.

Mol, Annemarie. "Care and Its Values: Good Food in the Nursing Home." In Mol, Moser, and Pols, *Care in Practice*, 215−34.

Mol, Annemarie. "Dit is geen programma: Over empirische filosofie." *Krisis* 1, no. 1 (2000): 6−26.

Mol, Annemarie. "I Eat an Apple: On Theorizing Subjectivities." *Subjectivity* 22, no. 1 (2008): 28−37.

Mol, Annemarie. "Language Trails: 'Lekker' and Its Pleasures." *Theory, Culture and Society* 31, nos. 2−3 (2014): 93−119.

Mol, Annemarie. "Layers or Versions? Human Bodies and the Love of Bitterness." In *The Routledge Handbook of Body Studies*, edited by Bryan S. Turner, 119−29. Abingdon, UK: Routledge, 2012.

Mol, Annemarie. *The Logic of Care: Health and the Problem of Patient Choice*. London: Routledge, 2008.

Mol, Annemarie. "Mind Your Plate! The Ontonorms of Dutch Dieting." *Social Studies of Science* 43, no. 3 (2013): 379–96.

Mol, Annemarie. "Natures in Tension." In *Natures in Modern Society, Now and in the Future,* edited by Ed Dammers, 88–98. The Hague: Netherlands Environmental Assessment Agency, 2017. https://www.pbl.nl/en/publications /nature-in-modern-society.

Mol, Annemarie. "Ondertonen en boventonen: Over empirische filosofie." In *Burgers en Vreemdelingen,* edited by Dick Pels and Gerard de Vries, 77–84. Amsterdam: Van Gennep, 1994.

Mol, Annemarie. "Who Knows What a Woman Is . . . : On the Differences and the Relations between the Sciences." *Medicine, Anthropology, Theory* 2, no. 1 (2015): 57–75.

Mol, Annemarie, and John Law. "Regions, Networks and Fluids: Anaemia and Social Topology." *Social Studies of Science* 24, no. 4 (1994): 641–71.

Mol, Annemarie, Ingunn Moser, and Jeannette Pols. "Care: Putting Practice into Theory." In Mol, Moser, and Pols, *Care in Practice,* 7–27.

Mol, Annemarie, Ingunn Moser, and Jeannette Pols, eds. *Care in Practice: On Tinkering in Clinics, Homes and Farms.* Bielefeld, Germany: Transcript Verlag, 2010.

Monteiro, Carlos A. "Nutrition and Health: The Issue Is Not Food, nor Nutrients, So Much as Processing." *Public Health Nutrition* 12, no. 5 (2009): 729–31.

Moser, Ingunn. "On Becoming Disabled and Articulating Alternatives: The Multiple Modes of Ordering Disability and Their Interferences." *Cultural Studies* 19, no. 6 (2005): 667–700.

Moser, Ingunn. "Perhaps Tears Should Not Be Counted but Wiped Away: On Quality and Improvement in Dementia Care." In Mol, Moser, and Pols, *Care in Practice,* 277–300.

Mouffe, Chantal. *Agonistics: Thinking the World Politically.* London: Verso, 2013.

Mouffe, Chantal. *The Return of the Political.* London: Verso, 2005.

Müller, Sophie M. "Distributed Corporeality: Anatomy, Knowledge and the Technological Reconfiguration of Bodies in Ballet." *Social Studies of Science* 48, no. 6 (2018): 869–90.

Müller, Sophie M. "Ways of Relating." In *Moving Bodies in Interaction—Interacting Bodies in Motion: Intercorporeality, Interkinesthesia, and Enaction in Sports,* edited by Christian Meyer and Ulrich V. Wedelstaedt. Amsterdam: John Benjamins, 2017.

Murcott, Anne. "Cooking and the Cooked: A Note on the Domestic Preparation of Meals." In *The Sociology of Food and Eating,* edited by Anne Murcott, 178–85. Farnham, UK: Gower, 1983.

Nanninga, Christa S., Louise Meijering, Klaas Postema, Marleen Schönherr, and Ant Lettinga. "Unpacking Community Mobility: A Preliminary Study into the Embodied Experiences of Stroke Survivors." *Disability and Rehabilitation* 40, no. 17 (2018): 2015–24.

Nauta, Lolle W. "De subcultuur van de wijsbegeerte: Een privé geschiedenis van de filosofie." *Krisis* 38 (2006): 5—19.

Nestle, Marion. *Food Politics: How the Food Industry Influences Nutrition and Health.* Berkeley: University of California Press, 2013.

Niewöhner, Jörg, and Margaret Lock. "Situating Local Biologies: Anthropological Perspectives on Environment/Human Entanglements." *BioSocieties* 13, no. 4 (2018): 681—97.

Noë, Alva. *Out of Our Heads: Why You Are Not Your Brain, and Other Lessons from the Biology of Consciousness.* New York: Hill and Wang, 2009.

O'Rand, Angela M., and Margaret L. Krecker. "Concepts of the Life Cycle: Their History, Meanings, and Uses in the Social Sciences." *Annual Review of Sociology* 16, no. 1 (1990): 241—62.

Otis, Laura. *Membranes: Metaphors of Invasion in Nineteenth-Century Literature, Science, and Politics.* Baltimore: Johns Hopkins University Press, 2000.

Paxson, Heather. *The Life of Cheese: Crafting Food and Value in America.* Berkeley: University of California Press, 2012.

Peet, Richard, Paul Robbins, and Michael Watts, eds. *Global Political Ecology.* Abingdon, UK: Routledge, 2011.

Pels, Peter, and Oscar Salemink, eds. *Colonial Subjects: Essays on the Practical History of Anthropology.* Ann Arbor: University of Michigan Press, 2000.

Phillips, Catherine. *Saving More Than Seeds: Practices and Politics of Seed Saving.* London: Routledge, 2016.

Pickering, Andrew. *The Cybernetic Brain: Sketches of Another Future.* Chicago: University of Chicago Press, 2010.

Pinch, Trevor, and Karin Bijsterveld, eds. *The Oxford Handbook of Sound Studies.* Oxford: Oxford University Press, 2010.

Pitt, Hannah. "An Apprenticeship in Plant Thinking." In *Participatory Research in More-Than-Human Worlds,* edited by Michelle Bastian, Owain Jones, Niamh Moore, and Emma Roe, 106—20. London: Routledge, 2016.

Plumwood, Valerie. *Environmental Culture: The Ecological Crisis of Reason.* London: Routledge, 2002.

Plumwood, Valerie. *Feminism and the Mastery of Nature.* London: Routledge, 1993.

Pollan, Michael. *The Botany of Desire: A Plant's-Eye View of the World.* New York: Random House, 2002.

Polletta, Francesca. *It Was Like a Fever: Storytelling in Protest and Politics.* Chicago: University of Chicago Press, 2006.

Pols, Jeannette, and Sarah Limburg. "A Matter of Taste? Quality of Life in Day-to-Day Living with ALS and a Feeding Tube." *Culture, Medicine, and Psychiatry* 40, no. 3 (2016): 361—82.

Probyn, Elspeth. *Eating the Ocean.* Durham, NC: Duke University Press, 2016.

Raffles, Hugh. *Insectopedia.* New York: Vintage Books, 2010.

Raffles, Hugh. "Twenty-Five Years Is a Long Time." *Cultural Anthropology* 27, no. 3 (2012): 526–34.

Rawls, John. *A Theory of Justice*. 1971. Reprint, Cambridge, MA: Harvard University Press, 2009.

Rebanks, James. *The Shepherd's Life: A Tale of the Lake District*. London: Penguin, 2015.

Reno, Joshua. "Waste and Waste Management." *Annual Review of Anthropology* 44 (2015): 557–72.

Rice, Robert. "Noble Goals and Challenging Terrain: Organic and Fair Trade Coffee Movements in the Global Marketplace." *Journal of Agricultural and Environmental Ethics* 14, no. 1 (2001): 39 66.

Richards, Audrey I. *Hunger and Work in a Savage Tribe: A Functional Study of Nutrition among the Southern Bantu*. 1932. Reprint, London: Routledge, 2013.

Roe, Emma J. "Things Becoming Food and the Embodied, Material Practices of an Organic Food Consumer." *Sociologia Ruralis* 46, no. 2 (2006): 104–21.

Rozin, Paul, Maureen Markwith, and Caryn Stoess. "Moralization and Becoming a Vegetarian: The Transformation of Preferences into Values and the Recruitment of Disgust." *Psychological Science* 8, no. 2 (1997): 67–73.

Sanabria, Emilia, and Emily Yates-Doerr. "Alimentary Uncertainties: From Contested Evidence to Policy." *BioSocieties* 10, no. 2 (2015): 117–24.

Schneider, Daniel. *Hybrid Nature: Sewage Treatment and the Contradictions of the Industrial Ecosystem*. Cambridge, MA: MIT Press, 2011.

Schrempp, Gregory. "Catching Wrangham: On the Mythology and the Science of Fire, Cooking, and Becoming Human." *Journal of Folklore Research* 48, no. 2 (2011): 109–32.

Serres, Michel. *The Parasite*. Minneapolis: University of Minnesota Press, 2013.

Serres, Michel. *Le Passage du Nord-Ouest*. Paris: Éditions du Minuit, 1980.

Serres, Michel, and Bruno Latour. *Conversations on Science, Culture, and Time*. Ann Arbor: University of Michigan Press, 1995.

Sexton, Alexandra E. "Eating for the Post-Anthropocene: Alternative Proteins and the Biopolitics of Edibility." *Transactions of the Institute of British Geographers* 43, no. 4 (2018): 586–600.

Shapin, Steven. "Descartes the Doctor: Rationalism and Its Therapies." *British Journal for the History of Science* 33, no. 2 (2000): 131–54.

Shapin, Steven. "The Sciences of Subjectivity." *Social Studies of Science* 42, no. 2 (2012): 170–84.

Shepherd, Gordon M. *Neurogastronomy: How the Brain Creates Flavor and Why It Matters*. New York: Columbia University Press, 2011.

Simms, Eva-Maria. "Eating One's Mother: Female Embodiment in a Toxic World." *Environmental Ethics* 31, no. 3 (2009): 263–77.

Skodje, Gry I., Vikas Sarna, Ingunn Minelle, Kjersti Rolfsen, Jane Muir, Peter Gibson, Marit Veierød, Christine Henriksen, and Knut Lundin. "Fructan,

Rather Than Gluten, Induces Symptoms in Patients with Self-Reported Non-celiac Gluten Sensitivity." *Gastroenterology* 154, no. 3 (2018): 529–39.

Sneijder, Petra, and Hedwig F. M. te Molder. "Disputing Taste: Food Pleasure as an Achievement in Interaction." *Appetite* 46, no. 1 (2006): 107–16.

Sneijder, Petra, and Hedwig F. M. te Molder. "Normalizing Ideological Food Choice and Eating Practices: Identity Work in Online Discussions on Veganism." *Appetite* 52, no. 3 (2009): 621–30.

Solomon, Harris. *Metabolic Living: Food, Fat, and the Absorption of Illness in India*. Durham, NC: Duke University Press, 2016.

Spang, Rebecca. *The Invention of the Restaurant*. Cambridge, MA: Harvard University Press, 2001.

Stengers, Isabelle. *In Catastrophic Times: Resisting the Coming Barbarism*. London: Open Humanities Press, 2015.

Sterckx, Roel. *Food, Sacrifice, and Sagehood in Early China*. Cambridge: Cambridge University Press, 2011.

Stoller, Paul. *The Taste of Ethnographic Things: The Senses in Anthropology*. Philadelphia: University of Pennsylvania Press, 1989.

Strathern, Marilyn. *After Nature: English Kinship in the Late Twentieth Century*. New York: Cambridge University Press, 1992.

Strathern, Marilyn. "Eating (and Feeding)." *Cambridge Journal of Anthropology* 30, no. 2 (2012): 1–14.

Strathern, Marilyn. "The Limits of Auto-Ethnography." In *Anthropology at Home*, edited by Anthony Jackson, 59–67. London: Tavistock, 1987.

Strathern, Marilyn. *Partial Connections*. Updated ed. Savage, MD: Rowman & Littlefield, 2004.

Struhkamp, Rita M. "Patient Autonomy: A View from the Kitchen." *Medicine, Health Care and Philosophy* 8, no. 1 (2005): 105–14.

Struhkamp, Rita M., Annemarie Mol, and Tsjalling Swierstra. "Dealing with In/Dependence: Doctoring in Physical Rehabilitation Practice." *Science, Technology, and Human Values* 34, no. 1 (2009): 55–76.

Sutton, David E. *Remembrance of Repasts: An Anthropology of Food and Memory*. 2nd ed. Oxford: Berg, 2001.

Swierstra, Tsjalling. *De sofocratische verleiding: Het ondemocratische karakter van een aantal moderne rationaliteitsconcepties*. Kampen, Netherlands: Kok/ Agora, 1998.

Taylor, Jean Gelman. *The Social World of Batavia: European and Eurasian in Dutch Asia*. Madison: University of Wisconsin Press, 1983.

Teil, Geneviève, and Antoine Hennion. "Discovering Quality or Performing Taste? A Sociology of the Amateur." In *Qualities of Food: Alternative Theoretical and Empirical Approaches*, edited by Mark Harvey, Andrew Mc-Meekin, and Alan Warde, 19–37. Manchester, UK: Manchester University Press, 2004.

Thompson, Charis. "When Elephants Stand for Competing Philosophies of Nature: Amboseli National Parc, Kenya." In *Complexities,* edited by John Law and Annemarie Mol, 166−90. Durham, NC: Duke University Press, 2002.

Tresch, John. *The Romantic Machine: Utopian Science and Technology after Napoleon.* Chicago: University of Chicago Press, 2012.

Tsing, Anna L. *Friction: An Ethnography of Global Connection.* Princeton, NJ: Princeton University Press, 2004.

Tsing, Anna L. *The Mushroom at the End of the World: On the Possibility of Life in Capitalist Ruins.* Princeton, NJ: Princeton University Press, 2015.

Tsing, Anna L., Heather Swanson, Elaine Gan, and Nils Bubandt, eds. *Arts of Living on a Damaged Planet: Ghosts and Monsters of the Anthropocene.* Minneapolis: University of Minnesota Press, 2017.

Van de Port, Mattijs, and Annemarie Mol. "Chupar Frutas in Salvador da Bahia: A Case of Practice-Specific Alterities." *Journal of the Royal Anthropological Institute* 21, no. 1 (2015): 165−80.

Van der Horst, Hilje, Stefano Pascucci, and Wilma Bol. "The 'Dark Side' of Food Banks? Exploring Emotional Responses of Food Bank Receivers in the Netherlands." *British Food Journal* 116, no. 9 (2014): 1506−20.

van Dooren, Thom. *Flight Ways: Life and Loss at the Edge of Extinction.* New York: Columbia University Press, 2014.

Van Huis, Arnold, Marcel Dicke, and Joop J. A. van Loon. "Insects to Feed the World." *Journal of Insects as Food and Feed* 1, no. 1 (2015): 3−5.

Vilaça, Aparecida. "Relations between Funerary Cannibalism and Warfare Cannibalism: The Question of Predation." *Ethnos* 65, no. 1 (2000): 83–106.

Visser, Margaret. *The Rituals of Dinner: The Origins, Evolution, Eccentricities, and Meaning of Table Manners.* 1991. Reprint, New York: Open Road Media, 2015.

Viveiros de Castro, Eduardo. *Cannibal Metaphysics.* Edited and translated by P. Skafish. Minneapolis: University of Minnesota Press, 2015.

Viveiros de Castro, Eduardo. "Exchanging Perspectives: The Transformation of Objects into Subjects in Amerindian Ontologies." *Common Knowledge* 10, no. 3 (2019): 463−84.

Viveiros de Castro, Eduardo. "Perspectival Anthropology and the Method of Controlled Equivocation." *Tipití* 2, no. 1 (2004): 3−22.

Voedingscentrum. "Dioxines." Accessed June 24, 2019. https://www.voedings centrum.nl/encyclopedie/dioxines.aspx.

Voedingscentrum. "Eiwitten." Accessed August 2016. http://www.voedings centrum.nl/encyclopedie/eiwitten.aspx.

Voedingscentrum. "Hoeveel en wat kan ik per dag eten?" Accessed August 2016. http://www.voedingscentrum.nl/nl/schijf-van-vijf/eet-gevarieerd.aspx.

Voedingscentrum. "Missie en visie." Accessed August 2016. http://www.voedings centrum.nl/nl/service/over-ons/hoe-werkt-het-voedingscentrum-precies /missie-en-visie-voedingscentrum.aspx.

Voedingscentrum. "Nitraat." Accessed August 2016. http://www.voedingscentrum
.nl/nl/nieuws/voedingscentrum-herziet-adviezen-voor-nitraatinname.aspx.

Voedingscentrum. "Schijf van Vijf." Accessed August 2016. http://www.voedings
centrum.nl/nl/schijf-van-vijf/schijf.aspx.

Vogel, Else. "Clinical Specificities in Obesity Care: The Transformations and Dissolution of 'Will' and 'Drives.'" *Health Care Analysis* 24, no. 4 (2016): 321–37.

Vogel, Else. "Hungers That Need Feeding: On the Normativity of Mindful Nourishment." *Anthropology and Medicine* 24, no. 2 (2017): 159–73.

Vogel, Else. "Metabolism and Movement: Calculating Food and Exercise or Activating Bodies in Dutch Weight Management." *BioSocieties* 13, no. 2 (2018):
389–407.

Vogel, Else, and Annemarie Mol. "Enjoy Your Food: On Losing Weight and Taking Pleasure." *Sociology of Health and Illness* 36, no. 2 (2014): 305–17.

Warde, Alan. *The Practice of Eating.* Hoboken, NJ: John Wiley & Sons, 2016.

Watson, James, ed. *Golden Arches East: McDonald's in East Asia.* Redwood City,
CA: Stanford University Press, 2006.

Watson, James, and Melissa Caldwell, eds. *The Cultural Politics of Food and Eating: A Reader.* Malden, MA: Blackwell, 2005.

Wiggins, Sally. "Talking with Your Mouth Full: Gustatory Mmms and the Embodiment of Pleasure." *Research on Language and Social Interaction* 35, no. 3
(2002): 311–36.

Wiggins, Sally, and Jonathan Potter. "Attitudes and Evaluative Practices: Category
vs. Item and Subjective vs. Objective Constructions in Everyday Food Assessments." *British Journal of Social Psychology* 42, no. 4 (2003): 513–31.

Willems, Dick. "Inhaling Drugs and Making Worlds: The Proliferation of Lungs
and Asthmas." In *Differences in Medicine: Unravelling Practices, Techniques
and Bodies,* edited by Marc Berg and Annemarie Mol, 105–18. Durham, NC:
Duke University Press, 1998.

Wittgenstein, Ludwig. *Philosophical Investigations.* 1953. Reprint, Hoboken, NJ:
John Wiley & Sons, 2009.

Wittgenstein, Ludwig. *Tractatus Logico-Philosophicus.* 1921. Reprint, London:
Routledge, 2013.

Wrangham, Richard. *Catching Fire: How Cooking Made Us Human.* New York:
Basic Books, 2009.

Wylie, John. "A Single Day's Walking: Narrating Self and Landscape on the South
West Coast Path." *Transactions of the Institute of British Geographers* 30, no. 2
(2005): 234–47.

Yanow, Dvora, Marleen van der Haar, and Karlijn Völke. "Troubled Taxonomies and
the Calculating State: Everyday Categorizing and 'Race-Ethnicity'—the Netherlands
Case." *Journal of Race, Ethnicity and Politics* 1, no. 2 (2016): 187–226.

Yates-Doerr, Emily. "Counting Bodies? On Future Engagements with Science
Studies in Medical Anthropology." *Anthropology and Medicine* 24, no. 2
(2017): 142–58.

Yates-Doerr, Emily. "Intervals of Confidence: Uncertain Accounts of Global Hunger." *BioSocieties* 10, no. 2 (April 2015): 229–46.

Yates-Doerr, Emily. "The Opacity of Reduction: Nutritional Black-Boxing and the Meanings of Nourishment." *Food, Culture and Society* 15, no. 2 (2012): 293–313.

Yates-Doerr, Emily. *The Weight of Obesity: Hunger and Global Health in Postwar Guatemala*. Berkeley: University of California Press, 2015.

Yates-Doerr, Emily. "The World in a Box? Food Security, Edible Insects, and 'One World, One Health' Collaboration." *Social Science and Medicine* 129 (2015): 106–12.

Young, Robert J. *Colonial Desire. Hybridity in Theory, Culture and Race*. London: Routledge, 2005.

Zaman, Shahaduz, Nasima Selim, and Taufiq Joarder. "McDonaldization without a McDonald's: Globalization and Food Culture as Social Determinants of Health in Urban Bangladesh." *Food, Culture and Society* 16, no. 4 (2013): 551–68.

Note: Page numbers for terms that appear in sidelines are placed within brackets

money, [29], [33], [35], [63], [59], 69, 83, [84], 85–87, 96, 120
mother, 63–65, 73, [87], [91], 95, 103–6, [105–7], 114–15, 119–20, 140
multiple, 6, 21, [103], 154n34
multiplicity, 20, 154n34, 154n35

naturalism, 9, 11
nature, [4–6], 11, [12], 13, [29–31], [37], [44], 53, 80, 96, 127–131, 136, 139
nausea, 60–61, 71, 73, 142
Nauta, Lolle, [8], 16, 18
Nazis, 13, 31, 95, 99, 102, 106, 151n18
Netherlands, 3, 6–7, 13, 19, 23, 41, 47, 68, 77, 97–98, 119, 123, [130–32], 131, 139
neurology, 30–32, 48, 55
neuromuscular, 2, 30–32, 36, 45, 48
norm, 11, 15–18, 97
normativity, 5–9, 14–17, 23, 95, 98, 127, 143, 154n35, 163n8

observing, 6, 18, 26, 34, 39, 69, 80, [114], [132]
orchestrating, 4, 23, 54, 56, 77, 80, 82–83, 101, 114, 134, 137, 153n26
otherness, [72], 77, 106, [118], [128], [132], [138–40], 153n31. See also difference
others, 14, [29–35], [46], [55], 76–77, 88, 95, 103–4, [105], 106, 110, 119, 123–24, 128, [128], 129, [134], 139, [140], 141–43
overweight, [76–78], [87], [95], 96, [138]

pancake, 27, 29, 41, 67, [112]
perceiving, 1, 4, 29–32, [33], 44–45, 50–61, [53], 65, 73, 95, 103, 142
perception, 3, 28, 30–32, 48, 50–62, 73, 95, 142, 160n24
phenomenology, 29–32, 44, 48, 50–51
philosophy, [4], 6–8, 12, 14, 15, 19–20; empirical, 1, 5–6, 15–16, 23
pizza, 84–85, 87, 119, 123, [15], 165n23
plant, 11, 40, [40], 44, 75, 78, 93–97, 99, 101, 109, 111–12, 115–17, 122–24, 127, 132, 139
pleasure, 5–6, 10, 28, 58, 60, 64, [64], [70–74], 72–74, 97, [105–9], 133–34, 137, [140], 141–42, 161n31

political, 2, [6–10], 7–10, 14–15, 76, 78, [82], 116, 127, 129–35
politics, 4, 7, 8, 14, 21, [53], 77, [82], 126–37
protein, [31], 42–43, 79–85, [87], 97, 117, 131–32, 141, 173n6

race, 12–13, [27–33], [40–44], 151n18
relating, 4–5, 25, 102–4, 106, 112, [112–18], 114, 119–24, [123], 126–28, [128–34], 141, 143, 162n42
relation, 4, 19, 24, [35], 41, 51, [53], 54, [59], 60, 63, 66–67, 71–74, 76, 82, 102–5, [103–9], 109–10, [112–18], 114–25, 155n11, 169n12, 170n21, 172n40
research, 2, 4, 13–15, 20–21, 24, 56, 78–86, [78], 90, 118, 131–33, 139, 154n37, 160n24, 164n17, 167n45, 170n20
restaurant, 24, 27–29, 45, 69–72, [93], 106, 118–19, 123, 162n40, 162n41
revalue, 11, 25, 52, 140. See also value

satisfaction, 24, 58–60, [63], [72], 73–74, [84], 106, 112, 160n23
scarcity, 48, 137
seeing, 50–54, [66], [70], 75, 92, 108, [114], 119, 133
sensation, 53–60, [59–61], 65, [68], 71, 73, 108
senses, 3, 50–56, [53], 60, [64], [68–72], 70, 73, 159n9, 159n17, 160n25, 167n45
Serres, Michel, 16, 19–20, 153n30
smell, 3, 42–43, 47, 51–56, 64, 67, 70–71, 88
smelling, 4, 58
social sciences, 3, 24–25, 45, 152n22, 159n9
socio-material, 4–5, 17, 22, 30, 58, 93, 96–97, 100, 128, 131–32, 137
son, 32, 103, 106, 115, 119
speech therapist, 34, 48
spitting, 54–55, 71, [114], [121–23]
subject, 4, 24–25, 28–30, 36, 44, 48–50, [51], 52–60, 65–66, 69–74, 80–83, 86, 103–105, [111–12], 114–15, 118–19, 130–31, 142, 162n43, 173n9
subjectivity, 2, 26, 28, 53
swallowing, 4, 24, 33–38, 55–58, 71, 73, 83, 91, [103], 110, 156n16, 162n42